THE WITNESS OF THE JEWS TO GOD

Edited by
David W. Torrance

'The Lord said to Abram,... "I will bless those who bless you, and him who curses you I will curse; and in you all the families of the earth will be blessed"' (Gen. 12:1–3)

'Pray for the peace of Jerusalem' (Ps. 122:6)

'Through their trespass salvation has come to the Gentiles,.... Now if their trespass means riches for the world, and if their failure means riches for the Gentiles, how much more will their full inclusion mean!' (Rom. 11:11, 12)

The Witness of the Jews to God

DAVID H. S. LYON
DAVID W. TORRANCE
GEORGE W. ANDERSON
C. E. B. CRANFIELD
GEORGE A. F. KNIGHT
JOHN K. S. REID
JAKOB JOCZ
MURDO A. MACLEOD
HENRY L. ELLISON
THOMAS F. TORRANCE
MARK KINZER
JOHANNA-RUTH DOBSCHINER

Edited by
DAVID W. TORRANCE

The Handsel Press
1982

Published by
The Handsel Press Ltd.
33 Montgomery Street, Edinburgh
Paperback ISBN 0 905312 18 X

First published 1982
© 1982 The Handsel Press Ltd.

Printed in Great Britain by Bell & Bain Ltd., Glasgow

Contents

Preface

THE suggestion for this book arose in the Overseas Council of the Church of Scotland, after discussion of a report submitted to the Church and Israel Committee. This report was concerned with the ways and means whereby the Church could exercise her responsibility to the Jews more effectively, as well as learn to share and be seen to share in Israel's mission to the world. In order to deepen understanding on the part of the Christian Church and of Israel, which will lead to participation in Israel's mission, the report calls for the creation and publication of a relevant literature. (See Appendix A(2): Report for Church/Israel Committee.)

The Overseas Council, however, is not responsible for this book or for the views expressed in it.

A number of people from different backgrounds and experience have been invited to contribute. Four are Hebrew Christians. All who have contributed are persuaded of the importance of the witness of the Jews to God and of the importance of a deeper understanding of the nature of that witness. Readers will discern differences in biblical interpretation and theological outlook. It is not the aim of a symposium of this kind to present only one interpretation of issues, some of which are difficult to understand and in the understanding of which Christians are divided. No contributor is committed to what is stated by another contributor or by the editor, and likewise the editor is not committed to the viewpoint expressed by any contributor. The aim of this symposium is to seek to stimulate readers to search for and to endeavour to find what God is saying today to Christians and Jews, through his Word. It is our hope and prayer that this book will help toward a deeper understanding of what God is saying and doing in his world today, and so lead to a deeper participation, by Jews and Christians, in Christ's one mission to the world.

I express my warm gratitude to the Rev. Dr. Iain R. Torrance and to the Rev. James B. Walker for their assistance in the reading and checking of manuscripts and to the Rev. David H. S. Lyon for contributing the Foreword.

D.W.T.

Foreword

This is a very important book that may be expected, if read as widely as it deserves, to influence profoundly attitudes to contemporary events and the ways in which the purpose of God in world history is understood. Although it is a book about the Jews, written in order to encourage meaningful Christian/Jewish dialogue, it is to be hoped that it will be read not only by those with a specialist interest in that subject. It focuses long overdue attention on the determinative place of the Jews in the economy of God, and many who may not have given thought to the Jewish people at a level affecting Christian belief and practice may well have their eyes opened by it to basic and crucial questions to which they have been virtually blind.

It is a book of essays written from several different standpoints, but all with one major thrust. The writers all share the conviction that the Jewish people have a decisive place in God's creative and redemptive purpose for his world, that the fact that Jesus was a Jew is a central matter for faith, and that it is decisive for effective witness to the Kingdom that the Christian Church draw near to the Jews in thoughtful and humble dialogue.

There is disagreement among the writers at many points, not least where questions relating to the Land arise. Their differing approaches, however, and their varying interpretations of current events make the reading of this book more profitable than it would have been if all the writers had followed one consistent line alone. The reader will be led into an ongoing conversation in which, although he may not be given all the answers, he will certainly be faced with the challenge of the Jewish reality, and be given impetus to study afresh the Scriptures that belong to the Christian and the Jew alike, and to look again at the New Testament in the light of them.

DAVID H. S. LYON

The witness of the Jews to God (their purpose in history)[1]

DAVID W. TORRANCE

When Zimmerman, private physician to Frederick the Great of Germany, said to his Majesty that the Jews constitute a proof for the existence of God, he was affirming what is perhaps generally accepted by Biblical scholars.

The very existence of the Jews in history, together with all that has happened to them in their long turbulent history, is proof that there is a God present and active, through his Holy Spirit, in history. By all normal laws of geography, history and ethnography, they ought as a distinct race to have disappeared long ago, like so many other larger and greater nations. As a nation they were broken up first by Assyrians and Babylonians, then by Greeks and Romans. Yet they returned and continued as a nation. In A.D. 70 Jerusalem was destroyed by fire and the Jews were scattered throughout the world. Despite the countries in whose midst they dwelt, with their vastly varying cultures, they were not absorbed. Despite wars, persecutions and repeated attempts to obliterate them, they have kept their peculiar identity. They have remained a people apart from the other nations of the world, a testimony to the preserving hand of God. 'For I the Lord do not change; therefore, you, O sons of Jacob, are not consumed' (Mal. 3:6, see also Lam. 3:22 and the parable of the fig tree in Matt. 24:32–35; Mark 13:28–31; Luke 21:29–33, where our Lord makes clear that the fig tree, the Jewish people, will be there at the end of history). Now from every corner of the earth and from at least 87 countries, a substantial remnant has returned to the ancient land promised within the covenant to Israel, a proof, for all who have eyes to see, of the truth of the living God witnessed to in the Bible (cf. Ps. 105:7–11; Gen. 13:14–15), and

1

giving to us and to the people of the world, our only true knowledge of God (John 4:22).

What is this knowledge of God that only Israel is able to unfold?

1. *Israel is a witness to God's continuing covenant of grace with Israel and the world.* God made a covenant of grace with Israel. This covenant made with Abraham was often reaffirmed to patriarchs, prophets and kings. Through it God promised to be their God and affirmed that they were his people, set apart for God, and thereby set apart from all the nations of the world. He promised to preserve them and bless them and through them to preserve and bless the world. God's covenant of grace with Israel was made within his wider covenant of grace with the world confirmed in the days of Noah. This wider covenant of grace was with man and all creation. God's universal covenant, which goes back to creation, was reflected and confirmed in his promises to Noah as given in Genesis (9:8–17). God's covenant of grace, with Israel and all mankind, and through mankind with all creation, was confirmed and sealed in Jesus Christ, who was himself a Jew and the complete embodiment of Israel. God took the initiative in making this covenant and therefore its continuance depends entirely on God. Its continuance does not depend on man. It is not a covenant of works (and the Bible knows nothing of a covenant of works between God and man). It is a covenant of grace. Israel by her continued presence today testifies that God is faithful. He does keep his covenant of grace with Israel and therefore with the world, despite Israel's and the world's continued sin and rebellion against him. He will never break his covenant with mankind even as he does not, and never will, break his covenant with Israel. He remains patient and merciful. His purposes of love and redemption remain. (For a full exposition of the Election of God and the Covenant see Barth's *Church Dogmatics*, vol. 2, part 2, pages 3–506, particularly pages 195–305: and vol. 4, part 1, pages 3–78: and for the relation of Creation and Covenant see vol. 3, part 1, pages 42–329.)

2. *Israel witnesses to the historical nature of divine revelation.* Her very presence today as a particular people on this earth amidst the other nations recalls us to her own early history and reminds us that our knowledge of God is given to us in an historical way, through the Jews. So often the Church has tried to link revelation with the insight of reason, as if we could discover God through our minds alone. So often a church has tried to order her worship, her life and her administration without careful

reference to God's historical revelation to Israel. She has not patterned her life and work strictly in accord with the Word of God witnessed to by the Jews in Scripture. In all such cases the Church has gone sadly wrong.

Again, many have tried to interpret the New Testament without any reference to the Old Testament, that is, without any reference to the historical revelation of God to Israel. The result has been a misinterpretation of the New Testament. Israel is a perpetual reminder that we can only understand God in the way that he has given himself to be known historically through Israel.

Both prophets and apostles witness through history to the incarnation of Jesus Christ, at a particular time, in a particular place, on this earth. The historic event of the incarnation has sealed the historic witness of both prophets and apostles and given to their witness that uniqueness, whereby the Bible, which is their written witness, is a Book marked off, and different from, any other book in the world. The Bible has been given to us by the Jews. They are in a remarkable way the people of the Book. The Bible, including the Old and New Testaments, is their Book. Whereas we can only understand the Jews through the Bible, so we can only rightly understand the Bible through our understanding of the Jews and their continuing rôle in history today. If we detach our understanding of the Bible from our understanding of the Jews, as scholars have so often tried to do, then our understanding of the Bible is not, as it were, earthed. We fail to understand the relevance of the Bible to society, nations and this world's needs, in the way in which God intends. We only rightly understand the coming of God into this world in Jesus Christ and his continuing presence in the world in mercy and judgement and saving power, as we understand God's historic revelation to Israel, together with Israel's continuing witness to God today. Her very presence recalls us to this fact.

Very often the Church has failed to recognise how much she needs the ongoing witness of Israel as she engages in Christ's mission to the world. In the great era of world mission, from the early years of last century, the Gospel has been taken, largely by gentile Christians, to every part of the world. A great deal has been accomplished in the expansion of Christ's Kingdom on earth. As the Gospel penetrates men's minds and reaches down into the roots of society and challenges the structures of society, great problems emerge. The world everywhere is thrown into ferment, because of the presence of the Gospel, the leaven in the lump (Matt. 13:33; Luke 13:20–21). Hence today we hear in world missionary circles a great deal about 'liberation theology' and the call for Christians to be involved in politics. This is put forward as the urgent claims of the Gospel. Hence there tends to arise a division in understanding and in approach between, on the one hand, those who wish to emphasise the spiritual aspects of the Gospel, its temporal and eternal dimensions, as involving deliverance from the power of sin and death, resurrection, the gift of a new life in Christ and the joy of the Kingdom of Heaven and those, on the other hand, who wish to emphasise that the Gospel is not just otherwordly. It is concerned with this world and with society as we know it today, and with the policies of nations. It is concerned with justice and political freedom and the enjoyment of God's material blessings. Many would affirm that these two viewpoints are not necessarily conflicting and that both reflect important aspects of the Gospel. Still, differences remain, dividing Christians and churches, to the hurt and hindrance of world mission. It is only by taking seriously the historic revelation of God to the Jews and through an understanding of the Jews' witness to God today and with the help of their witness, that the church, in her understanding, and in her engagement in mission, can preserve the wholeness of the Gospel in all its dimensions and present a united witness to the world.

Again, many attempts are being made throughout the countries of the world to create new social orders. Nation after nation is experiencing upheaval and revolution. The claim of each new government is, generally, to promote law and order, justice and freedom for its people and improved international relations. In so far as each new attempt is detached from Israel and God's revelation to Israel, the result is injustice and unrest that is often violent. There exists no set of laws and no political structure which can prevent a nation, no matter how democratically ordered, from slipping into anarchy, or a government from slipping into dictatorship. The only restraining influences which will prevent such happenings are the actual people within that nation or government. The fear of the Lord, an understanding of his will, and the knowledge that we must all render account to him, can alone restrain such happenings to a nation or government. Israel's presence is a reminder of God's presence in the world today. She recalls men and women and nations and governments to the revelation of God's will for the world which he has made known through Israel. Israel is a living reminder that all must give account to God today.

3. *Israel witnesses by her inner testimony, through prophets and*

apostles, and by her own life, through the long years of her history, to salvation as a gift of God's grace. Jesus the Messiah is the servant of God. Those New Testament scholars who have affirmed this interpretation are surely correct. He is the one foreshadowed by the Old Testament prophets and anticipated in the servant songs (Isa. 42:1–4; 49:1–6; 50:4–9; 52:13–53:12. See also Isa. 41:8 f., Jer. 30:10 and Ezek. 28:25). Jesus appears to have had such passages as these in mind when he spoke of his person and his mission through suffering (Mark 8:31–38; 9:30–32; 10:32–34, etc.). Israel, God's people, is also God's servant. This, the normal Jewish interpretation, is also surely correct. The servant is called out and set apart by God, not for Israel's sake alone, but for the salvation of the world. He is called to suffer and die for the sins of others and then to rise from death and be exalted by God, so that those who had rejected him are compelled to recognise that he suffered for their sins and for their salvation. What is required of him, as God deals with him in mercy and in judgement on behalf of others, is that he should respond to God in love and humble submission and obedience. He must be one with the people for whom he suffers and dies. He must in every way be their representative. Yet, at the same time, in order to be the instrument of God for their salvation, he must be in perfect harmony with God, fully yielded to him in love and obedience.

Israel in her weakness, stubbornness and sin is unable to respond to God's grace in a way that is effective for salvation. She is therefore unable in herself to fulfil the servant rôle to which she is called and therefore testifies that as she cannot, so no created man can. Salvation is not an act of man and cannot be achieved by an act of man, either by an individual or by a nation. It is entirely an act of God, a gift of grace. So Israel looks to the Messiah, as the one who alone can accomplish salvation and witness to salvation as a gift of grace.

Jesus, the Messiah, is alone able to fulfil the servant rôle. He is God himself come down to earth, entered into our humanity and taken to himself our flesh and blood. He alone is able to fulfil the divine mission on behalf of Israel and all mankind. He alone as man is able on behalf of all to respond to the Father in perfect love and faith and obedience and so to accomplish salvation for Israel and for all mankind. This salvation he accomplishes in what he says and does and above all in his own person, through suffering and triumphant resurrection. This salvation he bestows as a gift to all, Jew and Gentile, who come to him in faith.

Israel, despite her unbelief in Jesus as the Messiah, continues as the people of God to witness to the uniqueness of God's saving grace in Christ. All that has ever happened to her throughout ner history, her rejection by the nations, her incalculable suffering unto death, her deliverance and resurrection, witnesses to the fact that help, deliverance and salvation are from God alone and are a gift of grace through Jesus Christ. Israel, by her unbelief as a people and her rejection of God's call, has not lost the servant rôle to which God has called her. The nature of her witness has altered but not the fact of her witness. God's call to her does not alter. Hence through her divine calling and unique relationship with God and through her unique relationship with Jesus Christ who both fulfilled and confirmed her call, Israel, unknown to herself, witnesses to the nature of Christ's mission. Israel's rejection by the nations portrays Christ's rejection, her appalling suffering portrays Christ's suffering to the death of the Cross, even as her remarkable delivery from the Holocaust and restoration to the Promised Land portrays Christ's resurrection and is intimately related to it.

Israel, by God's over-ruling grace, witnesses to God's grace in Christ Jesus, by her unbelief and rejection of the Messiah, so that by God's over-ruling the very form of her present witness and even her rejection of Jesus as Messiah, have become part of God's call for her. This belongs to the mystery of God's call to Israel. In Peter's sermon in Acts, chapter 2, we read that Jesus was delivered up to be crucified 'according to the definite plan and foreknowledge of God' (v. 23). At the same time it is stated that the people in their own freedom crucified and killed him, so that they are summoned to repent and to be baptised in the name of Jesus (vv. 23 and 28). We cannot put these two statements concerning God's election of Christ and man's freedom to crucify Christ, logically together. We hold them together only in faith. Man's sin was in no sense God's will. Even so, it belongs to God's election plan in Christ to arouse sin to its utmost limit so that he might take it upon himself, condemn it and take it away and, thereby, at the point of greatest alienation make peace between God and man. In the crucifying of Jesus all sin boiled over. This was the most desperate act of wickedness where man in his freedom rose up in revolt against God and tried to destroy him. God took this same most sinful act of man, over-ruled it, and by Grace, made it his saving act for the world and not only so but his saving act from all eternity. So man's very rejection of Christ at the cross, by God's over-ruling grace, is made to perfect God's redemption of man and to work to God's glory. So Paul, in Romans, chapter 11, says of Israel's witness, 'Through their trespass, salvation has come to the Gentiles' (v. 11) and again, 'a hardening has come upon part of Israel, until the full number of the Gentiles come in, and so all Israel will be saved' (vv. 25, 26), and again, 'As regards the Gospel they are enemies of God, for your sake; but as regards election they are beloved...' (v. 28).

Jesus suffered for us and the Jews have suffered for us and continue to suffer. When we ponder the fact that they have suffered for us as our representatives and for our salvation, how necessary that as a Church we repent of all the church's past and shameful treatment of the Jews! How necessary it is for our faith, for our entry into Christ's salvation, for our witness to Christ, that we learn to understand the Jews, to sorrow when they sorrow, to weep when they weep, to love them and in love to help them to faith in Jesus as the Messiah! Then as the elected community of God, Jews and Church together, we shall witness, not only to the shadow side of the cross but to the resurrection and to the praise and glory of Christ.

4. *Israel witnesses to man's antagonism to, and rebellion against, God.* God chose Israel to be the representative of the human race, in and through whom he would work out his purposes of love and redemption. As the representative of the human race, men are able to see in God's dealings with Israel, the way in which God deals with the world. Likewise they see in Israel, in her attitude to God and his love, their own attitude to God and his love. Israel is a mirror in which we see God, in his dealings with men, and we see man, in his attitude to God. The closer God draws to man and the more God draws man into relationship with himself, the more man's behaviour and attitude to God are thrown into relief and writ large. That is to say, all that is noble and good and all that is evil in natural man are writ large in Israel. In her long history of resistance to God and his purposes of love and redemption in Christ, Israel witnesses to natural man's antagonism to, and rebellion against, God.

5. *Israel witnesses to God's mercy and judgement.* God made his covenant of grace with Israel and the world. Israel repeatedly broke the obligations of the covenant. She broke those commands which were given as signs of the covenant, but God's covenant with Israel remains. Hence all that has happened to Israel, her preservation through appalling suffering, exceeding the suffering of any other nation in history, her preservation through the horrors of the Holocaust of Nazi-dominated Europe, and the restoration of a remnant to the Promised Land, testifies to God's faithfulness

and mercy to Israel. As God's covenant of grace with Israel mirrors his covenant of grace with all mankind, so Israel witnesses to God's faithfulness and mercy not only to Israel but to the world. Israel can turn away from Christ. The world can turn away from Christ. As God will not let Israel go, so God will not let the world go. He remains merciful and today is actively engaged in mercy in the world through his Spirit. Israel witnesses to God's mercy.

Likewise Israel's appalling suffering witnesses to God's judgement. Because of her disobedience Israel has suffered under God, over and above her other sufferings. There is evil in the world, and therefore suffering which is unrelated to man's evil. Evil reaches out in a mysterious way far beyond the will and existence of man and defies explanation: and much of Israel's suffering defies explanation. Again much of Israel's suffering belongs to her peculiar rôle in the world as God's servant for the saving of the nations. Even so, there is that within Israel's suffering which relates to her disobedience to God and which witnesses to God's judgement. Furthermore, her sufferings, which are the world's sufferings 'writ large', testify that there is that within the world's suffering that relates to man's sin and rebellion against God. God is a God of judgement as well as of mercy. Israel witnesses to God's judgement.

Again, Israel's sufferings point forward to a greater judgement to come, to a final day of judgement and of mercy. God takes seriously the sin and rebellion of this world and he takes seriously all the evil in this world. Those who finally resist his offer of grace and mercy and salvation will be condemned. All evil will be finally swept away and in mercy he will renew this world so that it becomes the new creation of our God and his people who love him, he will make to dwell with him.

6. *Israel witnesses to God as person whom we consider today in history.* Israel witnesses to a personal God who actively intervenes in history and actively confronts men and nations today, compelling them into a position of decision where they decide for him or against him, where they choose life or death.

So often people today talk about the Christian faith as if there is no personal God to whom we must render account. They talk as if all that matters is a way of life, a certain standard of moral conduct, a system of belief. So often people speak as if God does not call us to decision. The whole question of evangelism and the need for personal decision is often unpopular in certain circles. The very presence of the Jews reminds us that we have to do with a personal God, who encounters us and who compels us to choose for him or against him, life or death.

Again, nations and governments often act as if God is distant and is not concerned about the way nations behave today. They often act as if God does not exist. The presence of the Jews and their restoration to the Promised Land remind us that God does exist and remind us that God is concerned about what nations are doing. He actively intervenes in history and every nation must give account to him. He is Lord of all history.

7 *Israel frequently is the focus of man's anger with God and thereby highlights that anger.* Natural man does not want God to reign over him. He wants to be like God, to have all power, to be master of his own life and the world. He would like to remove God from the earth and to forget God. Yet he cannot. The Jews, God's chosen people, remind him of the living and only true God. Their presence disturbs his conscience. He wants to remove this reminder of the living God and so, again and again, he tries to destroy the Jews. He excuses his anger against the Jews because of the many faults of the Jews, although the faults which he sees in them are really his own writ large, and because of the complexity of the situations in which the Jews are placed. He wrongly blames the Jews for all his problems. He imagines, sinfully, that his own survival, his mastery of his own destiny and the world, depend on the removal of the Jews. Yet, every decision he makes in regard to the Jews as Jews reflects the decisions he makes in regard to God. His anger with the Jews as Jews directly reflects his anger with God. Therefore the Jews, God's chosen people and instrument of God's salvation for the world, have suffered and their sufferings highlight natural man's real attitude to God.

8. *Israel witnesses to the fact that there is a hidden process of judgement going on all through history and that all nations are held in continuous account to God.* In calling Israel to be his servant and instrument for the redeeming of the world, God related himself to Israel in a way in which he did not relate himself to any other nation. As his representative in the world, the other peoples of the world, in their encounter with Israel, encounter God and their treatment of Israel reflects their desired treatment of God and indicates, in some measure, their acceptance or rejection of his plan as salvation for mankind. From such encounters with God there flow the inevitable consequences of divine blessing or judgement. Through succeeding generations in history, the rise and fall of many nations and individuals testify to

this fact. In loving Israel they have been blessed and in hating and persecuting Israel they have encountered God's displeasure. God's word to Abraham (Gen. 12:3, see also Gen. 27:29; Num. 24:9), which was fulfilled and sealed in Jesus Christ the Lord and Judge of all, has been, and is being, remarkably confirmed.

In promoting the Holocaust, Hitler promised the final solution of the Jewish problem, with the extinction of the Jews. Hitler fell and in a short space of time the Jewish people, delivered from the gates of death, became a nation restored to the Promised Land. What a witness to the hand of God! (Amos 10:14–15.)

Under the hand of God, Israel has been placed at the heart of world politics and repeatedly is the focus of world attention. Israel, through her conflict with the Arabs, lies at the heart of the energy crisis and the disruption of the world economy. What of the remarkable victories of Israel through successive wars? God's hand is upon Israel confronting the nations of the world and calling them to account. 'Lo I am about to make Jerusalem a cup of reeling to all the people round about; it will be against Judah also in the siege against Jerusalem. On that day I will make Jerusalem a heavy stone for all the peoples; all who lift it shall grievously hurt themselves. And all the nations of the earth will come together against it.... The inhabitants of Jerusalem have strength through the Lord of Hosts, their God.... On that day the Lord shall put a shield about the inhabitants of Jerusalem.... And on that day I will seek to destroy all the nations that come against Jerusalem' (Zech. 12:2, 3, 5, 8, 9.)

Israel is not more righteous than the other nations. God said of old, 'Thou art a stiffnecked people' (Deut. 9:6; also 9:13; 10:16 and see 7:7–9). It is a matter of her calling as an instrument for God's saving of the nations. Israel, by her presence and through all that concerns her, is made by God to witness to God in the midst of his world today. Every action, by every nation, concerning her is a moral action and every decision concerning her a spiritual decision, through which governments and nations are being confronted by God and tested by him. 'He has showed you, o man, what is good: and what does the Lord require of you but to do justice and to love kindness and to walk humbly with your God?' (Micah 6:8).

Sometimes people think of the Judgement of God as something which relates only to the last day. Jesus in his teaching concerning the Judgement (Matt. 25:31–46) makes clear that this is not so. There is today, in our encounter with the poor and needy, the sick and imprisoned, a hidden process of judgement

which is going on all the time, for in each of these encounters we
are encountering the Lord. On the last day God's verdict is
declared and made manifest, but the judgement is taking place
today. In a similar way the peoples and nations of the world in
their encounter with Israel are encountering God and are being
judged by God. Who has been so poor and needy or suffered
more than the Lord's servant (Is. 52:13–53)? Israel witnesses to
this continuing judgement.

Very often people speak as if the greatest danger facing this
world today lies in the confrontation of East and West and in a
possible nuclear war. They stress that man has in his hand the
power to destroy this world. This is not so. The power is in God's
hands and the greatest danger facing the nations of the world is
their blindness and antagonism to him who is the Lord of all
history and who is working out his purpose of grace and
salvation in the midst of the nations. The destiny of the world is
for ever wrapped up with the destiny of the Jews who witness, by
God's grace, to that Jew who lived, died on a cross and rose
again to be Lord and Judge of all history and the Saviour of the
world.

9. *Israel witnesses to the coming day of the Lord and to a
positive new creation.* Isreal recalls us to her past, to the great
things that God has done in and through his people and therefore
arouses our attention to what God is doing in the world today.
Israel also arouses our expectation as to what God will yet do on
this earth. She points forward to the coming day of the Lord,
when Christ will return to this world that he has redeemed and
when all things will be transformed and renewed and made to
become the new creation of our God. The restoration of a
remnant to the Promised Land, in itself the fulfilment of
prophecy, points forward to the fulfilment of those greater
prophecies concerning the new creation, to the renewal and
perfection of all God's people living on an earth renewed and
made perfect.

We cannot separate Jesus, the Son of Man, from the Jewish
people. Jesus is for ever a Jew. So then we cannot separate the
resurrection of Jesus from the restoration, in some form, of the
Jews: and we cannot separate the resurrection of Jesus and the
restoration of the Jews from the coming restoration, in some form,
of all mankind. Likewise, since the restoration of the Jews as a
people cannot be separated from the Promised Land on which
they were destined to dwell, it would seem that the present
restoration of the land, the causing of the wilderness to blossom

like a rose, must be regarded as a foretaste of the coming renewal of heaven and earth. As the resurrection of Jesus, the Son of Man and the complete Jew, is a foretaste and pledge of the coming resurrection of Israel and of all who believe, so the restoration of Israel and of the land on which they dwell is a foretaste and pledge of the new creation, as a genuine happening.

Israel's presence in the world today is a witness to a living hope. Christ is the only and certain hope of this world. Israel witnesses to that hope in Christ. Apart from Christ, this world is so often overcast with clouds of hatred and fear, sorrow and suffering, and nuclear war and, at times, seems shrouded in darkness. Israel and all that concerns her is a light shining in the darkness and a witness before the nations of the world, to the hope of the Living God. This world is in the hand of God who came in redeeming love and power in Jesus Christ.

10. *Israel, by her presence in the Promised Land, witnesses to the fact that God is about to do something great and dramatic in history.* What God will do will be in preparation for the coming day of the Lord. Israel, however, does not tell us what God will do, but only that he will act soon and in a powerful and awe-inspiring way, in a way in which the nations will be compelled to decide for or against God and when what happens will be seen ever more clearly to be of God. Prophecy does not chart out the future as a map, else we would walk by sight. Rather we are compelled to walk by faith in expectation that God will assuredly fulfil the word that he has spoken and when his word is fulfilled then through the Holy Spirit, we are made to recognise that this is the fulfilment of the word that God has spoken. Israel is a living prophetic message that God is about to do something big and dramatic on this earth. He, the Lord of all history, is calling the nations of the world today to reckon with God. He is warning them that at the last, which may even be tomorrow, they must give account to him, who is Redeemer, Judge and King.

NOTE

1. This article was first published in a shortened form in *Renewal* (no. 82, August/September 1979, Fountain Trust). By kind permission it is published here, in a developed and expanded form.

Israel, people of God: the Old Testament evidence

GEORGE W. ANDERSON

The name 'Israel' expresses one of the great theological themes of the Old Testament, and, indeed, of the New Testament also. The Bible is not only a book about God; it is a book about God and his people. It is in the relationship between the two that much of the theological content of the Bible is to be found. The present study is an attempt to explore what the Old Testament has to say about that relationship, the terms in which it is expressed, and its implications for God's purpose for the human race.

Such an inquiry inevitably has a bearing on other religious themes in the Old Testament; but it also involves some consideration of what would nowadays be called Israel's secular experience, her political and military strength and weakness, the social and economic developments through which she passed, her national aspirations and prejudices. Ancient Israel was a religious community. She was also a nation; and it would be a mistake to suppose that her national life was irrelevant to the theological interpretation of her existence as a religious community. It is precisely as Israel is seen as the people of God, living in the context of political, military, social, economic, national, and racial influences that the theological implications of her self-understanding as the people of God are clarified and emphasised. In the course of the development of biblical thought the concept of the people of God becomes universal in its range, transcending (as I believe it did in its origins) national and racial limits. But in Scripture the people of God is always in some sense Israel and the biblical meaning of the expression 'people of God' can never properly be entirely disconnected from the Old Testament applications of the word 'Israel' or from the historical experience of the community so designated. Nor can it be fully understood unless we recognise the significant relationship between community and individual which is expressed in varying ways in the development of Israel's self-consciousness as people of God.

The name 'Israel' provides no sure clue to the nature of the community. Its meaning is one of the most perplexing philological conundrums in the Old Testament. At least ten different explanations have been offered, none of which can with certainty be regarded as correct. According to the story in Gen. 32:22–32, the name was given to the patriarch Jacob when he wrestled with his mysterious adversary at Peniel. The interpretation given in that passage seems to be 'he who strives with God', or, 'perseveres with God', or, 'is strong with God'. There are philological difficulties here and it may well be that what is provided is a popular or theological interpretation similar to those given for the names 'Babel' (Gen. 11:9), 'Abraham' (Gen. 17:5), and 'Samuel' (1 Sam. 1:20), rather than a philologically accurate etymology. It is more to the point to ask, 'To whom or to what is the name "Israel" applied in the Old Testament?' To that question the Old Testament provides several answers. 'Israel' is the name of a patriarch and also of the community which derived its life from him. In early times the community was a tribal confederacy. Later it became a united kingdom. When the kingdom was divided, the name 'Israel' was applied primarily but not exclusively to its larger and northern part. After the destruction of the northern kingdom, the name survived as a designation of Judah (note Ezekiel's frequent use of 'house of Israel' in this way), marking it out as heir to the status and privileges of the ancient undivided community. This development is both a pointer backwards to the essentially religious implications of the name 'Israel' and also a token of the post-exilic emphasis on the religious rather than the political character of the community.

'Israel' is the name not only of a community but also of an individual, otherwise known as Jacob. Indeed, in the biblical record it is the name of an individual before it is the name of a community; but whatever conclusions we may draw concerning the historical existence of the individual Jacob-Israel, there can be little doubt that some at least of the stories about him are records of communal experience presented in individual terms. These are instances of that oscillation in thought between the individual and the communal which reappears elsewhere in the Old Testament and has both psychological and theological significance. The life of the community is understood and presented in individual and personal terms. It is viewed not simply as the sum total of the individuals of which it is composed but as having its own organic life. The unity of that life not only exists at any given time but extends from the ancestor or founder of the community through successive generations. In the particular instance which we are considering, the life of the man Jacob-Israel is continued in the life of the community Israel. This is true, not only in the obvious genealogical sense, but (for Old Testament thought) in the sense of an identity of life and experience. There is a vivid example of this understanding of the relationship between the representative individual and the community in Hos. 12:2–6, where the sin of the patriarch in supplanting his brother and the sin of the prophet's contemporaries are so presented that, as one commentator has aptly put it, 'the people *now* is in a real sense identical with Jacob *then*' (P. R. Ackroyd in *Peake's Commentary on the Bible*, ed. M. Black and H. H. Rowley, 537e). This concept expresses something more than a genealogical relationship and is not confined to such a relationship. On the one hand, the life of the community is often represented in individual terms; on the other, the representative individual, such as the king or other leader, may sum up in himself the life of the community, so that he is, in a profound sense, Israel. This provides a probable explanation of the striking oscillation between individual and communal traits in the descriptions of the Servant of the Lord in Isaiah 40–55. As we shall see, this relationship between the community and the representative individual provides not only a link with the past but a pointer to the future.

Important as is the link with the patriarch Jacob-Israel, it is on its relationship to God that the character and unity of Israel are primarily based. This relationship is initiated by election and expressed in covenant.

Statements that Yahweh *chose* Israel or that Israel is Yahweh's *chosen* are relatively late, being prominent first in the Deuteronomic literature; but this terminology is used to give clearer definition to a thought which is already present in earlier traditions but not expressed by means of the vocabulary of choice or election: the thought of Yahweh's initiative in saving Israel. The decisive saving act was the historic deliverance from Egypt, to which the prophets frequently refer in language and in contexts which demonstrate its fundamental importance. 'When Israel was a child, I loved him and out of Egypt I called my son' (Hos. 11:1). As N. H. Snaith has impressively shown, the love here referred to is not *hesedh*, the 'steadfast love' or 'devotion' which is appropriate to the covenant bond, but the unconditioned 'election love' (*'ahābhah*) which leads to the covenant bond (*The Distinctive*

Ideas of the Old Testament, chapters 5 and 6). Similarly, the rich personal content of the Hebrew verb *yadha'*, 'to know' (which can express much more than intellectual knowledge) is used by Amos to describe the same fact: 'You only have I known of all the families of the earth' (3:2), which the *New International Version* boldly renders, 'You only have I chosen'. In such passages the *fact* of election is implied, though the precise Hebrew vocabulary is not used. In some other passages the divine initiative is represented as having been made in God's dealings with the patriarchs and in the promises made to them (Gen. 12:1–3; Josh. 24:3 f.). In view of what has already been said about the relationship between a representative individual and the community, it is evident that such acts and promises are presented as determinative for the Israel of later times.

The emphasis on the divine initiative which is implicit in all such statements is more sharply defined by the introduction of the vocabulary of choice or election; and it is significant that in Deuteronomy this is done in relation to what Snaith has called the 'election love' of God: 'It was not because you were more numerous than any other people that Yahweh set his affection on you, and chose you, for you were the least of all peoples; but it was because Yahweh loved you and kept the oath which Yahweh swore to your ancestors that Yahweh brought you out with mighty power and redeemed you from the land of slavery, from the power of Pharaoh king of Egypt' (Deut. 7:7 f.). The community was given its special status, not because of any particular quality or importance which it possessed, but as a result of the love, choice, and action of Yahweh. Thus the terminology of choice or election, so often thought to imply inherent superiority and to be a stimulus for spiritual pride, was introduced precisely to exclude pride and to emphasise that the life of the community originated in the loving will of Yahweh.

Election leads to covenant. No single theme in the Old Testament has been subjected to such intensive and varying exposition during the past half century as that of covenant. W. Eichrodt chose it as the dominating concept in his *Theology of the Old Testament*. In an abundant flow of articles and monographs its formal characteristics and divergent types have been examined in relation to ancient Near Eastern treaty formulas. More recently it has been argued that the use of the term 'covenant' (*bĕrith*) to express the relationship between Yahweh and Israel is a Deuteronomic innovation, a view which W. Zimmerli rightly describes as 'an unmistakable foreshortening of the perspective' (*Tradition and Interpretation*, ed. G. W. Anderson, p. 380). The need for brevity precludes both the exposition and the critical appraisal of such studies. It must suffice (at the risk of appearing uncritically dogmatic) to state my own view, that the theme of covenant as applied to Yahweh's relation to Israel is ancient, that the term is used to denote not only a contract but a personal relationship analogous to that of kinship, and that its essential formulation is succinctly expressed in the words, 'I will take you as my people, and I will be your God' (Exod. 6:7). The echo of that formula in Jeremiah's prophecy of the New Covenant (31:31–34, see v. 33) serves to demonstrate that Jeremiah foresees a future which is continuous with Israel's past.

The New Covenant passage refers retrospectively to 'the covenant which I made with their ancestors when I took them by the hand to bring them out of the land of Egypt, my covenant which they broke, though I was their husband' (v. 32). Though the closing phrase has been otherwise translated ('I was their master'), the occurrence in Jeremiah and in other prophets of the marriage metaphor to express the relationship between Yahweh and Israel tells in favour of the above translation. Marriage is an appropriate figure for the covenant relationship. Jeremiah uses it expressively of the serene beginning of the bond between Yahweh and Israel: 'I remember the devotion (ḥesedh) of your youth, your love ('ahăbhah) as a bride, how you followed me in the wilderness, in a land unsown' (2:2). The breach of that bond is poignantly expressed by Hosea (chapters 1–3) in terms of his own broken marriage; and the same thought probably underlies the Song of the Vineyard in Isa. 5:1–7. The Song is a love song (v. 1), the unfruitful vineyard representing an ungrateful wife who, in turn, represents the bride of Yahweh, his ungrateful and disobedient people.

The figure of the Vine or Vineyard, derived from Canaanite culture, is used in several passages to express Israel's special relationship to Yahweh, most notably, perhaps, in Ps. 80:10–16, where it is associated with a theme far removed from Canaanite culture and religion, the deliverance of Israel from Egypt and the making of the people of Yahweh. As we have just noted, the figure appears at one level of the thought of Isa. 5:1–7 in a context of judgement (cf. Jer. 2:21; Ezek. 15:1–8; 19:10–14; Hos. 10:1).

In describing Israel's disloyalty to Yahweh Hosea uses not only the figure of the unfaithful wife (chapters 1–3) but also that of the rebellious and disobedient son, cared for in his early years but later defying the loving direction of his father (11:1–4). Hosea's association of this father-son relationship with the deliverance from Egypt ('out of Egypt I called my son') is paralleled in the Exodus narrative itself (Exod. 4:22f.). In Isa. 1:2 the figure is again used to emphasise the enormity of Israel's sin: 'Children have I reared and brought up, but as for them, they have rebelled against me.'

In these three figures, the Bride, the Vine or Vineyard, and the Son, Israel's special relationship to Yahweh is expressed in terms which depict the life of the community in individual terms (note, however, the plural in Isa. 1:2). All are used in relation to God's saving work by which Israel came into existence as his people; two at least (the Bride and the Son) imply the covenant relationship; and all three are used to give particular point to the prophetic proclamation of judgement.

Three other terms, which are applied to Israel as God's people, are communal rather than individual. All three may be used of other groups and in quite secular senses; but in the Old Testament the majority of occurrences relate to Israel. The terms are *'edhah, qahal,* and *'am.* As terms for Israel, the first two occur mainly in later passages. Both mean 'congregation' or 'assembly', *'edhah* indicating a company meeting at the appointed time and place and *qahal* denoting a group assembled in response to a summons. Both are applied to Israel when it is assembled for cultic or judicial purposes; but, whereas *qahal* may also be used of Israel assembled for war, *'edhah* is never so used. Both terms remind us that Israel is meant to be a worshipping community. *'am* means 'people' (usually to be distinguished from *goy* which means 'nation') and may carry the suggestion of kinship (Gen. 19:38; Hos. 1:9), though this sense is by no means always present. It may also indicate Israel assembled for war (1 Kings 20:15). It is applied to other nations (*e.g.,* Num. 21:25; Amos 1:5); but with one significant exception, only Israel is designated by Yahweh 'my people'. Israel is 'the people of Yahweh', the people of 'God', 'a people chosen for his own possession' (Deut. 7:6; 14:2; 26:18), 'a people which is God's heritage' (Deut. 4:20; 9:26, 29; Ps. 28:9), 'a holy people' (Deut. 7:6), 'called to be a kingdom of priests and a holy nation' (Exod. 19:6). Some of these phrases indicate the separateness of Israel, a separateness which arises from its special relationship to God and which, in its practical expression at certain periods (*e.g.,* the time of Ezra and Nehemiah) was essential for the maintenance of Israel's distinctive tradition. In

one notable passage of prophetic vision, however, we find that it
is not only Israel that may be called God's people: 'In that day
Israel will be the third with Egypt and Assyria, a blessing in the
midst of the earth. The LORD of Hosts will bless them, saying,
"Blessed be Egypt my people, and Assyria the work of my hands,
and Israel my inheritance"' (Isa. 19:24f.).

When Israel ceased to be a tribal confederacy and became a
monarchy, the change had religious as well as political and social
consequences. Elsewhere in the ancient Near East, kingship was a
religious as well as a political institution. This was true in Israel
also, yet with significant differences which arose from the
distinctive character of Israel's religion. The accounts of how
David brought up the Ark to Jerusalem, of how Solomon
provided for the Temple and presided at its dedication, of
Jeroboam's religious policies (tendentious though the account
may be) and of Josiah's reforms (2 Sam. 6:12–15; 1 Kings 7–8;
12:26–33; 2 Kings 22–23; 2 Chron. 34:3–33; 35:1–19) indicate that
the kings not only had responsibility for worship but took a
leading part in it. What is more relevant for our present purpose
is the evidence in the Royal Psalms of the relationship of the king
to Yahweh on the one hand and to the people on the other. The
evidence relates specifically to the Davidic king. Yahweh had
chosen David and entered into covenant with him (Ps. 89:1–4,
19–37; 132:11f.; *cf.* 2 Sam. 7, where, however, the word 'covenant'
is not used). In virtue of this covenant, the king was the son of
Yahweh, not by generation but by adoption on the day of his
accession (Ps. 2:7). In election, covenant, and sonship, the parallel
between king and people seems obvious. It has been widely held,
however, that the royal covenant, being a covenant of
unconditional divine promise and therefore everlasting (Ps. 89:28–
37), differed from the Sinaitic covenant with the people, which
was conditional. The contrast should not be exaggerated. There is
more than a hint that the royal covenant was not wholly free
from conditions (Ps. 132:12). Such difference as there was between
the Sinaitic and Davidic covenants was probably one of emphasis
rather than of essential character.

The elect and covenanted king represented in his own person
the life of Israel and in virtue of his special relationship to
Yahweh was a link between Yahweh and the people. If his
relationship to Yahweh was right, then he would be a channel of
divine blessing for the people, ensuring material and moral
well-being and good order in the community (Ps. 72).

This conception of the religious status and functions of

monarchy influenced Israel's future hope in two ways. When the Davidic dynasty had ceased to rule as a result of the Babylonian overthrow of Judah, Deutero-Isaiah applied to Israel as a whole the covenant promises made to David, assuring God's people of a religious influence over other nations comparable to the military and political influence which David had exercised (Isa. 55:3f.). This brings to concise expression the thought which runs through much of Isaiah 40–55, that Israel is promised deliverance and restoration in a new Exodus experience and also, as Servant of Yahweh, entrusted with a mission to the nations. The perspective is even broader. God's action in creating and renewing his people is said to be part of his cosmic purpose: 'I have put my words in your mouth, and hid you in the shadow of my hand, stretching out [Heb. 'planting'] the heavens and laying the foundations of the earth, and saying to Zion, "You are my people"' (Isa. 51:15f.).

The second point is that in the later hope of new order, when Israel will again be delivered from foreign domination, the covenant renewed, and the land restored, one element in the transformation of Israel's life as people of God will be the presence of a righteous king, Yahweh's Messiah. This hope is found in embryonic form in the Old Testament (Isa. 9:2–7; 11:1–8; Jer. 23:5f.; Ezek. 34:23f.; Micah 5:2–4; Zech. 9:9f.). In later writing it was amplified and elaborated.

There is, however, another aspect of the nature of God's people which must be considered, namely the concept of the Remnant. In the fact that the covenant with God's people is conditional, there lies the possibility of disobedience and apostasy, followed by judgement. The fact of judgement and the painful consequences for Israel are presented with stern emphasis in the prophets. Indeed, Amos says that it is precisely because of the special relationship between Yahweh and Israel that the divine punishment will be severe (3:2). In the prophetic message, however, there is another element, even in face of judgement. There is in Israel a nucleus of faithful men and women whose very existence is a token that God's promises will yet be fulfilled and that beyond judgement there lies renewal. The presence of this idea is not as widespread as the older English versions suggest. Not every occurrence of the word 'remnant' in them expresses this idea of a nucleus whose existence points to a hopeful future. The thought is present in God's word to Elijah on Mount Horeb, when the prophet is reminded that he does not stand alone. In Isaiah, not only is the thought present in the prophet's words but

the reality exists in the group of his disciples who respond in faith
when the mass of the people fail to do so (8:16–18). The thought
reappears frequently elsewhere in the prophetic literature; and
what is fundamental to it is the element of faith or faithfulness. So
it is that Isaiah sees the renewed people of God as a building
which Yahweh is erecting on Zion, with faith as its foundation
(28:16f.).

Thus in the life of the people of God in the Old Testament
there are two interlocking elements: the faithfulness of the Saviour
God, whose promises are sure, and the faith of his people. At the
beginning of the story, when mankind had been divided by the
disaster of the Tower of Babel, there emerged Abraham, to whom
the promises of God were made, the man of faith *par excellence*;
and in him there emerged, for the renewal of mankind, Israel, the
people of God, the Remnant in whom the promises are
proclaimed and through whom the promises are fulfilled.

Light from St. Paul on Christian–Jewish relations

C. E. B. CRANFIELD

In this short essay I shall try to draw out what seem to me to be the main implications for Christian–Jewish relations today of Paul's teaching as I understand it. For the sake of clarity I shall number my sections.

1. We may start from Paul's strikingly emphatic and solemn declaration of his grief in Rom. 9:1–5 ('I speak the truth in Christ, I do not lie—my conscience bears me witness in the Holy Spirit—*when I declare* that I have great grief and continual anguish in my heart. For I would pray that I might be accursed *and cut off* from Christ on behalf of my brethren, my kinsfolk according to the flesh ...').[1] It attests his clear recognition that the central point at issue between Christians (whether Jewish or Gentile) and non-Christian Jews is of transcendent importance. The fact that the great majority of his fellow-Jews reject Him who is, Paul is convinced, the true Messiah of Israel, is proper cause for deep anguish. The first point with regard to Christian–Jewish relations to be learned from Paul is, we submit, that we should recognise with full frankness the reality of the chasm which separates us and not indulge in any attempt to paper it over.

2. But the same passage shows something else, Paul's equally clear recognition that the unbelieving Jews are still his 'brethren', still 'Israelites' (note the present tense, *eisin*, in v. 4), still fellow-members of the people of God's choice. If we would be true to Paul's teaching, we must surely repudiate altogether the notion, which is very widespread among Christians and has often been expressed by theologians (including—God forgive him!—the present writer), that the Jewish people, having rejected Jesus Christ, has been dispossessed of its election and simply replaced by God by a new Israel, namely, the Christian Church. The whole of Rom. 11 bears this out, set as it is under the sign of v. 2a, 'God

has not cast off his people whom he foreknew'.[2] Addressing the Gentiles among the Roman Christians Paul says concerning the at present unbelieving Jews in vv. 28 f.: 'As regards *the progress of* the gospel they are enemies for your sake, but as regards the election they are beloved for the sake of the fathers; for the gifts and the call of God are irrevocable'. We may compare Rom. 3:3 f. ('What then? If some have failed to respond with faith, shall their lack of faith render God's faithfulness ineffective? God forbid! We confess rather that God is true, and all men liars...').

Paul does indeed recognise that 'not all who are of Israel are Israel' in the sense of standing in a positive relationship to the accomplishment of God's purpose, but that does not mean that only part of Israel is the elect people of God. All Jews, 'all who are of Israel' (Rom. 9:6), are members of God's elect people, members of that community which is Jesus Christ's environment, all without exception witnesses to God's grace and faithfulness; but not all of them are Israel in the narrower sense of being the company of relatively understanding, willing, grateful witnesses to that grace and faithfulness. Barth was surely right to see in Rom. 9–11 the recognition that the people of God exists in two forms in history, on the one hand, as the believing element of the people in Old Testament times, the Israel within Israel, and (continuous with it) the Church consisting of both believing Jews and believing Gentiles, and, on the other hand, that bulk of Israel which is not the inner Israel and (continuous with it) the still unbelieving Jews.[3] While it is only in its existence in one of these forms that the people of God bears a testimony to Jesus Christ which is positive, conscious, voluntary and joyful, even in its existence in the other it cannot help bearing witness to Him, and its witness, though negative, unconscious, involuntary and joyless, is in its own peculiar way impressively eloquent.

3. In Rom. 10:1 Paul declares that the desire of his heart and his prayer to God for his unbelieving fellow-Jews are 'that they may be saved', and his declaration indicates a continuing duty of the Christian Church, a duty which includes seriously and wholeheartedly willing, earnestly and faithfully praying for, and therefore also persistently but at the same time humbly, graciously and in a truly brotherly fashion working for,[4] the salvation of the Jews. It would seem to be an indication of the feebleness of faith and absence of serious engagement with Holy Scripture which appear to be characteristic of present-day British Church life that one so seldom hears in public worship any specific prayer for the salvation of non-Christian Jews.

4. In the following verse, the last four words of which give expression to very grave criticism, Paul pays to his still unbelieving kinsmen a most notable tribute: 'I bear them witness that they have zeal for God'. Both 'zeal' and 'for God' are significant. He acknowledges that their zeal has the right object: it is zeal for the one true God. And he acknowledges that it is indeed zeal. It is a double acknowledgement which the Church ought always to remember. It should both encourage a brotherly and open attitude towards the Jews on the Church's part and also contribute to a salutary disturbance of Christian self-complacency (for of how much of the churches' own membership could it be stated with equal confidence that the object of its worship is really the living God and not one or other of the various idols of an acquisitive, spendthrift, corrupt society, and, even where the churches' members are concerned with the true God, how much of their concern could be described with any accuracy by so strong a term as 'zeal'?).

5. We take a look next at the last words of Rom. 10:2. The meaning of the words 'yet not according to knowledge' is that, in spite of the earnestness of the still unbelieving Jews' zeal and the fact that their zeal is really zeal for the true God, it contains a grievous flaw—it is 'not according to knowledge'. That does not mean that the persons concerned do not know God: they certainly do know Him (*cf.* v. 19). But they will not know Him as He really wants to be known, as He really is. There is an incomprehension at the heart of their knowledge and in the centre of their dedicated and meticulous obedience a stubborn disobedience (*cf.* Mark 4:12). Paul goes on in v. 3 to explain that their ignorance consists in their failure to acknowledge God's righteousness, that is, the status of righteousness before Him which He Himself offers as a gift, and—what is the other side of this failure—their obstinate determination to establish their own righteousness, that is, their claim to be counted righteous before God by virtue of their own deserts. This is indeed a failure to know God as He really is—in His mercy and faithfulness and in the seriousness of His claims. The disobedience which results from this ignorance is their refusal to 'submit to the righteousness of God', that is, to humble themselves to accept it as an undeserved gift of God's mercy.

6. The meaning of the last four words of Rom. 10:2 and the following verse can be properly seen only in the light of their context. From 9:30–32a we learn that Israel, that is, the great majority of the people of Israel, failed to attain to the law of

righteousness 'because *they pursued it* not on the basis of faith but as on the basis of works'. They misunderstood that law which God had given them in His graciousness. Instead of recognising the seriousness of its claims upon them and so allowing themselves to be led to put their trust in God's forgiving mercy and to respond to it by giving themselves to Him in thankfulness and humility (that is, of pursuing it 'on the basis of faith'), they had cherished the illusion that they could so adequately fulfil its commandments as to put God in their debt (that is, they had pursued it 'as on the basis of works'). From vv. 32b and 33 we learn the Christological dimension of Israel's ignorance and disobedience: 'They stumbled against the stone of stumbling, even as it is written: "Behold, I lay in Zion a stone of stumbling and a rock of offence, and he who believes on him shall not be put to shame"'. Verses 30–33 as a whole indicate the intimate and essentially positive relation between the law and Christ, which is clinched by the words 'For Christ is the end of the law' in 10:4, in which (in spite of many recent confident assertions to the contrary) 'end' (Greek: *telos*) must surely have the sense of 'goal', 'substance', 'innermost meaning'. Israel has failed to recognise its Messiah because it has failed truly to come to grips with its own law, and it can never understand its law aright until it recognises and accepts Him who is the very substance and inmost meaning of the law. So the Messiah, who has been given for Israel's and the world's salvation, can only be, so long as Israel's stubborn perverseness persists, the occasion of Israel's undoing.

7. The guilt of Israel is rendered abundantly clear by Rom. 9:30–10:13: it is guilty because it has failed to heed properly its own law for which in its uncomprehending way it has been so zealous. But the fact that it has been given the law, the goal and inmost substance of which is Jesus Christ, does not by itself constitute such a full opportunity to invoke the name of the Lord in the sense of Rom. 10:12 and 13 as would render Israel altogether and unquestionably without excuse. For that fullness of opportunity to have been given it was necessary that the message that the divine promises have now been fulfilled should have been proclaimed by messengers duly commissioned by God Himself. So, before going on in Rom. 11 to give the assurance that, all human ignorance and disobedience notwithstanding, God has not cast off His chosen people, Paul is concerned to drive home in 10:14 ff. with final, incontrovertible decisiveness the fact that still unbelieving Israel is altogether without excuse by showing that such a proclamation has indeed taken place. Paul will have it

B

clear beyond any shadow of doubt that the salvation of Jews no less than that of Gentiles is a matter of sheer mercy, without the least handhold for human merit.

8. Jesus Christ, who is the occasion of the deep and grievous division between Jews and Christians which may not be concealed, is also the One who unites them. He, who is the acknowledged Saviour and Lord of all who believe in Him, is Himself a Jew, the Jew *par excellence*. The supreme privilege and dignity of the Jews is the fact that He is, so far as His human nature is concerned, a member of their race (*cf.* Rom. 9:5); and this, their surpassing dignity, can never be taken away from them. To despise them is to despise and dishonour Him, in whom alone there is salvation for men. The Jewishness of Jesus of Nazareth is the final and irrevocable condemnation of every form of antisemitism, whether it be blatant and brutal or subtle and even more or less unconscious, and the unbroken bond between believing Christian and unbelieving Jew.

9. Closely related to this bond between Christian and Jew which Jesus Christ Himself is in His own person is the bond consisting of the Old Testament which bears witness to Him. If the Church heeds St. Paul, it will recognise that truly to believe in Jesus is to believe in Him according to the fullness of the Old Testament's attestation of Him, which certainly includes believing in Him as the Messiah of Israel. It will recognise too, surely, that statements representing Christ and the Old Testament law as opposed to each other (common though they have been in recent decades among New Testament scholars) are mistaken and should be repudiated, and that the law should be seen as an essential part of the Old Testament's testimony to Christ, by which Church and Synagogue are bound together. It will recognise that, though at present a veil does indeed lie on the Jews' hearts, when they hear or read the law, it is nevertheless true that in all their engagement with the law, they are, objectively though unconsciously, having to do with Jesus Christ Himself, who is its substance and meaning and who is speaking to them through it, and it will look forward with eagerness to the time when their hearts will turn to Him and the veil be taken away (*cf.* 2 Cor. 3:14–16).[5]

10. If Christians and Jews are united by their special relatedness to Christ and by their common commitment to, and engagement with, the Old Testament, they are also further united by the special clarity with which by reason of these things their sinfulness is made manifest and by the specially serious character,

which their sinfulness possesses. According to Rom. 5:12ff., sin was already present and active in the world before the giving of the law, but it was as yet nowhere absolutely clearly visible and sharply defined. If sin was ever to be decisively defeated and sinners forgiven in a way that is worthy of the altogether good, merciful and faithful God, sin must first be made to increase somewhere in the sense of being rendered clearly manifest. So the law was given, 'in order that in one people (for their own sake and also for the sake of all others) sin might be known as sin. But ... when the advent of the law makes sin increase in the sense of becoming manifest as sin, it also makes it increase in the sense of being made more sinful, since the law by showing men that what they are doing is contrary to God's will gives to their continuing to do it the character of conscious and wilful disobedience'.[6]

It is in Israel and in the Church, where God's grace and God's commandments are most fully known, that human sin is most exceedingly sinful. Nowhere else can it be so hateful. The same evil which, when perpetrated outside Israel and the Church, is monstrous, is, when perpetrated within Israel or the Church, immeasurably more monstrous. 'You only have I known of all the families of the earth: therefore I will visit upon you all your iniquities'—such is the warning of Amos 3:2; and similar is the significance of Luke 12:48 '... And to whomsoever much is given, of him shall much be required...'.

It is in this context that we should, I think, look at 1 Thess. 2:15f., where Paul says about the unbelieving Jews (according to the RV): 'who both killed the Lord Jesus and the prophets, and drave out us, and please not God, and are contrary to all men; forbidding us to speak to the Gentiles that they may be saved; to fill up their sins alway: but the wrath is come upon them to the uttermost'. The last sentence is the most difficult part of this. It is frequently understood as a declaration that there is now no hope for the unbelieving Jews. So in the New English Bible the original is rendered: 'and now retribution has overtaken them for good and all'. But, if this 'for good and all' really were an accurate representation of the sense of the Greek, it would be necessary to assume a very drastic change in Paul's thought with regard to the situation of the Jewish people between the writing of 1 Thess. 2 and Rom. 11; and, while such a change may be conceivable, it seems to us more likely, in view of what Paul says elsewhere, that the meaning of this sentence is that God's wrath has already come upon the Jews to the uttermost—in the event of the Cross. In the first words of v. 15 Paul is not forgetting the part played by the

Romans, but is underlining the special guilt of God's chosen people. In the event of the Cross the disobedience of God's people reached its hideous climax, and God revealed it in its true character with final and absolute clarity. And in that special guilt of the Jews the Christian Church should see itself as having a share. For is it not itself, in spite of all its overwhelming privileges, continually putting Christ to shame by its unfaithfulness and wilful disobedience? While the judgement of the Cross is, of course, God's judgement on all men without exception, it is the sinfulness of Christians and Jews which is most starkly revealed by it.[7]

11. Paradoxically, in view of what has been said above, and yet perhaps after all not altogether surprisingly, Church and Synagogue are united also in proneness to self-righteousness and complacency. In Rom. 2 Paul apostrophises the typical Jew who is sure of his own moral superiority over the Gentiles. Much of what he says could be applied to very many Christians. But this proneness to self-complacency common to Jews and Christians—though in a good many it has been, and is, to a considerable degree, counteracted by serious engagement with Holy Scripture—is so obvious a matter, particularly to observers from outside, that it need not be laboured here.

12. But the fact that Jesus Christ and the Old Testament, though it is over them that they are so deeply and grievously divided, nevertheless bind Christians and Jews together means that they are also bound together in hope. The importance of the place which hope has in the life of believers, according to Paul, is clear enough from such passages as Rom. 5:4f.; 8:17–39; 12:12; 15:4, 13. Rom. 11 shows that he saw the existence of the still unbelieving Jews also as set by the mercy of God under the sign of hope. To his own question, 'has God cast off his people?', he gives the firm reply, 'God has not cast off his people whom he foreknew' (Rom. 11:1–2); and he assures the Roman Gentile Christian that God can graft in again the branches of the cultivated olive-tree which have been broken off (vv. 23 and 24). But his hope for his non-Christian fellow-countrymen does not ignore the need for faith in Christ (v. 23 includes the words, 'if they do not remain in their unbelief'). The salvation of 'all Israel' mentioned in the course of vv. 25–27 would seem to be envisaged as an eschatological event, the coming of the Deliverer out of Zion probably being understood by Paul with reference to the Parousia of Christ. The relentless concentration of the composite Old Testament quotation in vv. 26f. on God's forgiveness and on

Israel's need of it dashes all Israel's illusory hopes of establishing a claim on God on the basis of its merit. There is hope for Jews as for Christians because for both alike the last word is with God's mercy on sinners.

13. Finally, we must say something with regard to the services which Jews and Christians do, as a matter of fact, whether consciously or unconsciously, render each other, and also with regard to those further services which they may or may not, but which we hope they will, render each other.

It may at once be said that to each of the two communities the very existence of the other continuing through the centuries is a valuable challenge to examine again and again itself, its own foundations and present life. That we ought to show each other, not (as we have too often done) hatred, contempt and cruelty, but brotherly affection, respect and kindness, should surely be absolutely clear without its having to be said. It surely also should be generally agreed that the possibility of blurring differences for the sake of easier and more comfortable relationships ought to be regarded as a temptation to be firmly resisted and that we ought to express to each other what we believe as clearly as possible with the utmost frankness and sincerity.

We shall suggest first a service additional to the services already mentioned (that rendered by our very existence and that indicated in 3 above), which the Church and individual Christians can and surely ought to render the Jews. We owe it to them always faithfully to try to recall them to the Law, the Prophets and the Writings, whensoever they seem to us to have forgotten them or to be in serious danger of forgetting them. We certainly have to do this very humbly indeed in view of all that we Gentile Christians have on our consciences in relation to them. We dare not forget the monstrous barbarities perpetrated by the Nazis and by many collaborators belonging to other nations, the shameful silence of those who did not wish to know what was being done in their midst, the disgraceful failure of those in power in the various western democracies to act promptly to do what could have been done to save many more Jews from the Holocaust, the long, long record of Christian persecution of Jews which preceded the hideous horror of the Hitler days, and the continuing shame of the existence of antisemitism today whether in cruder or in more subtle forms. But we should only be increasing that burden, if we were to allow it to inhibit us now and in the future from speaking frankly. And we need to be very specially on our guard against the insidious temptation (it may well usually be below the level of conscious decision) to try to settle for making amends for our own sins at others' expense by a sentimental and uncritical commitment to the Israeli state's aspirations, which takes little or no account of the rights of the Palestinians. To succumb to this temptation would assuredly be to add yet more to the great pile of wrongs already inflicted on the Jews by Christians.

We certainly do owe them the clear challenge to examine their national, and particularly their political national aspirations, critically in the light of the Law and the Prophets and the Writings. Are the scriptural foundations of those aspirations as firm and sure as is often assumed? Even the question whether they are wholly illusory ought to be honestly faced. Are there perhaps serious spiritual dangers in Zionism? Is it possible that a good many Jews in their present preoccupation with political national goals and in their determination to attain them — sometimes it seems at any cost — are in danger of losing their own souls? If Jews commit injustice against people whose families God has allowed, in some cases for very many centuries, to dwell in the land once given to Israel and if — O that the suspicions might be proved ungrounded! — they quite often descend to gross inhumanity, are they not trampling upon the Law and the Prophets?

With regard to the service which the Jews do as a matter of fact constantly render to Christians, we may add to what has already been said at the beginning of this section and in section 4, the point that their very survival until now in spite of all that they have suffered is a particularly cogent evidence of the reality and faithfulness of God, a precious testimony presented to us for which we should be thankful.

But there is a further service which they can do to us, and which we should desire to receive from them, and indeed urgently implore them to render us. It is that they should recall us to a proper engagement with the Old Testament — in fact, that they should do us the same service which we suggested that we owe to them. Thereby they would be conferring upon us immeasurable benefits; for the Church today suffers grievous damage from the various forms of Marcionism which afflict it, and where the Church fails to draw nourishment and instruction from the Old Testament it is, not surprisingly, stunted and enfeebled. Serious engagement with the Old Testament is necessary, if the Church is to sustain anything approaching an adequate Christology, a proper Trinitarian doctrine, an adequate soteriology, a satisfactory doctrine of creation, to mention just four examples. But our imploring the Jews to try to recall us to the Old Testament should surely include the earnest entreaty that they should never cease from pointing out to us with the utmost forthrightness and rigour our daily-repeated failures to judge ourselves by the standards of goodness which we and they together possess in the Law, the Prophets and the Writings, our persistent hypocrisy, our double standards, our despicable self-righteousness and complacency, our deliberate flouting of God's commandments, our inhumanity, our godlessness. They are in a specially good position to be perceptive, penetrating critics of the Church and of individual Christians. If they do criticise us in the light of those Scriptures which we hold in common and bring their criticism home to us relentlessly and fearlessly, they will put us for ever in their debt.

NOTES

1. I hope I may be forgiven both for using in the quotations from Romans my own translation from *A Critical and Exegetical Commentary on the Epistle to the Romans* ((Edinburgh, vol. 1, ³1980, and vol. 2, ²1981) — for giving me permission to do this I have to thank Messrs. T. & T. Clark, Ltd. — and also for referring the reader to that commentary for the detailed exegesis, which is the basis of much of what I shall say here.
2. The relative clause should not be taken as limiting the reference of 'his people' to those members who are objects of God's secret election (*pace* Calvin); for in v. 1, in the light of 10:21, 'his people' must surely denote the people of Israel as a whole, and it is unnatural to give it a different sense in v. 2.
3. Reference may be made to the section on God's election of grace in *Church Dogmatics* II/2, pp. 1–506, as a whole.
4. *Cf.*, *e.g.*, Rom. 11:13f.; also Acts 13:14ff.; 14:1; 17:1–3, 10, 17; 18:4f.; 19:8; 21:39f.; 22:1ff.; 28:17ff.
5. With regard to the substance of this paragraph reference may be made to Cranfield, *op. cit.*, especially pp. 845–70.
6. Cranfield, *op. cit.*, p. 293.
7. I am grateful to the Editor of *Irish Biblical Studies* for allowing me to use in this paragraph some phraseology from my 'A Study of 1 Thessalonians 2' published in *IBS* 1 (1979), pp. 215ff.

Israel—the land and resurrection

GEORGE A. F. KNIGHT

Israel's relationship to the land has to be seen alongside all the other elements that are bound up with her election. The relationship is to be understood as but one of God's promises for Israel's future through which God reveals himself and his purposes within the bonds of his covenant-making process. The theological expression of this work of Yahweh that renders him unique amongst all the gods of the ancient Near East, is expressed in Genesis chapter 9. There the onus of 'remembering' the covenant that God has made 'between me and all flesh that is upon the earth' (v. 17) rests upon God, and not upon man. Consequently the upholding of the covenant is a continuing act of grace on God's part.

In the Old Testament we discover that God has continued to reveal himself to his creature, man, through the channel of personal relationships. We see this reality clearly when God declared to Moses at the Burning Bush, 'I will become — *hayah* — *with* you' (Exod. 3:12), the Hebrew verb being the same as that used two verses later to describe God by his name. God's name, or his essence, as we might say, becomes known through his creative action within and through a member of the human race. But his relationship with all men is not the same as with Moses. What we find is that God makes covenant with one people alone. He does so by using Moses as his spokesman, or, if you like, the head of the body of Israel (Exod. 19:3–6). In answer to God's gift of covenant what is required of Israel on her part, basically, is obedience. So we begin to see, from the report of this early tradition of what took place at Mount Sinai, an example of that particularism that we continue to meet with in God's elective plan throughout all the centuries following.

This particularism is unique to the ways of Israel's God. It remains quite unacceptable to the religious thought of such religions as Hinduism in India or to most of the philosophies of modern, western man. There were those Old Testament theologians who contributed to the total picture of God's elective plan by declaring that, even in the days of saga, and of legend of old, God had acted likewise. For at the beginning of Israel's story God had chosen and made covenant with their ancestor Abraham (Gen. 12:1–3; 15:1–21; 17:1–21), the forefather of the whole People of God, and had then repeated his promise that he would be *with* each of the Patriarchs in turn.

It is interesting that the various theological schools and writers within the Old Testament should all agree about this particular element in revelation. Even the Wisdom school took the issue for granted. This is despite the fact that the school which emphasised the election of the line of David to be God's 'son' for ever (2 Sam. 7), may not have known of the tradition that affirmed the election of Israel as a whole to be the 'son' of God (Exod. 4:22). There was the tradition, emphasised by still others, of God's election of Jerusalem to be the Holy City, Zion, God's 'footstool' on earth. This tradition sought to root the theology of God's activity in ancient history (Gen. 14:18) at one particular spot on earth.

The selection of the site for the Temple by David was of divine leading (2 Sam. 24:18–25). 1 Kings 8, as part of the Deuteronomic tradition, records the great prayer of Solomon, who, when he dedicated the completed Temple, said: 'O Lord my God ... let thy eyes be open night and day towards this house, the place of which thou hast said "My name shall be there"'. So, as Ps. 26:8 puts it, the Temple became 'the place where thy glory dwells'.

Then we recall that Aaron, the 'ancestor' of the whole priestly class that was ordained to serve in the Temple at Jerusalem, had also been elect of God in the beginning. As an element in the whole revealed Torah, or 'Law' of God, which we read about in Leviticus, the priest was called of God to teach Israel to remain, what God intended her to be, his 'kingdom of priests' and a 'holy nation'.

It was through such particularism, peculiar to the Old Testament, therefore, that the purpose of God for all men was to be channelled, and through which it was to reach forth to the ends of the earth. For Israel herself, as shown her by her theological interpreters, the prophets, had been elect with the purpose in view of being God's servant. God would give Israel, to use the words of Isa. 49:6, as a light to the nations, 'that my salvation (my creative, saving love) may reach to the end of the earth'.

But *all* the above elements in God's elective purpose are dependent upon still one other factor, *viz.*, the land. Just as, in the beginning, God had to create 'the heavens and the earth' (really all one in Hebrew thinking) so that there might be a *place* where his Word could become Light (Gen. 1:3), so too with the election of Israel. God had redeemed Israel out of the 'chaos', the *tohu* of Gen. 1:2, which had become manifest in the particular social situation of life in ancient Egypt. What God had done was to redeem Israel *from* a land of chaos, *into* a land where Israel was to discover the very opposite of *tohu*, *viz.*, *shalom*, peace, wholeness of being, prosperity, holiness of living. Thus God's promise of the The Land, *ha-arets*, is absolutely basic to the fulfilment of all other promises made to Israel. *The Land* is the locus of them all, for it is on *The Land* that all these promises came together in Israel's thought and experience, like the strands of a rope which, unless they do come together, cannot comprise the one strong rope that they are intended to be. So we recognise that what we might call the 'spiritual' purposes of God could not have advanced or have been realised without such a *place* for them to become history.

The Holy Land therefore was God's place, in fact, it was 'the place of God's feet'. *The Land*, *ha-arets*, was that one factual element in the Old Testament revelation that could be regarded as being wholly objective and not dependent upon a subjective theologising in the minds of fallible people. Consequently, while all else might change and decay, *The Land* would remain 'whilst the earth remained'. The land was the objective and immovable symbol of the presence of the Lord whom no man can see. Thus it was the symbol of what the Psalmist says: 'God is in the midst of her; she shall not be moved' (Ps. 46:5). If we could borrow from Greek thinking for a moment, the land was like the physical element in the human body that gives the possibility for the various qualities of the human mind and spirit to be able to exercise themselves at all.

However, two distinct elements in the biblical faith relating to God's ongoing purpose through his covenant are still to be noted. (1) God's promises, as listed above, were dependent for their fulfilment on the co-operation of Israel. At the giving of the covenant God had bestowed his *ḥesed*, his covenant-love, upon Israel; in return Israel was to show her *ḥesed* to God; for only if she did so could the covenant be fruitful. But Israel continued to be disloyal and perverse, as Hosea, amongst others, insisted. She kept running after other gods instead of reflecting back to

Yahweh the *hesed* he had showed towards her when he chose her as his beloved bride.

(2) The biblical faith cannot be described or illustrated by the image of a slowly growing and maturing flower. It does not evolve, in the manner of the evolution of species in the natural world. God's work (his 'strange' work, as Isaiah called it — Isa. 28:21) goes forward, not in a smooth ascent, but by crises, by destruction and renewal, by death and by resurrection. The very ancient so-called 'Song of Moses' had glimpsed this reality even before Israel had inherited the land:

'See now that I, even I, am he,
    and there is no god beside me;
I kill and I make alive;
    I wound and I heal' we read at Deut. 32:39;

'And there is none that can deliver out of my hand', or as we might put it today, 'And there is no other way of understanding reality'.

Now, these two elements in the biblical revelation fused together in the year 587 B.C. That was the year of the fall of Jerusalem. Because of Israel's disloyalty to the God who had made covenant with her, in that year God acted upon her in judgement. For his purposes he employed 'my servant Nebuchadnezzar', to use Jeremiah's phrase, within the historical process which he himself controlled. Nebuchadnezzar, with whom God had made no covenant, now became the instrument of God's judgement upon his own chosen people. As a result of this action by God, each of the promises which he had made with Israel seemed to have been finally annulled; and so the conclusion that some in Israel were led to reach was that God was not in fact like what he had revealed himself to be of old; God was, one might even dare to declare, a liar. Not that God's promises were mere illusion, or that God himself was dead. Such ideas could not have entered the mind of ancient Israel, though they might be indicative of the mind of modern man. For today, post-Christian man completely disregards the significance of the biblical 'covenant'. He even compares and contrasts the faith of Israel in the 'Comparative Religion' classroom with the religions of the East! In doing so therefore he shows himself to be blind to the fact of Israel, the fact of the land, and the fact of Israel's experience of the covenant.

God had made two solemn declarations to Abraham: (1) 'I will make of you a great nation ... by you all families of the earth shall bless themselves'. But with the advent of Nebuchadnezzar 'this great nation' was no more a nation. It was merely a scattering of displaced persons struggling for a living under a foreign king. (2) Then again, God had said to Abraham: 'To your descendants I will give this land'. But the reality now was that the heathen king Nebuchadnezzar had dispossessed Israel of that Holy Land, and had even added it to his own dominions. Those two promises, we recall, had been presented in terms of a covenant, one element of which was that its Giver undertook never to break his promise (Gen. 15:18; 17:2). But broken it now certainly was.

The words introducing the giving of the Covenant to Israel at Sinai had been: 'You have seen ... how I bore you on eagles' wings and brought you to myself. Now therefore ...' But again the reality was that God was no longer carrying Israel. In fact, he had abandoned his people to the good graces of a ruthless foe.

An integral group within that People of God, whom God had abandoned to this foreign dictator, was the priestly class. These were now scattered, along with their people, over the Babylonian plain, and so were no longer able to fulfil the terms of their ordination. Their task had been to serve the altar at the Jerusalem Temple. But the Temple was now no more. It had been laid in the dust, and its holy vessels had been carried off in triumph by heathen hands. In a word, as Amos the prophet had long since proclaimed would happen: 'The end has come upon my people Israel' (Amos 8:2).

The horror of this collapse of all meaning in life was borne in upon the soul of one particular priest in exile, *viz.*, Ezekiel. It came home to him by means of a parable that incarnated itself in his experience of being a Son of Man. Ezekiel had been deported after the first siege of Jerusalem in 597 B.C. and was now awaiting in exile in fearfulness and dismay the outcome of events in 587 when Nebuchadnezzar returned to finish Jerusalem off. He had to go through grievous days as he sat by his wife watching her go down into the valley of the shadow of death. 'Son of man, behold, I am about to take the delight of your eyes away from you at a stroke ... but make no mourning for the dead ... At evening my wife died.' Next morning the word of the Lord came to me, Thus says the Lord God, Behold *I* will profane *my* sanctuary ...' (Ezek. 24:15–21). This 'sanctuary' was of course the place where God was accustomed to meet in total intimacy with his Bride, Israel, the People whom he had chosen for himself, even as a man chooses one woman to be his bride from all other possible women. So we continue, '... a man who had escaped from Jerusalem came to me and said, "The city has fallen"'. So the end had come at last, the 'death' of the people of God had become historical event.

No sooner had Ezekiel recovered from the blow he had suffered, than he preached a sermon virtually on the theme 'Those who take the sword shall perish by the sword'. Israel had gained *The Land* by violence in the days of Joshua. God had indeed used her violence, so that the conquest of Canaan could even be called by the name of 'The Wars of the Lord'. But such was the case only because God had chosen to involve himself in history. For by working *in* human events God can create new situations, or recreate them, situations of human folly and evil. The God of the Old Testament is always the God 'who makes all things new'. Once Israel had won the Holy Land and had settled there, she had necessarily to continue to *hold The Land* by violence. And, as Jacques Ellul points out, violence produces only one result — more violence.

Consequently God has eventually to do the humanly incredible thing to his own people. He has to reverse Israel's conquest of *The Land*. He has to lead a heathen power to undo the history of half a thousand years, and give the land, by violence!, to others. Hosea tells us of God's agonising decision in this regard (Hos. 11:8–9). So Israel has now to learn, not to *use* violence, but to *suffer* violence. What God does now through events is to declare to Israel his new thing, *viz.*, the *eschatological significance* of *The Land*, and let her see it in the light of his saving purpose, not just for Israel, but for all mankind. In other words, God must first kill, before he makes alive again, even when, as Psalm 137 declares 25 times over, his *ḥesed*, his covenant love endures for ever.

So then Ezekiel now discovers two basic realities about the God of the ancient Covenant. (1) Just as Ezekiel was bound up, even one flesh, with his beloved wife, 'the delight of his eyes', and so had known the darkness of *tohu* when finally his wife died, so God, 'one flesh' (the Old Testament dares to suggest) with his beloved Bride, Israel, came to know *in himself* the horror of the darkness that befell his own people when in judgement he had to profane his sanctuary on the day that the solemn words sounded forth down the centuries, 'The city has fallen'. (2) Immediately following news of the 'end' of Jerusalem God turns at once to Ezekiel with a new promise: 'I will make with them (Israel in exile) a covenant of peace', *shalom*, or rather, a 'total, comprehensive' covenant, one which we see from what follows is a re-creation of the covenant God had once and long ago made with Noah at the Flood. After the complete 'end' that had come upon all creation, God's *action* of re-creation follows at once upon the utterance of his *word* of promise. Ezekiel's vision of the Valley of Dry Bones, dead bones, very dead bones, into which God now breathes life (as he did to man in the beginning — Gen. 2:7), but now *all over again*, marks the second element in the turning point of God's redemptive action. To express it in metaphorical language therefore we might say that since the historical moment of 587 B.C. had marked for Ezekiel the 'death' of Israel, so now he could dream of the 'resurrection' of God's people. Moreover, this dream also became event at a moment in history, in the year 538 B.C. For it was in that year that King Cyrus issued his famous edict that allowed Israel, the poor prodigal son, to 'come to himself', to 'arise', and to go home to his Father's house.

By this 'resurrection' of Israel, God's covenant had of course been vindicated. Israel had learned that God had never abandoned her at all. The first shape of the covenant with its warlike content had now been transmuted, however, in that God himself, the warrior who had come forth 'trampling out the vintage where the grapes of wrath are stored', was now 'carrying' Israel once again by bearing the cost of the battle *alone*, and without her help, and by showing forth his glory as the red blood of redeeming love. Isaiah 63, which gives us this figure of God's redemptive activity, was penned *after* the 'resurrection' and return to Zion. 'Fear not, for I have redeemed you ... when you walk through fire you shall not be burned' (Isa. 43:1–2) were words that God had said to his people while they were still in exile to which they had been driven by God's judgement. There they had learned that, even while God had called his people 'my servant Israel', he had been *with* them all along, even as they suffered the fate recorded in Isa. 53.

So then, how does *The Land* fit into this new revelation? Israel returned in 538–537 B.C. to a Jerusalem and to a land that was now no longer theirs by right of conquest. The land was now merely a province of the Persian Empire. Some centuries later it changed ownership again, and became part of the empire of the Ptolemies, then of the Seleucids, and finally of the Romans. The Maccabean interlude when Jerusalem was governed by the Hasmonean priestly dynasty did nothing to change this situation, for most of *The Land* remained in alien hands. Should God's revelation of his will in what he did with Israel in respect to the Holy Land in

the day of Ezekiel not still apply in answer to the claim made by
the modern state of Israel to occupy *The Land* by right of
conquest? Not everyone would agree with the position of the
modern Zionist. The Land of Israel, won and then controlled by
violence, had now by 587 B.C. served its purpose in the plan of
God. Amongst others, the prophet Jeremiah, who lived through
those traumatic events of that year, recognised that the ancient
Covenant must, in God's good time, find a new *place* from which
to operate, and that place, he believed, would be the individual
human heart (Jer. 31:31–3).

The fall of Jerusalem with all that went with it was thus the
first step towards the winding up of the old Covenant in the form
it took when Israel was necessarily constituted as a political state.
In the Middle Ages the Church sought to regard the Holy Roman
Empire as the Kingdom of God *on earth*. It ought to have taken
warning from Israel's experience of old. Belief in this view of the
land of Europe lingered on even until the Second World War. For
up to 1939 no Jew was ever allowed to own any part of the soil
of Poland, or even to work it under the direction of a Christian
farmer, on the ground that, as an unbeliever, he was like a
Philistine of old, and so had no right to touch the soil that was
God's gift to his believing people through Christ.

We take these theological actualities and turn now to the New
Testament. There we find that the New Covenant spoken of in it
picks up all the strands of the rope that seemed to have been cut
in 587 B.C. and declares that God has now transformed them all,
because of what he did to Israel at that date. He did so in such a
way that they now all point to the person and work of Christ.

The New Testament now sees how Christ can be, not only king
in the line of David, but also King of kings and Lord of lords. It
sees why Jesus set his face steadfastly to go up to Jerusalem, 'for
all things must be accomplished there', and there only. When at
the moment of his death the 'veil of the Temple was rent in
twain', it sees how God has re-created the meaning of his
covenant that made use of the whole sacrificial system that had
been attended to by generations of priests. It sees how Israel as
God's first-born *son* has not been abandoned, but has been re-
created in him who is indeed Son of God. And so it sees how the
theology of the Cross can be expressed in terms of what *God has
done already* in judgement and re-creative power from 587 to 538
B.C.

But what happened about *The Land* in all this? We note how
the New Testament has nothing at all to say on this particular

promise of God. And so we ask — Why should this be so? The
answer lies surely in the manner in which both Testaments think
in terms of (1) The purposes of God as advancing till he makes
all things new, both heaven and earth together; and (2) How God
moves forward to this end, not in terms of evolution, but in terms
of crisis, or, to use our biblical symbols, by means of death and
resurrection.

As a modern pilgrim to the Holy Land, I went through what
most Christians experience when they first gaze upon the sacred
sites. This was an unexpected feeling of disappointment and even
of disillusion. Interesting it was, of course, to see the huge
foundation stones of the ancient Temple, to gaze at the hill-slope
where Goliath fell to David's pebble, and even to walk the streets
where *he* walked in days of old. But he was not there in my
experience that day, nor was he to be found even in the fishing
villages of the lovely Lake of Galilee. Of course he was not there;
and anyway, why was I seeking the living among the dead? 'He is
not here; for he has risen, as he has said', declared the angel to
the women at the empty tomb.

But who was this 'he'? 'He' was the focal point of all the
promises of God made within the bonds of the Covenant — and
one of those was God's promise of *The Land*. He had now lived
on it, walked on it, had never departed from it for any other land.
His body had been nurtured by the grain and the vegetables that
had grown out of that land, his thirst had been slaked by its
streams. A man is what he eats, says the physician today. The
land with all that it produced, this land of milk and honey, had
been a necessary element in God's plan for the life and person of
Jesus else as a human person he could not have lived as Son of
man. In the light of the whole argument above, therefore, what I
want to emphasise is that Jesus' physical body, composed of the
produce of *The Land*, and of that land only, now revealed finally
what the choice of that land was for. Jesus' body was now the
place of God's redemptive purpose.

'Behold my hands and my side', the resurrected Christ said to
Thomas. The religions of the world, almost without exception,
think in terms of natural progression. When a man dies, these
religions take for granted that his soul, and his soul alone,
progresses onwards into the world beyond. Not so with Israel,
either in her thought or in her literature. In the Old Testament
we find no reference to the idea of the soul as something that is
separable from the body. The word *nephesh* describes the totality
of a man's being; for man, Israel believed, cannot be a personality

without his stomach, brains, heart, and even his kidneys, as more than one Psalmist reminds us. Nor do we find in the Old Testament the idea that heaven is a place to which the departed soul proceeds at death. This is because God created heaven and earth as one. God made all creation as one, matter and spirit, heaven and earth, body and soul. The Old Testament knows of only one ultimate reality, that is God himself. All else is God's creation. So that when a man dies it is his wholeness of body, soul and spirit, built up from the food he has eaten, the books he has read, the places, the cities he has visited, that returns to God who gave him life. That then was the Old Testament vision.

But in the New Testament vision becomes miracle. It does so because of the reality of the revelation given us by the living God that is spoken of in the Song of Moses. God raised the *whole* Christ from the dead, St. Paul asserts, because it was the whole Christ who had died upon the Cross and descended into *tohu*, the chaos of death and 'hell'. Consequently the words of the risen Christ to doubting Thomas 'behold my hands and my side' refer to this miracle of re-creation, no matter what difficulties we have in grasping it because of our scientific education.

I felt empty of God's promise of the *The Land* when I discovered, on my visit to Palestine, that Tel Aviv could have been built in Utah, or Jaffa in southern France. This to me was no longer the Holy Land. And then it all came home to me why this was so. 'He is not here; he is risen!' And *in* him, I saw clearly, as I reviewed in my mind the on-going work of God, there had risen, not just the will and purpose of God, but also, in epitome and in a representative capacity, *The Land* itself, to become the first-fruits of the new heaven and the new *earth*, wherein dwelleth righteousness. And so I realised that the Risen Christ *is* the eschatological significance and ultimate outcome of God's ancient promise of *The Land*.

Israel—people, nation, state

JOHN K. S. REID

The attempt to reach academic precision in the terms used in this essay is a luxury that must be forgone, since both time and expertise are lacking. A more pragmatic approach must be adopted, and indeed serves the purpose very well.[1]

1. Introduction

No one will deny that the Jews for nearly 4000 years have been what must be called a people.[2] This character is a constant, always retained, never relinquished or lost. But during this long time this People experienced vicissitudes and from time to time acquired characteristics that transpose it into other categories. A glance at salient points in its history shows this.

(a) It was certainly a *people* that moved into Egypt and there endured the servitude inflicted by the Pharaohs. (b) With the exodus and under the leadership of Moses, the People acquired or resumed an independence they did not possess in Egypt: if not exactly sovereign, it is a People that is its own master. (c) Under Joshua the People entered a 'promised land' and in subsequent years possessed it, the original inhabitants being extruded. The People in possessing a land becomes a *nation*. (d) After the conquest, conflicting influences operate. While occupation is a cohesive factor, the manner of its eventual administration through judges is divisive, though stopping short of disruption. (e) About kingship there is difference of opinion (v. inf. 2.3). But it imparts a degree of unity hitherto unknown: the People equips itself with the apparatus of government and becomes a *state*. (f) This unity breaks up after Solomon: monarchy becomes dyarchy; and the People under the names of Judah and Israel pursues a divided life and meets different destinies. (g) The Northern Kingdom capitulates to Sargon and disappears; the Southern Kingdom collapses and is deported. The portion of the People in Babylon is divested of land and prospers; that left in Judea occupies land under Babylonian sufferance and in poverty. In both cases, statehood has gone; in Babylon the People continue as People, while in Judea, occupying land as it does, a nation may be said to persist. (*h*) Temple (515 B.C.) and walls (*c.* 433) are rebuilt. From this point until the days of the Romans, the fortunes of the People manifest no lasting change: it is a nation but not a state, subject to the control of five successive dynasties, though under the Maccabees resuming temporary control of its own affairs in a remarkable century of armed revolt. With its suppression and the destruction of the temple in A.D. 70 and consequent Dispersion, the People's pretensions to nationhood and statehood are extinguished for 2000 years, the Bar-Kochba insurrection (133–5) being a momentary spark among embers that declined to ignite. (*i*) So until recent times, without nationhood or statehood, the People persisted as People only. 'La marche tragique du peuple élu à travers l'histoire a provoqué au tour de Javhé un magnifique regroupement de toutes les énergies et de toutes les espérances.... Le peuple est devenu la communauté de ceux qui appartiennent à Javhé par l'observation de la Loi' (H. Michaud, art. 'Peuple', *Voc. biblique*, ed. J.-J. von Allmen, 1954).[3] (*j*) The reoccupation and repossession of Palestine by the People is a story on its own that falls into two parts.[4] From about 1881 onwards a series of Aliyahs takes place, in which Jews went to live and work in what is now called Israel. Settlements were planted: 1879 Petach Tikva (Gate of Hope) and Rishon le Zion 1882 (The First to Zion, *v.* Isa. 41:27), whose vivid names express the elation with which the People set out to constitute a new life in a movement regarded by it not as colonisation but as homecoming (*cf.* Amos Elon: *The Israelis, Founders and Sons*—London, Weidenfeld & Nicolson, 1971, p. 90). At first an instinctive and unorganised surge in search of sheer *Lebensraum*, especially to escape from repression in Russia, the movement became selfconscious and deliberate under the influence of Zionism. In its later stages it undoubtedly received additional impetus from the worldwide phenomenon of resurgent nationalism. By the Balfour Declaration 1917, the movement received official acknowledgment and the support of one of the Great Powers. At the same time it was obliged to operate under restrictions whose imposition the People found vexatious and the Great Power politically necessary. The second part of the story begins in 1939, when the Jewish influx into Palestine took on the character of life-or-death intensity. With the approval of the U.N. and several individual nations of the world, Ben Gurion on May 14, 1948 in Tel Aviv read the opening words of a Declaration:

'Eretz Israel was the birthplace of the Jewish people. Here their spiritual, religious and political identity was shaped. Here they first attained to statehood, created cultural values of national and universal significance, and gave to the world the eternal Book of books.' The Jewish People assumed at this historic moment the character and apparatus that transformed it once again into nation and state.

2. *Jewish assessment of the facts*

(2.1) People and nation — *am* and *goy* — O.T. uses both terms to designate a community, *people* emphasising the persons composing it, *i.e.*, the individual aspect, and *nation* the solidarity of the unity, *i.e.*, the corporate aspect. But more important is the different denotation with which it usually invests the terms. The overwhelming importance of the first is illustrated by the concordances: Young has to devote 16 columns to People, and only three to nation. (For N.T. Young devotes two columns to *laos*, and only a half-column to *ethnos*.) This constitutes a massive apparatus from which examples selected must be as representative as possible.

For the most part O.T. uses people to denote Israel or the Jews, and nation to denote the other peoples or communities round about. Thus Exod. 6:7: 'I will adopt you as my people, and I will become your God'; and predictably enough, Moses addresses Pharaoh (Exod. 8:1): 'Let my people go'.

The People is deliberately and regularly separated from the nations, as Lev. 20:24: 'I am the Lord your God: I have made a clear separation between you and the nations'; and the separation is paralleled by the ritual 'clear separation between clean beasts and unclean beasts and between unclean birds and clean birds'.

However, the usage is not quite uniform. Gen. 12:2 has 'I will make you into a great nation'. Similar lack of uniformity applies to nation, for which sometimes people does duty: Deut. 7:6 f., where A.V. has 'the Lord thy God has chosen thee to be a special people unto himself, above all people that are upon the face of the earth. The Lord did not set his love upon you nor choose you because you were more in number than any people, for ye were the fewest of all people.' Here N.E.B. sacrifices linguistic precision for the sake of accuracy of meaning and translates *am* as nation and nations.

Exod. 19:5 exhibits an unusual interchange of terms: 'If only you will now listen to me and keep my covenant, then out of all peoples you shall become my special possession.... You shall become my kingdom of priests, my holy nation.' Here the usual nations are designated peoples, and God's people a nation, albeit a holy nation. *Cf. p.c.* Deut. 26:18f., where the same sentiment is expressed in the more usual terminology.

(2.2) Possession of the land — two moments stand out as of supreme significance in the development of the People: the possession of the land, and the institution of the kingship. The People occupied and possessed the 'promised land' in full consciousness that it discharged a divine mission whose character was the covenant. If, as is here suggested, occupation of a country or land is constitutive of what is meant by nation, then the People deliberately enters upon nationhood believing it to be God's will and purpose for it. This conviction is based upon the covenant which included responsibilities and rewards: in Exod. 19:5 the responsibility is 'now listen to me and keep my covenant'; the privilege simply to 'become my special possession'. But in both early Abrahamic and in Sinaitic form, the covenant includes among the privileges possession of the land. Thus Gen. 22:17: 'This is the word of the Lord: By my own self I swear ... I will bless you abundantly and greatly multiply your descendants ... (and they shall) possess the cities of their enemies'; and Deut. 1:8: 'I have laid the land open before you: go in and occupy it, the land which I sware to give to your forefathers, Abraham, Isaac, and Jacob, and to their descendants after them'. So too Lev. 20:22: 'You shall keep all my rules and my laws and carry them out, that the land into which I am bringing you to live may not spew you out ... and I told you that you should occupy (the) land, and I would give you possession of it'. Similarly Josh. 1:11: 'Within three days you will be crossing Jordan to occupy the country which the Lord your God is giving to you to possess'.

(2.3) Kingship — the unanimity with which the People embarked on and accomplished the occupation of the land breaks down over the subsequent issue of the kingship. The two contrasting accounts in 1 Sam. may be presumed to express divergent contemporary views within the People: 1 Sam. 9, 10, 11, 13, 14 narrate the installation of Saul as king without disapproval; most of chapters 7 and 8 regard it as a grave offence; while Deut. 17:14f. is neutral as it prescribes the conditions to be met by anyone appointed to the office. There is a phrase of crucial importance in the narratives. When the People's wish to have a king is recorded, the reason given is to be 'like other nations'. Evidently this is the precise ground why Samuel condemns and resists the request. The People that is separate should not manifest inclination to assimilate to other nations. The phrase recurs in the neutral Deut. passage: 'let us appoint over us a king as all the surrounding nations do'. On the pragmatic definition adopted here, occupation of land makes a nation — and this on biblical grounds is unobjectionable; but kingship converts nation into state—and this provokes, according to some O.T. documents, or in some members of the People, bitter dissent. Here is an early and classic example of the tension apparent in all its history, whether to be or to renounce being 'like other nations'. In the later days of Dispersion, the tension manifests itself as a polarisation for and against 'assimilation'.

(2.4) How did the People regard the post-exilic return? That it was understood as a re-enactment of the covenanted promised land and its possession may be taken for granted. But what exactly was being re-enacted? It was not an exact reiteration ,of what happened earlier. According to *Voc. biblique* (*op. cit.*, pp. 225b f.), before Exile 'the people of the land' designated all the inhabitants, grouped as they were round the king (2 Kings 16:15) or the priests (Jer. 34:19); after the Exile it denoted the population of Palestine who did not observe the Mosaic Law (Neh. 10:31). Politically the People has an existence not different from the neighbours; only religiously does it differ. The kingship and cognate statehood have evidently been relinquished for good — but the People continued, grouped now round the Temple and the observance of the Law. With the final post-70 Dispersion, the land was forfeited, the centripetal factor of the temple was stripped away, and observance of the Mosaic Law was left as the sole evident constitutive characteristic.

(2.5) The disappearance of kingdom, temple, and land created a vacuum into which hope entered. What was the nature of the hope? It does not either then or now appear to embrace kingship. As for the temple, while a rebuilt temple certainly is the object of hope,[5] there is no inclination to restore the apparatus of priest and sacrifice.[6] But land remains a constant component of Jewish hope; and down the centuries unceasingly the greeting has echoed: Next year in Jerusalem. Land is the loadstone on which, wherever the People finds itself, the compass of its hope focuses. Occupation of the land is basic. Whether this occupation includes such sovereignty as constitutes statehood, or sufficient independence to constitute nationhood, is a matter of secondary importance on which opinion might differ. But decision is eventually taken. Zionism and the events of the 1930s and 40s tip the balance decisively, though even then not unanimously, in favour of nationhood and statehood (*v. inf.* 5).

3. Today

'Today Israel is a nation. For the first time since the destruction of Jerusalem in A.D. 70, the Jews have again a country, a state and a national existence' (S. Neill: *Christian Faith and Other Faiths* — OUP (1961), 1970, p. 25). As said above, the People has acquired a country and become a nation; it has fashioned articulate forms of independent self-government and is now again suddenly a state. What is to be made of this?[7]

The crucial question is: what right has the People to the land now again called Israel? Yaacov Herzog (*A People that Dwells Alone* — London, Weidenfeld & Nicolson, 1975, pp. 30ff.) replies to A. Toynbee's celebrated gibe that Jewish existence today is like a fossil which can be said neither to be dead nor alive, and in doing so addresses himself particularly to the charge that the Jews 'have no historical right' to the land they call Israel. (*a*) Jewish residence in Palestine has never at any time ceased. The People's independent and sovereign possession of land is a comparatively brief episode — less than 700 years, from conquest to exile, *c.* 1250 B.C. to *c.* 587 B.C. For another 600 years possession continued in a reduced and dependent manner under the suzerainty of the great powers which the tides of history swept one after another to pre-eminence. This condition ended abruptly in A.D. 70. But since then (or since 132), especially in Safed, Tiberias, Hebron and Jerusalem, some of the greatest religious thought and works of all time appeared, 'the Mishnah, the Jerusalem Talmud, the Midrash, the Targum, right down to the Shulhan Arukh, which is the basic code of Jewish law', during century after century of continuous residence. (*b*) During historical time, Palestine has been possessed by a nation and not merely occupied by people or nation, on only three occasions, twice under Jewish rule, and once by the Crusaders. For the rest, the land was dominated by a great succession of sovereign powers under whose suzerainty, benign or malevolent, the inhabitants of Palestine did no more than occupy or inhabit the land: under Hadrian, the Jews returned to Jerusalem and enjoyed tranquillity under Severus; 325: the advent of Christians, and Palestine fell into the Eastern half of the Roman Empire, Byzantium, a period marked by wars against the Persians and controversy between

Christian sects, *e.g.*, Athanasius and the Arians; 614: the Persians won control; 638: the Mohammedans ruled for 500 years, until the Crusaders (1100) for about a century; 1300: the Mameluke sovereignty; 1517: the Ottoman Turks brought a century of peace and corruption, until Napoleon[8] was defeated at Acre, the Turks were consolidated in power and Palestine was reduced to a desert (see Max I. Dimont: *Jews, God and History* — London, W. H. Allen, 1964, p. 393). (*c*) Throughout this long period of Dispersion, the People has cherished the hope and expectation of a return to the land — not equally in all Jews, but uninterruptedly by at least some. Here Toynbee's 'statute of limitations', which 'provides that a legal claim does expire after a certain time', simply does not apply. Such a 'statute' depends upon acquiescence of the parties concerned. This in other cases can be counted upon: Greeks lay no claim to the vast possessions of Alexander the Great, nor the Welsh to most of England; or for that matter the Algonquins to Quebec. In contrast, the Jews have never relinquished or diminished their claim to the land. So, when asked by the British Royal Commission headed by Lord Peel 1937: 'By what right do Jews claim possession of Palestine?', Chaim Weizmann replied simply: 'Memory is right — other nations too have occupied lands and then abandoned them: they did not remember; the Jews did and do' (Elon, *op. cit.*, p. 37). This uninterrupted bond between the People and the land is difficult to assess, principally because it is simply unique and defies categorisation with any other sociological or demographic phenomenon. But its existence cannot be denied. It is the reality that effectively distinguishes the People from other nations, and in particular from the kaleidoscope of Levantine groupings. (*d*) The validity of the claim of the People has received some degree of surprising acknowledgement. The series began with the Balfour Declaration 1917 and its promise of 'a home' for the Jewish People, understood by Weizmann as not meaning a 'state' and as not harming the rights and interests of the inhabitants (Herzog, *op. cit.*, p. 35). It continued in the action of the House of Lords, and then of the U.N. Arab acknowledgement can also be cited: Emir Feisal, undisputed leader of Arab nationalism, headed the Arab delegation to the Peace Conference at Versailles, and in a letter declared that he welcomed the Jews home.[9] (*e*) In a special class of justification must be placed the events of the 30s and 40s leading to the Holocaust. These injected a terrible urgency to the People's claim upon the land as a refuge, a startling clarity that only sovereign possession and statehood could safeguard that refuge, and a degree of consensus which, though not unanimous, rendered it a clearly majority view (see Herzog, *op. cit.*, p. 140; but the relevant literature is immense).

4. Theological or religious assessment

What has been said is a brief and incomplete survey of the secular evidence that supports the claim of the People to the land of Palestine today. There is, however, another range of evidence that needs to be reviewed: the People's claim is advocated also upon theological or religious grounds. 'If the nations of the world say to the Jews: Ye are robbers, you have stolen this land, then the Jews can reply: In the beginning God created the heaven and the earth: all the earth is the Lord's and he gave this land to Israel' (Herzog, *op. cit.*, borrowing from Rashi of Troyes (1040–1105), celebrated commentator on Bible and Talmud). With elemental simplicity this adds to the secular justification of the claim a divine dimension and so pleads the cause theologically: the presence of the People in Palestine today is *iure divino* (by Divine Right).[10]

(4.1) This theological justification of the claim does not deny the reality of secondary causes; nor is it impaired by the fact that about this justification Jewish opinion is deeply divided. First, the People saw the return to Jerusalem after the Exile as fulfilment of a divinely covenanted promise. But by another assessment it was contrived by Cyrus, who shrewdly calculated that a tribute-paying subject nation would be more profitable than an unproductive desert (see Dimont, *op. cit.*, p. 70). Bringing the matter up to date, the People shifted responsibility for the modern return to Palestine from God's shoulders to their own when, after 1800 years of passivity, Zionism deliberately put aside pacific waiting upon God and appealed to force and the arbitrament of war, and in 1948 (and earlier in a less decisive manner) took up arms to defend its existence in Palestine (see Dimont, *op. cit.*, p. 199). So Arthur Koestler (*Promise and Fulfilment, Palestine 1917–1949* — London, Macmillan, 1949, p. 220) believes that a single small-scale action determined 'whether a nation shall live or die' — not the divine intervention of God, but 'the knocking out of four [Egyptian] tanks [at the Gaza strip] at close quarters with primitive home-made explosives', which held up the Egyptian advance for 48 hours and denied them what would have been a decisive link-up with the other Arab armies advancing from the North. Christian belief similarly accommodates divine purpose and secondary causes: it holds with Peter (Acts 2:23) that Jesus of

Nazareth 'was given up' to the Jews 'by the deliberate will and plan of God', and that at the same time the Jews 'used heathen men to crucify and kill him'. Secondly, Jewish opinion is deeply divided on the issue whether a divine dimension is to be discerned in the return to Palestine; but neither does this difference impair the appeal to divine justification. One view certainly holds divine justification as bedrock conviction and fact, as in the already quoted 'the Lord gave this land to Israel' (*v. sup.*). The view is not confined to scholarly appreciation only: it is carried by Menachem Begin into the heart of political policy: 'Nobody has the right to tell me to stay in Judea or Samaria. The U.N. — what is that? international law — what is that? human rights — what is that? Right is divine, because it is given me by God, the Father of Abraham, Isaac and Jacob' (Christian Peace Conference, 'The Theological Background of the Middle East Conflict', I–II, 1980, p. 6). Another section of opinion simply denies the claim, and this on two quite different grounds. Kach, the right wing extremists of the 'Thus' movement, with a presence in Palestine but organised and financed from America, plead naked political expediency. In contrast, the Mea Shearim, the Naturei (or Neturei) Karta or Guardians of the City, argue quite differently. The divine dimension is by no means denied; but this particular manner of fulfilling the divine purpose is unacceptable, since it is not the Messiah that leads the advance. Of course too appeal to the divine dimension is also made with a frankly cynical or hypocritical pragmatism, in order to strengthen and absolutise a claim thought realistically to be based on purely secular grounds. But such division of opinion makes it no different from other people's differing views on issues of major importance: it argues decisively neither for nor against the validity of the appeal to *ius divinum*. Nor does cynicism introduce a decisive element: after all Kaiser Wilhelm's soldiers in World War I had 'Gott mit uns' engraved on their buttons; and as these lines are being written a slogan in the U.S. presidential election has just been coined and popularised: 'For God's sake vote for Reagan'.

(4.2) That affairs of this kind are interpreted in the light of a divine dimension must evoke the profound respect and admiration of Christians. Yaacov Herzog (*loc. cit.*, p. 54) continues: 'why should the rest of the world accept this evaluation? The answer is connected with one's outlook on history: whether it is an outlook of faith or a materialistic conception of history.' Here crystal clear is the affirmation that, beyond the natural world with its secular order and values, spiritual realities have their place, demanding recognition and appropriate implementation beyond all calculations of a materialistic or legal or even moral kind (*v. sup.* 4.1, Begin). Macaulay once said: 'whether injustice had or had not been committed was immaterial.... Just or unjust, (it) had taken place so long ago that to reverse it would be to unfix the foundations of society.' The aphorism could be used to dismiss summarily the claim of the People. But the force of this People's appeal to *ius divinum* derives its strength from springs more profound than Macaulay's pragmatism; and the spiritual values it invokes are not destroyed, reduced or diminished by the manifest inability of, *e.g.*, the Arabs to admit the argument based on them. Nor is greater credence to be accorded to the position outlined by Christian Peace Conference (*op. cit.*, p. 2), which bluntly declares: 'no theological significance is to be attributed to the State of Israel'. This is a defensible position. But its presentation here is predictably infested with anti-colonial, anti-imperialist, anti-capitalist claptrap that affronts reason and wearies patience. In any case, it operates with an outright rejection of any divine dimension: it argues (if argue it can be said to bother to do) that the People's occupation of Palestine is not *iure divino*, not because such a dimension is inapplicable to this particular case, but because no such dimension exists. The argument can be challenged only on grounds lying within a universe of discourse in which spiritual values and a divine dimension are recognised to have reality and a paramount place. This is a presupposition that Christians accept; and they accordingly ask: in this kind of universe of discourse, has the People's claim validity?

(4.3) The acquisition of land and sovereignty, and so of nationhood and statehood, evidently exposes the People to hazards and temptations. It is told (Herzog, *op. cit.*, p. 145) of Baron Rothschild that 'after winning his battle of many years to have the disabilities to members of the Jewish faith removed from the House of Lords, he slipped away from the hierarchy of Britain congratulating him on the achievement and was to be found prostrate in prayer in a small synagogue in the Whitechapel ghetto of East London, his lips murmuring: "Would that this freedom shall not mean the diminution of our faith"'. The hazard is that when a conviction admits props that are adventitious its proper and innate strength may be eroded and in the end replaced by reliance on the props; and when the passage of time renders the props insecure, the original conviction has the strength of only dry bones, until vivified by a new breath of life.

The history of the People illustrates the general principle. For the graph rises in a majestic curve from the beginnings in Egyptian slavery, through the vicissitudes of nomadism in the desert, to possession of the promised land and nationhood, and further with kingship to statehood. From that proud apex, the precipitous decline begins, arrested only partly and temporarily until final Dispersion.[11]

(4.4) It would appear incontestable that the initial occupation of the land was prescribed in the covenant and included in the purpose of God, and consequently that the assumption of nationhood by the People was divinely sanctioned. The evidence of Section 2 above cannot be read otherwise. It would further seem that the lesson this teaches is *either* that possession is to be reiterated with similar *ius divinum*; *or* the initial possession of the promised land is a temporary non-repeatable interlude, designed to demonstrate the frailty of adventitious props and their dispensability in the divine purpose.

(4.4.1) On the first interpretation, that the initial possession of land and acquisition of nationhood and statehood are to be repeated, the People's possession of Palestine today is such a divinely-willed repetition. The justification of this understanding that comes most easily to mind is simply that what God wills he eternally wills: with God there is 'no repentance'. It is, however, not easy to rest with so simple an appreciation of the facts. For one thing the argument might carry those who accept it unexpectedly far — farther than they would care to be taken. If there is to be repetition, possession today should mean the total exclusion of the 'Palestinians', together with the total possession of the area occupied in O.T. times, 'from Dan to Beersheba', and arguably Jerusalem and some trans-Jordan territory. The day before these lines were written, Menachem Begin uttered again the claim to possession of the Golan Heights. This consequence is welcomed by some and the militancy of much Israeli action gives fateful expression to it. But it is not easy to accept an interpretation that entails such painful consequences for, *e.g.*, the Palestinians.[12] Even if the Israelis stop short of putting the inhabitants to the sword, the severity with which they are treated and their expropriation operated and maintained is hard to justify morally.

There must also be noted an invincible imparity between the O.T. situation and the present day which makes impossible exact repetition. It cannot be doubted that possession of the homeland in Palestine means much to all Jews. This factor is of great importance, but an evident present-day feature makes the assessment of it extremely difficult. In contrast to the initial occupation of the promised land, present-day Palestine cannot contain all the People; nor in fact does by far the greater part of it have the faintest desire or intention to return. 'Next year in Jerusalem' — when once again the possibility of realising it is theirs, most of the People deliberately and contentedly ignore it. This consequence of Dispersion is irreversible.[13]

(4.4.2) The second interpretation sees in the initial divinely willed possession of the land a lesson to be learned, not an example to be followed. The phasing out of nationhood and of statehood left and leaves unimpaired the People as such. For most of its history the People has existed in this exposed and vulnerable condition, which Dispersion has not created but simply aggravated. The People persists, stripped to the bare essentials with which it began, and its reality is thereby enhanced. That it has today equipped itself again with land and sovereign statehood is theologically irrelevant. Something more must be said about this.

5. *God's purpose and the People*

The question: 'what part does the People play today in God's purpose?' cannot be discussed at length in this essay. The concern is with the tie between People and land, since this lies at the base of the complex designated by the title. But neither can the question be entirely ignored.

There is for the People today no discernible rôle that would require, or be enhanced by, or achieve richer fulfilment in, possession of the land and the assumption of nationhood and statehood implied. God's 'calling (is) irrevocable' (Rom. 11:39). This calling is to witness to God before the world and to Jesus Christ who is the action of God in the world. This calling is directed first to the People. With the advent of Jesus Christ, the Church emerges out of the heart of this People, and this calling is directed to the Church. But if the calling is irrevocable, the People is still encompassed by it. But its rôle now must be different both from that of its heir which is the Church, and also from that with which it was charged before the advent of Jesus Christ. The Church takes over the rôle of witness in a retrospective sense: the Messiah has come. The People's former witness: the Messiah will come, no longer has meaning and must change. The new rôle of the People can only be to witness to the condition of mankind without Christ.

About the rôle thus projected, three observations may be made. (a) The witness is not only anthropological: it is also christological, since it is precisely this condition that Christ assumed and remedied. The People witnesses still to God in his entirety — to God who judges and also, refractedly, to God who is gracious. It keeps before the eyes of the world a visible and earthly representation of the two haunting symbols from Old and New Testaments: the scapegoat of Lev. 3:12, 16:18, and the lamb slain from the foundation of the world of Rev. 5:6, 13:8. (b) Its anthropological witness is to the precariousness of man's existence from which he is always being rescued by the work of Jesus Christ. The People confronts the world with a living representation of the pilgrim character accorded by Heb. 11:13 to it, though unacknowledged by it, and to all men of faith. (c) It is evident that in saying this one runs the risk of being appallingly misunderstood — of being interpreted as rationalising, excusing, and even justifying the frightful and continuing chapter of the Christian story entitled anti-Semitism. To ward off this accusation, one can only appeal to the example of Peter (Acts 2:23), who has no intention of excusing the actions leading to the crucifixion when he places them within 'the deliberate will and plan of God'. It is better in this way to make sense of the inhumanity which Christians have inflicted upon the People than to envelop it in silence.[14]

6. What now?

Yaacov Herzog takes for his book a theme from Num. 23:9, where the outsider goy Balaam is inspired to expound the essential character of the Jews: 'I see a people that dwells alone'. The People has lived without intermission with the tension that description connotes: it has cherished the thought of dwelling alone, and it has hankered after being like other nations. The recurrent and unresolved issue of 'assimilation' is a clear example, even if it is on a lower key and lacks the heroic overtones of aspiration to be nation and state. For some the burden of dwelling alone is becoming too much. A. Koestler (op. cit., p. 332f.) utters a heart-rending cry, that to remain a separate race is an 'untenable anachronism': 'Now that the mission of the Wandering Jew is completed, he must discard the knapsack ("we seem to carry anti-Semitism in our knapsacks wherever we go") and cease to be an accomplice in his own destruction. If not for his own sake, then for that of his children and his children's children. The fumes of the death chambers still linger over

Europe: there must be an end to every Calvary.'[15] His judgement is that, as the physical Jewish characteristics are in process of disappearing, so 'within a generation or two Israel will have become an entirely "unJewish" country' (p. 330). If this were to happen, and if at the same time the process of 'assimilation' were to continue to its logical end, the world would be rid of a component of its life that both shames it of its ineradicable inhumanity and evokes that inhumanity. Mankind would be more at peace with itself. But in fact men have no right to a 'good conscience', as even 1 Pet. 3:16 rightly interpreted tells us.

With the eventual, perhaps eschatological, outcome of the 'Jewish question' this essay cannot concern itself.[16] But the People of the Jews has as above interpreted a present rôle in the purpose of God which provides it with a *raison d'être* clearer and more profoundly splendid than can be discerned for any other single people, nation, or state.

NOTES

1. *The People* will usually be employed to denote the Jews or Israel; *Palestine*, despite some anachronistic inaccuracy, will mean the 'promised land' or Israel. *Possess* will mean outright sovereign tenure of land; *occupy* will denote living in the land under alien sovereignty (*cf. p.c.* the more recent usage); *inhabit* will be used of peoples originally occupying or possessing the land whose status is altered by invaders.
2. Even this unpretentious statement is inexact. The Jewish scholar Georges Friedmann (*The End of the Jewish People?* — London, Hutchinson, 1962, pp. 226 f.) 'came to the conclusion that it was hardly possible to speak of a "Jewish people"' (see Lucas Grollenberg: *Palestine Comes First* — London, S.C.M. Press, 1980, pp. 113 f.). (Grollenberg is a Dutch Dominican.)
3. The tragic march of the chosen People precipitated round Jahve a splendid regrouping of all their energies and hopes.... The People has become the community of those who belong to Jahve by the observation of the Law.
4. For an angry repudiation of this view of the Jewish 'return', see E. W. Said: *The Question of Palestine* — London, Routledge & Kegan Paul, 1980, p. 87 *et passim*.
5. Menuhin's father reproached Yehudi for spending time in learning the recorder while the temple remained unrestored!
6. R. Menahem of Galilee (beginning of Christian era): 'One day all sacrifices will cease; only the thankoffering will not cease' (*Encyclopedia of Religion and Ethics*, art. 'Worship — Christian', p. 763b).
7. It seems that no question concerning the Jews can now be raised for the first time. The twelfth-century poet and philosopher Judah Halevi scrutinises the question of Israel and land in *Kuzari* — see F. E. Talmage: *Disputation and Dialogue* — New York, Ktav Publishing House, 1975, pp. 160 ff. for a summary.

8. Elon, *op. cit.*, p. 288, recalls that under the pyramids Napoleon exhorted his troops to remember the 4000 years of human history they signified; and that at a recent Massada commemoration the speaker reduced this to insignificance by claiming that it was 4000 years of Jewish history that were memorialised.

9. The authenticity and even the existence of this so-called 'Frankfurter letter' has been challenged (see Grollenberg, *op. cit.*, p. 37).

10. In the twelfth century Joseph Kimhi (*c.* 1110–*c.* 1170), a Provençal Jewish scholar, gave in his *Book of the Covenant* an account of his disputations with Christians on the theme — the first Jewish anti-Christian polemic to be written (see F. E. Talmage (ed.): *Disputation and Dialogue* — New York, Ktav Publishing House, 1975, pp. 9, 104, 159 ff.). The dispute centred on certain biblical texts, especially Gen. 49:10 and Dan. 9:24 ff., of which there were not only different interpretations but also variant versions. The form given to the question is the loss of Jewish sovereignty. Jewish interpretation as exemplified by Kimhi held that sovereignty was lost with David; the traditional Christian view, that it was terminated by the advent of Jesus. In this complicated interchange (in A. Posnanski: *Schiloh* — Leipzig, 1904, the account occupies two volumes!) the issue is not whether termination has taken place, but only how or with whom. But the larger issue lies dormant even here: if with David, then it is conceivable that sovereignty might by reversal of fortune be subsequently resumed; if with Jesus the Messiah, there can be no resumption. It was complained that Jerome used both interpretation and textual conjecture to prove that the land truly promised is not on earth but in heaven.

11. A close parallel in the history of the Church has been recently suggested (G. Noel: *The Anatomy of the Catholic Church* — London, Hodder & Stoughton, 1980). The book traces the Church's history through four stages: The Community that became the Church; The Church that became an empire; The Fascist Phase; and 'The Age of Constantine is dead'. Perhaps 'the pre-Constantine period deserves our continued reflection' (p. 15): the Church's future path may lie in the direction of a recovery of the simplicity of that earlier era. In any case the prognosis is that renewal will come, since, 'as at Vatican II, the Spirit can break through at the most unexpected junctures' (p. 274).

A parallel nearer home may be ventured. The Church of Scotland, perhaps in the exhaustion induced by prolonged internal and external strife, in 1707 made provision for its Establishment 'to continue without any alteration to all succeeding generations' and for the sovereign to promise maintenance of Presbyterianism in the Coronation oath; and in the area of doctrine in 1647 and again deliberately in 1921 and 1929 tied itself to the Westminster Confession of Faith as principal standard, subordinate only to Holy Scripture.

12. See E. W. Said, *op. cit. passim*, especially chapter II ii. His argument has great weight, but is flawed by the closely dependent relationship alleged of Zionism upon 'a European *mission civilisatrice*' and nineteenth-century colonialism (p. 18). So too Grollenberg (*op. cit.,* chapter 3) complains that the founding of the state is 'a "colonial" enterprise': 'The tragedy of the state of Israel is that it was planned and prepared for in a Europe which thought in colonial terms, but came into being in a world that had rejected colonialism' (p. 22). This appreciation must be rejected: in no ordinary sense can the new Israel be regarded as an exercise in colonialism. To colonise is to settle without right or invitation in a 'new

country' (O.E.D.), usually in order to exploit its resources or utilise facilities it makes available. There is no doubt that Britain fully realised the potential advantages of a Jewish occupation of Palestine and was accordingly glad to accept a U.N. mandate. Thus interests similar to those advanced by colonising were certainly being served. But the occupation by Jews of Palestine was quite unlike any other colonial enterprise in that they deemed themselves to have a right to return. That this right was not acknowledged by the Arabs makes no difference to the situation. One of the complexities is that it was precisely the coming of the Jews that initiated, or at least stimulated, an Arab nationalism in Palestine which could only see their coming as indistinguishable from colonialism. Here, as so often, the Jews trail an element of the incommensurable across the pathway of an uncomprehending and vaguely resentful world.

13. Such 'armchair Zionism' is no modern phenomenon. In the twelfth century the poet, philosopher and Rabbi Judah Halevi, in his masterpiece *Kuzari*, gives a romanticised account of the conversion to Judaism of the king of the Khazar nation in southern Russia. Halevi cunningly executes the indoctrination of the king, until he is ready to accept Judaism in principle. Then the Rabbi 'refers almost casually to Eretz Israel as God's country. The king is taken aback. He had, heaven knows, enough trouble with the concept of God's people: must he contend with God's country as well?' Then he turns the tables on the Rabbi and reproaches him: if 'sabbaths, festivals and numerous other commandements can be observed perfectly only in the Holy Land', why does he not go there? At the end of the work the Rabbi does indeed make the pilgrimage; and his 'exceeding tender hold upon the dust of Eretz Israel brought him more joy than all the gilded castles of Spain' (see F. E. Talmage, *op. cit.*, pp. 160 ff.).

14. K. Barth (*Church Dogmatics*, II 205 ff.) understands the People as witnessing to (*a*) the judgement of God, (*b*) the obduracy and misery of man, and (*c*) the sentence and punishment God himself endured. He can properly be criticised for allowing the judgement and the mercy of God to fall apart (like Calvin in the doctrine of predestination) and consequently appearing to represent the People's witness as only, or at least primarily, to God's judgement. This encourages the terrible misunderstanding mentioned above, as F. E. Talmage exemplifies (*op. cit.*, p. 38): 'it seems that as in the past... — the very misery and suffering of European Jewry is called upon as a witness to Christianity ... on this topic the thinking of a Christian anti-nazi and that of a Christian nazi are not very far apart'.

15. M. Buber offers a different appreciation. Retorting to Gerhard Kittel (see Talmage, *op. cit.*, pp. 53 f.) he declares that 'the "wandering Jew" is a figure of Christian legend, not a Jewish figure'; and he continues: 'Authentic Jewry is ever aware that *in the very next moment* the promise may be fulfilled and its wandering may end. It does not believe that it is ordered to affirm the Dispersion, but believes that it must prepare itself in the Dispersion for the ingathering. It knows of no "tragedy willed by God" which it must needs recognise, but knows only the mercy which calls man to his work.'

16. The alternative options are set out with fine clarity by S. Neill, *op. cit.*, pp. 23 ff.

C

Israel after Auschwitz

JAKOB JOCZ

In this paper 'Israel' signifies the whole Jewish people and not only the Israeli State. 'Auschwitz' is not a geographical location but stands for the mind-boggling tragedy which befell European Jewry under Hitler.

The extent of the tragedy in sheer magnitude must be regarded as the greatest calamity which overtook world-Jewry in its long and checkered history. There is hardly a Jewish family which has not been affected by the Holocaust either in personal loss of dear ones or in mental anguish.

Traditionally, *tisha be-Av* (9th day of Av) has come to be associated with the great calamities in Jewish history: the destruction of the first temple under Nebuchadnezzar (586 B.C.); the fall of Jerusalem and the destruction of the second temple in the Roman war (A.D. 70); the defeat of Bar Kokhba and the fall of Betar (A.D. 135). Even the expulsion from Spain in 1492 is sometimes associated with this fatal date. Pious Jews observe the day with a 24-hour fast and special prayers (*cf.* J. J. Petuchowski, 'The Ninth of Ab Today', *Jewish Chronicle*, July 20, 1960). But now an additional day of mourning has been added to the Jewish calendar: *Yom ha-Shoah* (The Day of Destruction). In the State of Israel it is observed as a national day of mourning for the victims of the Holocaust on 27 Nisan (the first month of the Jewish calendar, spring). It is also the Remembrance Day of the uprising of the Warsaw ghetto. (In the Diaspora the date is April 19.) In addition, the Israeli rabbinate has decreed that Tevet 10th (10th month of the calendar) be observed in memory of those numerous victims whose names remain unknown. In many instances whole families have perished so that there is no one left to recite the mourner's *kaddish* for them.

It is estimated that about six million Jewish men, women and children were massacred at the hands of the Germans. Even when allowing for hyperbole, the numbers are such as to stagger the imagination. The usual term 'to decimate' is here totally inapplicable as one third of world-Jewry has been wiped off the face of the earth under the most hair-raising circumstances. The nightmare is such as to make it unbelievable.

Walter Laqueur cites the case of the U.S.A. ambassador to Sweden, Hershel Johnson, who reported to Washington (April 5/1943) that of the 450,000 inhabitants of the Warsaw ghetto only 45,000 were left. 'So fantastic a story told by this German eye-witness to his friend, my informant, that I hesitate to make it an official report.' Laqueur finds the ambassador's apologetic tone puzzling: 'It is difficult to understand Johnson's hesitancy', he wrote (*Commentary*, Dec. 1979, 44). But is it?

Not only non-Jews but many Jews found the tales leaking out from occupied Europe incredible. Most people put it down to war propaganda. The German radio called it *Greuelmärchen* — fairy tales of cruelty to embarrass the enemy. Lying in wartime is a common practice. We know from diaries of Jewish victims that they themselves doubted their story would be believed by the world outside. Traditionally Jews held Germans in high esteem. They found it impossible to believe that the nation of Bach, Kant and Goethe could perpetrate such crimes as burning women and children. The facts are such as to make language fail. Elie Wiesel, himself an inmate, tells us that no novels, poems, films, plays, documentaries, are adequate to convey the real story of Auschwitz. We would need a new language to express the inexpressible (*A Jew Today*, 1978, pp. 197 f.). Wiesel insists that neither those who were not there, nor those who were in the camps are equipped to convey the 'shade of shades' that was Auschwitz: 'one would have to invent a new vocabulary, a new language to say what no human being has ever said' (*ibid.*, p. 200). Those who write on the subject have difficulty, hence they either trivialize or give the impression of hyperbole. Perhaps Walter Jens's description is the best-fitting: 'Nacht der Nächte, die Henkerzeit — the Night of Nights, the time of the hangman' (*Das Buch Nelly Sachs*, ed. H. Holmqvist, 1968, p. 381). Theodor Adorno's reaction to the story of Auschwitz is often quoted: 'nach Auschwitz kann man nicht dichten — after Auschwitz one can no more write poetry'.

The shock experienced by the Jewish community as a result of the Holocaust is still deeply felt; the more so as it happened in the twentieth century and was perpetrated by the most educated European nation. Many of the ring-leaders in the Nazi party were university graduates reared in German culture. This fact raises fundamental questions. Jews are in search of an answer to two basic problems: Where was God and where was man?

1. *Where was God*

The question regarding God's absence occurs in much of Jewish literature. Many Jewish writers have taken a radical position: God is not. A leader among the radicals is Richard L. Rubenstein, formerly a liberal rabbi and now professor of religion at Florida State University.

Rubenstein's reaction to Auschwitz is definite and uncompromising: to believe in God after Auschwitz is not only unreasonable but indecent: 'we have lost all hope, consolation and illusion'. History means chaos and the universe makes no sense. Man is left an orphan and the values he needs he must create for himself. There is no higher instance of appeal. This does not mean that religion is at an end. Man must reconstruct a religion without God. (*After Auschwitz*, 1960). There are many intellectuals who take a similar view.

An even more difficult problem arises for the still believing Jew. His quest of a theodicy after Auschwitz puts a heavy burden upon his conscience. The orthodox Jew is hard pressed to square the facts of Auschwitz with what he has been taught to believe about the God of Israel. Rabbi Eliezer Berkovits writes from an orthodox point of view. His theodicy is supposedly the first effort on the part of an orthodox Jew to justify God's ways before men (*Faith After the Holocaust*, 1973).

Rabbi Berkovits is sorely tried to account for the disaster which befell God's chosen people in view of His goodness and His omnipotence. In order to do so he falls back upon human freedom, but has to admit that this is insufficient to exonerate God from responsibility as Lord and Creator. Yet in spite of this he holds that no Jew dare doubt God's presence, 'though he is unable to set limits to the duration and intensity of his absence'. He admits, however, the difficulty to justify the ways of providence except by faith: 'even if no answer can be found, we would still be left with the only alternative with which Job was left, *i.e.*, contending with God while trusting Him, of questioning while believing, inquiring with our minds, yet knowing in our hearts' (*op. cit.*, p. 136). Rabbi Michael Wyschograd, another orthodox Jew, takes a similar position (*cf.* 'Auschwitz: Beginning of a New Era?', *Tradition,* Fall, 1977, pp. 63 ff.).

So heroic an act of faith, contradicted by experience, is not given to many.

An outstanding figure caught between faith and despair is Elie Wiesel. By reason of his personal experience of four concentration camps and his great literary ability he occupies an almost prophetic position in the spiritual crisis of our age.

Elie Wiesel was born at Sighet, a small Hungarian town, in 1928. He comes from an orthodox family and received his early education in a *Yeshiva* (Talmud School). At the age of 15 he was taken together with his father to Auschwitz. Both his parents and his younger sister perished at the camp. He was liberated from Buchenwald on April 11, 1945, and emigrated to France where he studied at the Sorbonne, concentrating on literature, psychology and philosophy. In France he became correspondent for an Israeli newspaper. Later he was sent to the United Nations headquarters in New York to work for the same paper. He was appointed professor of Jewish Studies at City College, New York in 1972 and four years later he assumed a professorship at Boston University. As a journalist he used to write in Hebrew. His books are written in French and translated by his wife.

The dominating ingredient in Wiesel's literary output is his experience of Auschwitz. Like Albert Camus, Wiesel is the rebel *par excellence*. He has a perennial quarrel with God. Wiesel has been well described as the Job of the twentieth century. One of his students, Michael Berenbaum, writes: 'Wiesel refuses to relieve God of his responsibility. Both Wiesel's love for Israel and his respect for the God that Israel revered precludes' the possibility of a theodicy. The traditional explanation *mipnei hata'enu* — because of our sins we are exiled (*cf.* Singer's Prayerbook, 264) is inapplicable in this case — the massacre of children cannot be justified under any circumstances. Thus the once God-fearing boy emerged from the concentration camp a tortured man confronting the Void. (*Cf.* Michael Berenbaum, *The Vision of the Void*, Theological Reflections on the Works of Elie Wiesel, 1979).

Berenbaum tells us that Wiesel's 'overwhelming despair' led him to adopt a radical position regarding God and man. He suggests a close kinship between Rubenstein and Wiesel. There is however a difference: though Wiesel is described as 'the theologian of the Void', his nihilism is not absolute. Wiesel's revolt is that of the disheartened believer and not of the renegade (*Cf. Souls of Fire*, 1972, p. 111).

There is reason to suspect that Berenbaum overstresses Wiesel's vision of the Void. Unlike Berkovits, Wiesel is unable to affirm the wisdom and providence of God. But this is not an outright denial of God's existence, only of His absence. Wiesel's deepest problem is the silence of God. He accuses God of indifference. Whereas Rubenstein offers a definitive answer: God is not; for Wiesel it remains an open question. This becomes evident from his play *The Trial of God*, 1979.

The setting is a small Russian town after a pogrom and the date is February 25, 1646, on the festival of Purim. The Jewish community has been massacred except the innkeeper and his daughter. She was raped by the mob. Three *purimspieler* arrive on the scene to make fun as is customary on the day of Purim, but the innkeeper is not in the mood for hilarity. At his suggestion they constitute themselves into a court of law to put God on trial. The innkeeper assumes the rôle of prosecutor but there is difficulty in finding somebody to act in defence of the accused. At last a stranger turns up by the name of Sam, who agrees to act as attorney.

Berish the innkeeper: 'I have resigned from God. Let Him look for another innkeeper, let Him find another people — I am through with Him!' The reason he offers: God is merciless and unreliable; he regards mentioning God's mercy as an insult: 'Speak of His cruelty instead'. For Berish, God is an enemy who takes sides with Israel's enemies. Here is the indictment: 'either He is responsible or He is not. If He is, let's judge Him; if He is not, let Him stop judging us.' Berish cannot understand a God who massacres 'His friends and allies.... He could have taken care of those who loved Him with all their hearts and believed in Him — in Him alone!' Berish is puzzled by His 'hostility, cruelty and indifference'. 'Either He dislikes His chosen people, or He does not care about them — period!'

Sam's defence is on traditional lines: 'If God chooses not to answer, He must have reasons. God is God, and His will is independent from ours — as is His reasoning.'

Meanwhile while the court is in session, a new storm is brewing, the village is preparing for a renewed pogrom, though there are no Jews left. A priest appears to warn of the danger. He vaguely suggests conversion as a means of escape but the innkeeper will not hear of it: 'My sons and my fathers perished without betraying their faith, I can do no less'.

Sam the attorney immediately reacts to the contradiction: 'You baffle me. You speak of faith, of sacrifice, of martyrdom. Have you forgotten what you said?...'

At this point the trial is interrupted by the shriek of the mob outside. The verdict is unannounced. The play is inconclusive. However there is an additional twist to it: Sam the stranger turns out to be Satan in disguise — an obvious hint to the book of Job.

Even the doubting, the rebelling Jew refuses to betray his faith. In another context Wiesel tells the story of a non-believing Jew who is being pressed by an officer at the concentration camp to blaspheme the Name of God and the non-believer refuses at the cost of his life (*cf. A Jew Today*, 1978, p. 130).

The Trial of God well dramatises the spiritual dilemma in which not only Wiesel but many thinking Jews find themselves. As for Wiesel, 'he stands at the brink with respect to God. He loves Him and hates Him, he fears Him and yet tries to live without Him'; Berenbaum adds: 'Wiesel is torn by the ambivalence as he confronts the void' (*op. cit., p.* 202).

Such 'ambivalence' is characteristic for a large section of Jewry today. There is total disorientation regarding Jewish destiny and the meaning of Jewish and world history. But it runs against the grain for Jews to accept Rubenstein's total nihilism: 'omnipotent nothingness is the Lord of all creation' (*cf. op. cit.,* pp. 154, 225; also his *Morality and Eros*, 1970, pp. 183 ff.). Even Wiesel cautions against despair and regards Israel's exile as a mystery which defies explanation. He writes: 'to me, the essence of Jewish history is mystical and not rational' (*A Jew Today*, p. 158).

2. *Where was man?*

The case with man is even worse. Traditionally Judaism leans heavily towards humanism. It takes the *imago Dei* concept seriously. Man is the bearer of the image of God. Judaism denies the concept of original sin. Man is born blameless and pure and with the ability to keep the Law. He therefore needs no salvation, only repentance. The keyword is *teshuvah* (turning to God) and not conversion in the Christian sense. Every man is his own redeemer. The secular form of self-redemption is aestheticism: emphasis upon education, culture, the fine arts. This was the characteristic mark of assimilated German Jewry. They adored German culture, music and literature. They felt at home with Goethe's dictum: 'edel ist der Mensch, hilfreich und gut — man is noble, helpful and good'. The collapse of faith in man equals the collapse of faith in God.

The museum of the Holocaust in Jerusalem, *Yad va-Shem* with its vast collection of photographs, documents and exhibits recording the tragedy called 'Auschwitz', stands as a devastating monument to human degradation. The dream which turned into a nightmare discredited once and for all every form of facile humanism. The lie about man, Wiesel expresses in the words of a father from beyond the grave addressing his son: 'we were naïve, innocent, so innocent that we refused to believe that evil exists. We were incapable of believing that human beings could fall so low' (*op. cit.*, p. 140). The rude awakening to the stark facts about man's capacity for evil is at the heart of the spiritual crisis which tears at the soul of contemporary man. Auschwitz is not merely a Jewish tragedy, it is the tragedy of mankind. Humanity is profoundly involved in the Holocaust. Those who perished in the gas ovens of Auschwitz were human beings put to death by other human beings. Richard Rubenstein is well aware of the impact of the tragedy: 'Although Jewish history is replete with disaster, none has been so radical in its total import as the Holocaust. Our images of God, man, and the moral order have been permanently impaired. No Jewish theology will possess even a remote degree of relevance to contemporary Jewish life if it ignores the question of God and the death camps' (*After Auschwitz*, p. X). The effect of Auschwitz stretches far beyond the Jewish people and affects the rest of humanity. Wiesel rightly says 'The Holocaust has left its mark on more than one generation, in a way mankind came close to suicide in Auschwitz' (*A Jew Today*, p. 183). He is aware that a radical change has taken place in the human situation; that the war against Jews is a war against mankind. 'Now we know that all hate means self-hate, that the annihilation of the Jews is bound to end in self-destruction' (*ibid.*, p. 182).

Nelly Sachs, a typical German Jewess, assimilated to German culture, found her way back to the Jewish people as a result of the persecution to become the threnodist of the holocaust. Her theme is Death — the death of her people. She says of herself: 'der Tod war mein Lehrmeister — death was my teacher'. Her elegy: *In the Habitations of Death* begins with the verse:

> O the chimneys
> Upon the cleverly devised habitations of death.

Her cultural retreat is indicated by the confession: 'In the choirs of others/ you have been singing/ one tone higher/ or one tone deeper'. She now discovered that neither she nor her people were in tune with the choir. Theirs was a song in a different key. The remarkable thing about Nelly Sachs is, that though singing about Death, she refuses to yield to total despair. Her motto is taken from the book of Job: 'and after my skin has been destroyed, then without my flesh I shall see God'. But she knows of the lonesomeness of man: 'So einsam ist der Mensch'. Her sadness is without bitterness and this itself is a triumph of the spirit: 'even death still celebrates life'. Her mystical faith has helped her over the precipice.

The case of Victor E. Frankl is equally unusual. Unlike Nelly Sachs, he went through the agonies and humiliation of a concentration camp, yet emerged unbroken in spirit. He met God in the camp and as a result discovered the importance of meaning for human life. As professor of psychiatry at Vienna he is the exponent of Logotherapy — healing by helping patients to discover meaning to their lives. In his therapeutic system suffering is an integral element. Others have not been so fortunate.

Jewish intellectuals agonize over the causes which led to the tragedy of Auschwitz. It is generally maintained that Christian anti-Semitism is the root of the Holocaust. The late professor of history, Jules Isaac, persuasively, proved that the Holocaust is the end result of the Church's teaching of contempt for the Jewish people. Such contempt predisposed Gentiles to look upon the Jew as an inferior being, a fact which was exploited by the Nazis for their own ends. Prof. Isaac reduces the traditional view to three main points: 1. The Jewish exile is the result of divine punishment; 2. Judaism is a degenerate religion; 3. the Jewish people is guilty of deicide.

It would be difficult to contradict Prof. Isaac's contention. Luther's outburst against the Jews was no small factor in influencing the populace against them. Julius Streicher, the fiend of Jew-baiting, made full use of Luther's anti-Jewish tracts. Hitler and his henchmen found well-prepared ground for the Final Solution. But it is a mistake to identify the motivation behind 'Christian' anti-Judaism with Nazi Jew-baiting. There is a frightening suspicion behind Hitler's extermination policy, namely that it was not ideologically motivated at all. In spite of all the racist mythology, sustained by German propaganda, the reason for the Final Solution was cool and calculated logic: the population in the occupied lands must give way to the expansion of the German race. The liquidation of redundant people began with the Jews, who are usually the first victims. Raul Hilberg and Hannah Arendt have seen more clearly than the rest of Jewish leaders the real reason behind the Holocaust. Berenbaum puts it like this: 'the Jews became chosen victims not only because of the tradition of anti-Semitism but also because they were economically superfluous to Germany.... One logical method of eliminating a superfluous population is by extermination' (*op. cit.*, p. 197). This frightening but logical conclusion gives substance to the old adage: *homo homini lupus* — man is to the other man a wolf. Cold-blooded, calculated murder, devoid of all ideological pretence, reveals the spectre of an abyss worse than hell. Auschwitz, therefore, confronts us with stark and unmitigated evil.

Jews were not the only victims. Poles, Ukrainians, Russians, Gypsies, communists; Jehovah's Witnesses, were all part of the extermination scheme. All this in the name of *Lebensraum* for the German people. To speak of anti-Semitism in the Nazi context is to misinterpret the facts. To reduce the evil of Auschwitz to mere 'anti-Semitism' is a refinement which makes it innocuous. Such depravity of human nature is difficult to contemplate. (*Cf.* David Stern, 'Imagining the Holocaust', *Commentary*, July, 1976.)

The absence of God and the absence of man are logically related. The believing Jew asks: Where was God? The secularised Jew asks: Where was man? Because man has abysmally failed God has become a casualty. The result is an encounter with evil as the overwhelming Jewish experience of our age. (*Cf.* Louis Jacobs, 'The Problem of Evil in our Time', *Judaism*, Summer, 1968, pp. 347 ff.). Not that Judaism was unfamiliar with evil before the Holocaust. But it believed that rational man can cope with it and control it (*cf.* Gen. 4:7). Since Auschwitz this is now in doubt. The ugly face of evil stares at modern man from every corner. Its influence is all-pervasive. Eugene B. Borowitz quotes a passage by Irving Kristol which well indicates the mood of our era. Kristol writes: 'the spiritual distress of the modern world does not arise merely because man perversely chooses to do evil rather than good. If it were so uncomplicated as all that, present day Judaism ... would have an answer right at hand. The horror that breathes into our faces is the realization that evil may come by doing good — not merely *intending* to do good, but by *doing* it' ('Crisis Theology in the Jewish Community', *Commentary*, July, 1961).

In such a world no one can be trusted. Israeli policy whether towards Arabs or allies reflects this crisis of trust. Berenbaum describes Wiesel's reflection on the State of Israel: 'Despair toward his fellow man and toward other nations has led the Israeli to a necessary self-reliance and may provide the only possibility for survival' (*op.* cit., pp. 159 ff.). Doubt in the trustworthiness of man is a sad and disturbing factor which sours human relationships. This is the way Wiesel sees the present situation: 'The bankruptcy of the West, the abdication of man, the betrayal of the liberals, the failure of culture, the silence of God' (*A Jew Today*, p. 41).

3. *The unresolved dilemma of guilt*

The game of identifying the culprit is a futile enterprise. Rubenstein blames God, if he exists. Wiesel blames both God and man including his own people who did not do enough to rescue the perishing. Berkovits puts the onus upon human freedom. There are Jews who blame themselves for their complacency and short-sightedness. Others simply blame the Germans as a nation of murderers who did what no other people in history has ever done — commit genocide.

To mark out the Germans as specially evil is to delude ourselves. We know from history and experience that given the circumstances similar crimes have been committed and are committed by other people the world over, though not with such precision and on such a scale. The philosopher Immanuel Kant recognised the fact that the propensity for evil is ever present in the best of men and that its power is universal. He says, evil is 'interwoven with human nature' (*cf.* also Gen. 6:5; Jer. 17:9). Man is a dangerous creature. The biochemist, Robert S. de Ropp, describes man as the fiercest killer in the animal world, *homo ferox*. He is the more dangerous because of his skill; he calls man 'an overbrained pest'. Man without God is capable of any crime his fevered imagination can devise. The real anguish arises when we discover that man with God is equally vulnerable. Wiesel asks what one is to make of the fact 'that there were those who went to confession between massacres'. He states that among the S.S. there was a large proportion of believers 'who remained faithful to their Christian ties to the end'. He puzzles over the fact that so many of the torturers came from Christian families. Their non-German collaborators, the Poles, Ukrainians, Lithuanians, White Russians, Hungarians, etc. had a Christian tradition behind them. All these lent a hand in the massacre of Jews (*op. cit.*, pp. 11 f.).

Auschwitz casts a dark shadow over traditional Christianity.

Admittedly there were faithful and heroic souls who risked their lives in the rescue of Jews. But their number was infinitesimal compared to the masses of so-called Christians. Wiesel pays tribute to the 'several dozen bishops and priests, (the) few hundred men and women in all of Europe', but bewails the fact that the majority of Christians stood aloof, either indifferent or hostile.

The late Michael Zylberberg, a survivor of the Warsaw ghetto, and a personal friend of this writer, relates listening to a sermon in Passion Week, 1944. He had taken refuge in a Church close to the ghetto. A Jesuit priest was in the pulpit describing the

sufferings Jews inflicted upon Jesus. There was not a hint of what
was taking place a few yards away, behind the ghetto walls (*A
Warsaw Diary*, 1969, pp. 150f.). It is impossible to account for this
kind of insensitivity. Auschwitz stands as an indictment not only
of Western culture but of traditional Christianity. There is bitter
irony embedded in our situation. While scholars, pastors and
priests expatiate on pharisaic hypocrisy, there seems to be little
effort made to apply it to our own condition as a Church. Yet
Auschwitz is too gruesome a fact to pass over in silence. The
Church in Germany had to face the issue but only for a while.
Roman Catholic circles have taken up the subject of Auschwitz
with considerable assiduity. On the whole, Anglo-Saxon
Protestants have shown less inclination to dabble in a mess not of
their making. Jews interpret such lack of concern as an act of
hostility. This became especially evident in the so-called Yom-
Kippur War (Oct. 1973). The sudden attack by the Arab forces of
Syria and Egypt put the Israeli State in peril. There were a few
days when it seemed that Jewish forces would buckle under.
Jewish communities outside Israel were shocked to discover the
lack of concern on the part of Christian leaders. Wiesel writes:
'Western Europe, with only rare exceptions, refused to help, and,
much worse, attempted to sabotage America's aid'. 'The world', he
adds, 'is indifferent to our death' (*op. cit.*, pp. 37f.). But from
Christians, especially from those engaged in friendly dialogue with
Jews, they expected a different attitude. The silence they met with
shook the Jewish community. Earl Raab spoke for many when he
wrote: 'On two flash occasions when Israel's life seemed to have
been in peril — 1967 and 1973 — official American Christian
leadership was gaudily silent. Some leading individual clergymen
spoke out on behalf of Israel, but a number of individual
clergymen who had been considered "friendly", and with whom
the Jews had much concourse, said nothing or were uncommitted,
as were most of the formal establishments of both Protestant and
Catholic churches.' (*Commentary*, Jan. 1974, p. 27.)

Some Jews withdrew from the Jewish–Christian Dialogue as a
result. For Christians the problem is a difficult one. On the one
hand there is the sense of guilt and the rightness of the Jewish
cause to secure a place under the sun where they are at home. On
the other hand, political Zionism seems to contradict Christian
ideals of a united humanity. In addition, the cause of Arab
refugees weighs heavily upon the Christian conscience. The late
A. C. Forrest, editor of the *United Church Observer* (Canada), got
himself in great trouble for pleading their cause (*cf. The Observer*,

March, 1972). It released a flood of letters to the press for and
against Forrest. The Forrest categorically denied any anti-Semitic
sentiments, but was most critical of Israeli policy regarding the
Palestinian Arabs (*Canadian Churchman*, May, 1969; also
Toronto *Globe & Mail*, Feb. 20, 1971). Prof. Willard G. Oxtaby
of Toronto pointed out some of the moral issues for Christians
arising from the aims of the Israeli State. One of these is that as
far as Christians are concerned Israel is a political fact; whereas
'for many Jews it is a profoundly religious fact' ('Christians in the
Middle East Crisis', reprinted in *Disputation and Dialogue*, ed. by
F. E. Talmage, 1975, pp. 220ff.; *cf.* also p. 185). The difficulty
arises from the fact that much can be said on behalf of both
contending parties — Arabs and Jews. Prof. Jacques Kornberg in
a letter to the Editor sees the conflict 'as a tragic clash of two
rights' (Toronto *Globe & Mail*, Aug. 21, 1976, p. 7).

Christian opinion is divided on the issue. A letter signed by 14
theologians to the Editor of the *Globe & Mail* strongly affirmed
support of Israel during the Yom Kippur crisis (Oct. 19, 1973).
Five days later 14 professors from the Department of Near
Eastern Studies, expressed the opposite view (Oct. 24, 1973). They
declared the first letter 'rife with prejudice'. They argued 'that
since the Christian world has been guilty of crimes against the
Jews, it is therefore obligated to support Zionism willy-nilly — to
the utter disregard of the wrongs done in the process to the
Arabs, the original innocent by-standers'. To them this is a
fallacious conclusion.

The problem is full of pitfalls. Such is the human predicament.
Israel needs a home, but Israel's home means homelessness for
others. Jews expect Christians to stand by them. Any criticism is
regarded as hostility and branded as anti-Semitism. There seems
to be no easy way out of the situation, except perhaps by a
humble acknowledgement of guilt. However, the French author,
François Mauriac has shown that there is a possible way out of
the maze. Here is the story as told by Elie Wiesel:

Wiesel met Mauriac at the author's home for the first time.
Mauriac, a devout Roman Catholic, spoke of his love for Israel,
for the Bible and for Jesus. Listening to the sufferings of Jesus,
Wiesel became irritated and burst out, why dwell on the suffering
of one who died so many years ago, while 'not far from here, I
knew Jewish children every one of whom suffered a thousand
times more, six thousand times more, than Christ on the cross.
And we don't speak of them.' Wiesel was so upset that he left the
apartment. Mauriac brought him back, sat him down and made

him tell his story. While listening to Wiesel, Mauriac burst into tears. This is how Wiesel describes the scene: 'The tears were streaming down his face, and he did nothing to stop them, to wipe them away' (*A Jew Today*, p. 18).

It was this outburst of compassion which became the bond of friendship between the Christian and the Jew. It was thanks to Mauriac's encouragement that Wiesel took up the pen and began to tell the unspeakable story of Auschwitz.

It would be futile to expect the mass of so-called Christians to meet Jews in the same spirit; this can only be done by individuals who are prepared to identify with Christian guilt and Jewish anguish and thus become messengers of reconciliation.

The witness of the Church to the Jewish People

MURDO A. MACLEOD

No matter how much Israel may wish to remain separate from the Church of Jesus Christ, it cannot be excluded from the church's concern and responsibility. The desire of many Jews that the church should concern herself with her own worship of God and leave Israel to its own understanding and worship is impossible. The modern Jewish writer, Pinchas Lapide, says: 'It is ... no exaggeration to say that a pious Jewish recluse might spend all his religious life practising the 613 precepts of his faith without ever finding out that Christianity exists. Not so the pious Christian, who cannot open his Sacred Scriptures without confrontation with what the Church chooses to call "the mystery of Israel"' (*The Last Three Popes and the Jews*: Pinchas Lapide).

The roots of the church lie within Israel, the structure of the church was built upon Israel, and the hope of the church is intimately bound up with Israel. The church is incomplete without Israel. The Hebrew Scriptures are of fundamental importance to the understanding and proclamation of the Christian message. Without them Christianity is inexplicable. The classic formulation of this relationship is, of course, to be found in that most profound and crucial passage of the letter to the Romans, chapters 9 to 11, written by one who was himself a Hebrew of the Hebrews and a servant of Jesus Christ. It was to Israel that God Incarnate first revealed Himself, and it was to Israel that He first offered Himself as the Messiah of God. When they rejected Him, He wept over them. Being rejected by them, He did not reject them. Before His ascension, when He commissioned His disciples, Christ charged them to begin the preaching of the gospel at Jerusalem. If the church were to disobey this command to preach Jesus Christ to the Jewish people, she would be guilty of infidelity to her Lord and of a most virulent anti-semitism. To

71

withhold the gospel, the good news, from the Jewish people would be most culpable.

There can be no doubt that Christ commissioned His church to go out into the world, the whole world, with a programme of evangelism. 'Go ... and make disciples of all nations, baptising them ...' (Matt. 28:19). Such is the commission as recorded by Matthew. Luke adds 'that repentance and forgiveness of sins should be preached in his name to all nations' (Luke 24:47). As John Stott points out, 'The cumulative emphasis seems clear. It is placed on preaching, witnessing and making disciples, and many deduce from this that the mission of the church, according to the specification of the risen Lord, is exclusively a preaching, converting and teaching mission' (*Christian Mission in the Modern World*: John R. W. Stott).

This immediately raises the emotive word 'mission'. To many Jewish people this concept is anathema. The opposition to this concept is in a large measure understandable in view of the history of 'Christian anti-semitism' which has blighted the history of Christendom for nigh on two thousand years. Reference will be made to this later. For the moment we must use the term in its strict etymological sense. A mission is the fulfilling of a duty on which one is sent. That the church has been commissioned by Christ as a missionary agency is evident from the Johannine version of the great commission. 'As the Father has sent me, even so I send you' (John 20:21). He made His mission the pattern for His church.

We must, therefore, understand the church's mission from our understanding of the mission of Christ. His mission was to submit Himself to the will of the Father and to proclaim the good news that derived from His obedience. 'I must preach ... to the other cities also; for I was sent for this purpose' (Luke 4:43). The *mission* of the church is the comprehensive name of its function. *Evangelisation*, the preaching of the good news, is one particular expression of the church's mission. In the New Testament to evangelise does not necessarily mean to win converts. It is pre-eminently the announcement of the good news irrespective of the results. Compare Acts 14:7, 8:4, 8:12, 8:25, 40. So the evangelistic ministry of the church is the continuation of the ministry of Christ who claimed to be the sent messenger of God, fulfilling the Isaianic prophecies:

> How beautiful on the mountains,
> are the feet of *one who brings good news*

who heralds peace, *brings happiness*,
proclaims salvation,
and tells Zion:
Your God is King. (Isa. 52:7 J.B.)

The roots, therefore, of the church's mission go back even beyond the apostles and Christ Himself to the prophetic message of the Tenach. The message of the good news is none other than Christ Himself. In his Pentecost address to the men of Israel the first word of Peter's message was 'Jesus' (Acts 2:22). When Philip evangelised the Ethiopian official, his message was 'Jesus' (Acts 8:35). When Paul defined his message it was, 'Christ we proclaim' (Col. 1:28).

The indissoluble unity between the church of Jesus Christ and the people of Israel may be viewed in another light. The covenant made with Israel was 'I will take you for my people, and I will be your God' (Exod. 6:7). The new covenant in Jer. 31:33 was 'I will be their God, and they shall be my people'. It was, as John Calvin insists, a new covenant in administration not in substance. This new covenant, promised through Jeremiah, was affirmed by the writer to the Hebrews to be that inaugurated in the blood of Christ and was of similar content. 'I will be their God, and they shall be my people' (Heb. 8:10). The relationship that exists between Christ and His people is the motive for their purity: 'What agreement has the temple of God with idols? For we are the temple of the living God; as God said, "I will live in them and move among them, and I will be their God, and they shall be my people".' (2 Cor. 6:16). When the Apostle John saw the vision of the new heaven and new earth it was as God's dwelling place established with men, and the ancient covenant promise is repeated 'they shall be his people, and God himself will be with them' (Rev. 21:3).

We can see, therefore, that far from being a disposable option, the church must concern itself with Israel as a priority. 'They are Israelites, and to them belong the sonship, the glory, the covenants ... and of their race, according to the flesh, is the Christ. God who is overall be blessed for ever. Amen' (Rom. 9:4, 5). When Paul says that the gospel is the power of God unto salvation, to the Jew first, he assigns his due place of priority, not superiority. John Duncan has succinctly stated it: 'He is *primus inter pares* from which position he should neither be by Gentile pride degraded nor by the voluntary humility of Gentile obsequiency, exalted.' (*Rich Gleanings from Rabbi Duncan*:

Sinclair.) To be a Jew does not give any standing in the sight of God, but nevertheless it is a privilege that we dare not despise.

The Apostle Paul poses the question 'Then what advantage has the Jew?' and he answers it most emphatically 'Much in every way' (Rom. 3:1, 2). He will not allow any to depreciate a divinely ordained distinction. It is not sufficient to regard the priority to which Paul refers as being merely a temporary one. The whole context is against such a limitation. 'The implication appears to be rather that the power of God unto salvation through faith has primary relevance to the Jew, and the analogy of Scripture would indicate that this peculiar relevance to the Jew arises from the fact that the Jew had been chosen by God to be the recipient of the promise of the gospel and that to him were committed the oracles of God. Salvation was of the Jews.... The lines of preparation for the full revelation of the gospel were laid in Israel and for that reason the gospel is pre-eminently the gospel for the Jew' (*Commentary on the Epistle to the Romans*: John Murray).

The priority in evangelism carries a solemn corollary. In the final administration of rewards while the Jew still has priority in the endowment of glory, he will also have priority in the allotment of retribution (Rom. 2:9, 10) for there is no partiality with God (Rom. 2:11). There was a priority in the apostolic proclamation. There is to be a priority in the final assessment of the last day. We have no warrant for cancelling that priority in the interim. The practical expression of this priority, however, remains to be determined in each local situation.

It is sometimes asked why there needs to be a particular proclamation of the gospel to the Jew. Can he not be included in the witness to the nations among whom his race is scattered? There is, of course, no excuse for passing them by. To do so would, as we have said, be anti-semitism of the worst kind, denying to the Jews what the church considers the greatest good on earth and in heaven, too, and the accusation of racism could then be most legitimately levelled at her. The Scriptural mandate leaves us with no alternative but that there should be a continuing witness distinctly to the Jews. It was the explicit command of our Lord before and after His resurrection. The apostles also agreed that the proclamation of the gospel should continue to them in a distinct way. When the apostles saw 'that I [Paul] had been entrusted with the gospel to the uncircumcised, just as Peter had been entrusted with the gospel to the circumcised ... they gave to me and Barnabas the right hand of fellowship, that we should go to the Gentiles and they to the circumcised' (Gal. 2:7, 9). This does not mean that there are two gospels. There is one gospel for Jew and Gentile, but there are different ways of proclaiming the same gospel. A study of the sermons in the book of The Acts of the Apostles would seem to indicate that there was a distinct difference between the proclamation of the message to the Gentiles in which the forthcoming judgement of God was the emphasis, and the message proclaimed to the Jews which looked back to the revelation made 'in many and various ways ... to our fathers by the prophets' (Heb. 1:1).

In our proclamation of the gospel to Israel we must not only emphasise the unity of our doctrine and that of the Tenach, we must underline the unity of the church and Israel. We Gentile believers are, in a sense, proselytes of believing Israel. That is borne out by the figure of the wild olive tree which Paul uses in Rom. chapter 11. The church is not a creation *de novo*. It is the universalising and fulfilling of the election which began in Eden. The church has not taken the place of Israel; it has been grafted into Israel. But still ethnic Israel and the church of Christ yet remain distinct entities. There was a tension in the covenant originally made with Abraham. There were those elements which related specifically to the physical seed of Abraham, such as the promise of the land. There were those parts that applied to his seed, which is Christ, and his seed which are the children of Abraham by faith. Those who are grafted into the stock of Abraham partake of the promise as his seed according to faith. He is, in this sense, the father of the faithful. This is not an artificial dichotomy. There is the seed of Abraham according to the flesh; Paul says: 'I myself am an Israelite, a descendant of Abraham, a member of the tribe of Benjamin' (Rom. 11:1). But he also goes on to say: 'So you see that it is men of faith who are the sons of Abraham' (Gal. 3:7).

While the church in her witness to Israel must emphasise her unity with Israel, she must also at the same time not arrogate to herself prerogatives that belong peculiarly to Israel, such as the promise of the land, nor must she spiritualise away such promises. The land of Israel was the cradle of the redemptive acts and the question concerning it cannot be lightly dismissed. The problem of the land of Israel as a Jewish national home is a peculiarly modern one. However, it has loomed on the horizon of eschatological studies since the days of the early church. The Jews themselves have also been concerned with the idea of a return, and attempts to do so have always been in their minds and purpose. Chaim Weizmann, the first President of the State of Israel, said in 1936 that if we would 'take the trouble to study the post-Roman period of the Jews and the life of the Jews in Palestine, we would find that, during the nineteen centuries which have passed since the destruction of Palestine as a Jewish political entity there was not a single century in which the Jews did not attempt to come back'. (*The Jewish people in Palestine*; Royal Commission on Palestine, 1936.)

It is difficult to be dogmatic concerning the present return of the Jewish people to Israel and to say that it is the fulfilment of prophecy. We must note, however, that God promised the land to Abraham and his seed. Paul would appear to indicate that nations are divinely created entities, and indeed the sovereignty of God over His world would necessitate such a view. God 'made from one every nation of men to live on all the face of the earth, having determined allotted periods and the boundaries of their habitation' (Acts 17:26). The nation, its geographical boundaries, and its appointed time of existence are set by God. The one cannot be divorced from the other. According to the King James Version of Deut. 32:8 'When the Most High divided to the nations their inheritance, when he separated the sons of Adam, he set the bounds of the people according to the number of the children of Israel'. As long as the nation endures, the land appointed to them by God is theirs until the time appointed by God that the nation should be no more. According to the clear teaching of Rom. chapter 11 the Jewish nation will remain a nation, scattered and persecuted it may be, but nevertheless a people, and they will remain such at least until Israel returns to Christ. It would appear, therefore, that the land is theirs. God has not revoked His act in creating them a nation, nor has He revoked His gift to them of the land wherein they should dwell. If, therefore, in the overruling providence of God, out of the conflict of the nations, their home has again been established in the land of Israel it is our Christian duty to recognise this as the Lord's doing and wonderful in our eyes. It is also our Christian duty to recognise in the restoration of the people of Israel to the land of Israel the faithfulness of God to His own promises. That there are injustices existing in the dispossession of certain Arab dwellers in Palestine is unquestionable, and it is also our Christian duty, in our witness to Israel, to plead that they, with all other nations, are to 'do justice, and to love kindness, and to walk humbly with your God' (Micah 6:8).

In recent years the Christian church has sought to find new

nomenclature in describing its relationship with the Jewish people. We have observed earlier that the term 'mission' is a concept loaded with all the history of forced conversion and barbarous treatment of the Jewish people. Many churches and organisations which previously used the term 'mission' now speak of 'gospel proclamation among the people of Israel', or ministry to the Jews, or witness to Israel. It is interesting to observe that the adoption of such a description of the church's responsibility to Israel was that used in the early part of the nineteenth century when, for example, in England the two major organisations representing the Anglican church and the non-conformist churches were known as The London Society for promoting Christianity amongst the Jews (now The Church's Ministry among the Jews), and The British Society for the Propagation of the Gospel among the Jews (now Christian Witness to Israel). The concept inherent in these former titles is a more Biblical understanding of the church's relationship to Israel. It distinguishes between the duty to evangelise, proclaim the good news, and the mission of total obedience to Christ's commands.

Some Christian theologians have gone even further, and have denied the right of the church to preach the gospel, or proclaim the good news, to the Jewish people. This is either based upon a non-Christian attitude to the authority of Christ or because of what is termed a post-Holocaust situation where the church has forfeited its right to speak to Israel. Neither of these positions can be entertained. For example, the reformed churches of The Netherlands (G.K.N.) in their Declaration of Principles governing the Christian kibbutz Nes Ammim state that 'The goal of the kibbutz is to renounce both practically and in principle any pretention to engage in missionary proselytism (that is, efforts to make Jews members of the Church)'. Johannes Verkuyl writes, 'I must register my disagreement, for it strikes me that it calls Christians to do something which is principally impossible and never allowable. No Christian community may ever vow to give up its missionary activity'. (*Contemporary Missiology*: Johannes Verkuyl.)

With this we heartily concur. To identify in any way the unspeakable atrocities of the Holocaust with the Christian Faith is stretching credulity too far. Without question the Christian church is guilty of not raising its voice more clearly and forcibly during the terrible years of the thirties, but it cannot be denied that wherever the true Christian gospel was known, loved and practised, the church sought to make its voice heard. It is not the first time that the voice of righteousness has been a voice crying in the wilderness.

As an alternative strategy such modern theologians, more prominently James Parkes, Reinhold Niebuhr and Paul Tillich, have sought to promote a concept of dialogue which is in opposition to mission, by which they mean evangelisation. This tension, indeed opposition, that has been created between dialogue and mission is a purely artificial one. The term 'dialogue' is difficult to define as used by many modern theologians in this connection. It is very much a Humpty Dumpty word. 'When I use a word', Humpty Dumpty said in a rather scornful tone, 'it means just what I choose it to mean, neither more nor less.' 'The question is', said Alice, 'whether you *can* make words mean different things.' (*Alice through the Looking Glass.*)

Generalisations are generally misleading. But perhaps it may be true to say that the consensus view of dialogue among many ecumenical scholars such as those referred to above is that Christ is already present everywhere and what we must do first is to 'find the Christ already there'. Most recently this view was enunciated by Pope John Paul II in his last address in the Philippines when he stated that the Church should sit down with the proponents of other Faiths and seek to find Christ in these. Such a concept is given plausibility from Peter's words to Cornelius 'Truly I perceive that God shows no partiality, but in every nation any one who fears him and does what is right is acceptable to him' (Acts 10:34, 35). However, such words cannot bear the weight that is laid upon them, for later Peter informed the church in Jerusalem that God's promise to Cornelius concerning Peter was that 'he will declare to you a.message by which you will be saved' (Acts 11:14). So in whatever sense Cornelius was 'acceptable' to God before his conversion he had neither 'salvation' nor 'life'. The biblical usage of *dialegomai* has been the matter of some controversy but according to Kittel and Arndt-Gingrich the usage would seem to imply religious lectures or sermons or simply preaching which may or may not end in disputation.

So if by dialogue it is meant that truth is a search to which all may contribute, none having more authority than the other, then this is a concept to which a Christian cannot agree. No matter how unpalatable it may be, there is a Divine intolerance in the Christian Faith. Jesus said: 'I am the way, I am the truth' (John 14:6). However, if by dialogue it is intended that disagreeing parties should sit down together and enunciate their differences freely and courteously, seeking conjointly to understand where each other stands and how the one perceives the other, this can only be welcomed. When Jesus first visited the Temple He was found sitting with the Rabbinic scholars *listening to them* and asking them questions.

There is growing in certain areas of Christian/Jewish relationships an encouraging atmosphere of sincere seeking to understand what the other is saying. The Christian church is becoming more and more conscious of the indispensable nature of the Old Testament for the understanding of its own message. In the Lutheran church in Germany there has recently been issued a declaration on this very subject. Coming from a church in which the Scripture readings were only from the Gospels and the Epistles, this cannot but be welcomed with enthusiasm. On the other hand there is also a growing willingness on the part of many Jewish writers to recognise the Jewishness of Jesus. Professor Klausner wrote: 'Jesus was the most Jewish of all Jews, more Jewish even than the great teacher Hillel' (*Jesus of Nazareth*: Joseph Klausner). Jakob Jocz writes: 'The Jewish effort is directed to reclaiming Jesus the Jew from the Gentile church and to reinstate him to a place of honour in Jewish history. This process of reclamation has continued for over a century and has been greatly accelerated in recent years' (*The Jewish People and Jesus Christ*: Jakob Jocz).

While we may welcome this increasing openness to the Prophet of Nazareth, the words of Jakob Jocz remain true today: 'The Jewish or the Christian attitude can neither be the result of history or of race, but entirely depends upon the personal response to Jesus Christ. Christian theology is the result of faith in Jesus of Nazareth, the Son of God. Jewish theology is the negation of that faith. The dividing line is not between Jews and Gentiles in the racial sense, but between men who accept and men who reject the Christian claim. The division between Jews and Christians on a historical basis is thus fictitious. There is only one division: between the man who in his actual, existential situation says yes and the man who in his actual, existential situation says no to the challenge which Jesus Christ presents.' (*The Jewish People and Jesus Christ*: Jakob Jocz.)

The controversy and the conflict must ultimately be resolved in the acceptance of the person of Jesus Christ. The question is, and must ever be, What think ye of Christ? Whose Son is He? If the answer is only that given by the Pharisees, 'The Son of David', it falls short of the claim of the Man of Nazareth in His further reply to the Pharisees, and in His claim 'I and the Father are one'

(John 10:30). The Jewish scholar, Dr. David Daube, states that 'the conflict between Synagogue and Church always was and still is about the question of the divinity of Jesus, not about any minor issues'. (Preface to *The Jewish People and Jesus Christ*: Jakob Jocz.)

The Witness to God of the Covenant People

HENRY L. ELLISON

The story is well known how King Frederick the Great of Prussia, deeply influenced by the atheism of the French 'Enlightenment', turned mockingly to his court physician and said, 'Can you prove the existence of God to me in a couple of words?'. The doctor, well known as a devout Christian, bowed deeply and said, 'The Jews, Sire', to which no royal answer has been recorded.

It is not so long ago that many historians regarded God as the controller of human destiny with human history moving towards a goal of his setting. The typical Victorian historian would probably willingly have echoed the words with which Lord Tennyson closed his 'In Memoriam',

> One God, one law, one element
> and one far-off divine event,
> to which the whole creation moves,

or even more the affirmation in Locksley Hall:

> Yet I doubt not through the ages one increasing purpose runs,
> And the thoughts of men are widen'd with the process of the suns.

The modern historian, however, is far more likely to respond to H. A. L. Fisher's remark in his Introduction to his justly famous *History of Europe*: 'Men more wise and learned than I have discerned in history a plot, a rhythm, a predetermined pattern. Those harmonies are concealed from me. I can see only one emergency following upon another as wave follows upon wave, only one great fact with respect to which, since it is unique, there

81

can be no generalisation, only one safe rule for the historian: that he should recognise in the development of human destinies the play of the contingent and the unforeseen.'

But just as intellectual man was settling down to the comfortable conviction that international affairs depended on human wisdom and institutions like the League of Nations, quite apart from the basic facts of men and guns, this optimism was increasingly challenged by the growing plight of the Jews, which grew ever more desperate. This was at first not due to German anti-semitism, but was a by-product of Polish economic problems.

It is often alleged that a major factor in anti-semitism is the Jewish claim to belong to an elect race. This has probably played a much smaller part than is often thought, but it is a claim based on a belief that God has a vital rôle in human history.

The Holocaust, with a third of the Jewish nation as its victims, seemed to be a decisive refutation of the Jewish claim, leading many Jews to question God's existence. The coming into existence of the State of Israel and its subsequent history convinced many Jews and non-Jews alike that it was a result of divine intervention.

For many years leading theologians, especially in Europe and North America, were drifting increasingly into what can only be called a Marcionite position, seeing in the Old Testament no more than an ethical handbook of no major theological value. In fact the Greek contribution to Christian theology was by many Continental theologians placed considerably higher than that of the Hebrew element. The Jew was generally written off as having no present or future significance.

The setting up of the State of Israel proved a real bombshell to many in these circles. It was a leading New Testament professor in Germany, who said at a small study-conference called by the W.C.C. shortly after the last war at the Château de Bossey near Geneva, that many German theologians had realised that Rom. 9–11 provided the essential key to the understanding of the New Testament and indeed of theology generally.

The undeniable fact is that, if we take the history of the Jewish people seriously — something that is all too rare among Christians — in conjunction with the Scriptural statements about it, we are virtually compelled to accept the concept of a purposeful Creator. Such an acceptance need not rule out the concept of evolutionary development, but subjects it to an overruling creatorial intellect and purpose. In addition this purpose must be seen as ethical and moral, Here again this cuts at the root of evolutionary ethics. The moral system imposed by the Creator is based on higher principles than purely transient self-interest. Not only is there a Creator, but we also see him intervening in human history, not by reversing the normal channels of human behaviour and their consequences, but by the raising up of exceptional men as deliverers, and by the controlling of natural phenomena at the vital moment, including unexpected and often inexplicable acts of preservation. The miracles of the Old Testament, which are such a stumbling block to many modern men of science, would lose much of their unacceptability, were it more widely realised that apart from a handful of inexplicable happenings scattered through the story they are normally concentrated round events of crucial importance.

Jewish history shows the working out of God's purposes by a process of choice or election, which, unlike human, does not involve rejection of the unchosen: 'You shall be my own possession among all peoples, for all the earth is mine' (Exod. 19:5) is God's statement. Even the unchosen are under his control and answerable to him for their behaviour. 'Did I not bring up Israel from the land of Egypt, and the Philistines from Caphtor and the Syrians from Kir?' (Amos 9:7, and *cf.* Amos 1:3–2:3, and the prophecies against the nations in most of the canonical prophets). In addition, however, election privilege always implies moral responsibility. 'You only have I known of all the families of the earth; therefore I will punish you for all your iniquities' (Amos 3:2). This is something that tends to be overlooked in some Christian circles that lay great stress on predestination.

Great suffering and divine punishment were always relieved by the light of the Messianic hope, the confidence that the kingdom of God, his sovereign rule, would yet fill the earth and transform it. While other reasons could be mentioned, it is perhaps above all the growing dim of this hope in the Church that has held back many Jews from faith in Jesus. The 'crown rights' of Christ are all too often ignored in the Church today; few Christians seem to know anything of being seated in the heavenlies with Christ (Eph. 2:6, Col. 3:1); the Sermon on the Mount is honoured less by observance and more by being ignored. In addition, while it is easy to show how ridiculous the traditional observance of the Torah (law) can be, it, at least, insists that there should be no separation of the secular and religious.

We may be grateful too for consistent Jewish stress on God's unity. Apart from it, the Church might well have compromised and acquiesced in the virtual tritheism of popular theology. It challenges the virtual dualism that underlies the undue respect shown to Satan and his emissaries in some circles today.

Possibly the most valuable contribution of the Jew to our thinking in recent years has come from what we have learnt to call the Holocaust. For a time there was a tendency in some countries to wash one's hands of responsibility for the terrible things that happened in Germany and those countries which had been overrun. But then it was realised more and more that the Final Solution was made possible by the indifference of virtually all Western countries. The success of a handful who risked concentration camp and death to save Jews they knew showed what could have been done had more been willing to take the risk. The doctrine of original sin has always been the most unpopular for the humanist, and for long there has been a growing tendency in the Church to ignore it and to believe that a general improvement in morality has set in. The suffering of the Jew has reminded us that in God's sight we are all sinners and all our righteousness is as a filthy rag in his sight.

The Church's traditional criticism of Judaism, more often than not based on ignorance, has tended to hide from its eyes the far more valid criticisms that the Synagogue has been able to make of the Church.

The Church, because of her normal expectation that the Jewish Christian will become assimilated into his new Gentile environment, instead of her being willing to integrate him and welcome him for whatever riches of understanding of God he may have brought with him, has been impoverished. It could well be that just as the Holy Spirit used mainly Jewish Christians to interpret the riches of Christ to the infant Church, so he may well use their descendants today to bring us a richer understanding of those riches.

The divine vocation and destiny of Israel in world history

THOMAS F. TORRANCE

The people of Israel are charged with a divine destiny which was not of their own choosing and are called to fulfil a definite function in God's purpose of love and salvation for all peoples and nations. Far from having only a temporary significance which came to its end with the emergence of the Christian Church, Israel continues to play an all-important if often a hidden rôle in the mysterious decisions of God which will become fully manifest only in the consummation of his Kingdom at the end-time. That God does not go back upon his distinctive covenant with Israel or change his mind about his special gifts to Israel or revoke his calling of Israel for universal mission, is central not only to the message of the Old Testament but to the message of the New Testament as well. This is made indubitably clear in several chapters of St. Paul's epistles of the most far-reaching significance, Rom. 9–11 and Eph. 2.

With these passages particularly in mind, let me state the main theme of this contribution, and then go on to say three things about Israel which Christians need to ponder much more deeply and three things about what we may learn today from and through Israel.

My main theme is that the people of Israel have been given a vicarious mission to fulfil which is of critical significance not only for the Christian Church but for all mankind. The universality in God's saving purpose for the human race informed the intimate communion which he established with Israel from the very beginning of their history, but after the long spiritual and historical ordeal of Israel's struggle with God, it became finally

85

and fully embodied in human existence with the incarnation in
Jesus Christ of the one Word of God by whom all men are made
and in whom they have their being. In a decisive manner Jesus
gathers up in himself the whole history of Israel in its ever-
deepening communion with God and fans it out through his
death and resurrection and ascension in an expansive movement
toward the coming world community or *oikoumene* (Heb. 2:5),
the all-embracing People of God. In spite of this catholicising or
universalising of Israel's mission through the Christ-event, which
shattered the earthly securities and broke open the ossified
patterns of Jewish institutions, the place of Israel in salvation-
history remains central to the organic framework of the Kingdom
and People of God. The recognition of this fact by the Christian
Church was sealed by the basic place they were constrained to
give to the Old Testament as Holy Scripture, for the Apostolic
Community regarded themselves as incorporate within the one
People of God only so far as through Christ they were 'grafted on
to the trunk' of Israel, the Israel of the Covenant Promises and
divine Oracles. That is surely how we must continue to regard
our brethren the Jews: as belonging in the profoundest sense to
the one Church of God and as continuing to hold the secret of
the unity of mankind in God's redemptive purpose for the world.
As the appointed instrument of God's self-communication and
self-commitment to humanity, Israel constitutes the critical centre
in the human race, and, in human history, of God's will 'to gather
together into one the scattered children of God', as the high priest
Caiaphas expressed it in his remarkable prophecy on the eve of
Jesus' crucifixion (John 11: 49–52). That is the peculiar destiny
and status of Israel as a people (*laos*) and not just as a nation
(*ethnos*), the people who through their relation to God and the
universality of his purpose are called to transcend ethnic divisions
and open up the way for the one undivided Kingdom of God
among men.

Strange as it may seem from a theological perspective, this is
not a destiny to which the people of Israel have ever been fully
reconciled. From the rise of the kingdom under King Saul, when
the Children of Israel wanted to become a nation like other
nations and a kingdom like other kingdoms, to the present State
of Israel, the Jews have resisted their divine calling to be a people
of God in the full sense. The deep-seated tension between their
laic destiny and their *ethnic* actuality has always been embedded
in their spiritual and historical struggle to serve God and to exist
as a national entity, and it remains basic to the stubborn problem

of Israel in Israel today. This has not been helped by a long tradition in Western Christianity which has regarded Israel as people of God only in a carnal and not in a spiritual sense and therefore as a people whose destiny was replaced by the Church of Jesus Christ — a tradition, of course, which is in sharp conflict with the Holy Scriptures of the New as well as the Old Testaments. It is of the utmost importance that Christians today should recover the apostolic perspective, in accordance with which the Jewish Church and the Christian Church belong inseparably together in the one People of God within which Israel in their 'laic' status as God's People have ontological and not just historical priority as the 'mother' of faith in the living God. Gentile Churches and the nations in which they have developed are not without serious difficulties of their own, deriving from their different 'ethnic' characters, in recognising the imprint of divine Providence upon Israel as 'People of God' or 'Church', which does not help modern Israel to respond, as it might, to God's purpose with it among the nations. But it must be pointed out that any breach on their part with Israel would mean a breaking away from the centre of God's order of redemptive recreation and reunification of mankind. Schism between Christians and Jews is the deepest schism and the root cause of all other schism in the one People of God, while rebellion against the reconciling purpose of God being worked out through Israel cannot but bring fragmentation among the peoples and nations of mankind, for it detaches them from their creative centre in God's providential activity in history, when they are thrown back upon their separated existences and cultures as national entities. Nationalism of this kind can only take the form of group-egoism or ethnic sin, which is the poisonous root of all racism. It is not difficult to show how in modern times racism and anti-semitism go together, whether we look at the situation in Germany before and after the Second World War or the situation in the Middle East in the conflict between Arab and Jewish relations, although behind all anti-semitism there is at work a perverted animosity against God and the way he has taken among the nations for the salvation of the human race. Anti-semitism is, after all, a rebellion against the peculiar vocation and destiny of Israel, especially against its vicarious mission, but for that very reason it is also a deep-seated rebellion against the vicarious mission of Jesus Christ himself. That is to say, anti-semitism is a manifestation of what the New Testament calls 'anti-Christ'.

It is of course in the light of the fulfilment of God's self-revealing and self-giving in Jesus Christ, and from the perspective of his atoning passion and mediation, that we dare to speak in this way about the crucial part given to Israel throughout history in the working out of God's redemptive will, and indeed about the eschatological import of Israel for the future of the world. There is much here that quite baffles us, but there are three points about the vocation and destiny of Israel which we must surely stress.

1. *Israel is the unique partner of divine revelation*

What ultimately stamps the People of Israel as so distinctive is that they are the people chosen from among the human race for the special purpose of being God's instrument in the mediation of divine revelation and reconciliation to all peoples and nations. To use Jeremiah's analogy, Israel is the vessel of clay in the hands of the divine Potter. Just as a lump of clay is taken by a human potter to be moulded for a special purpose and is broken down again and again and reshaped until the potter is satisfied that it will be an adequate vessel to convey what is intended, so Israel is moulded and shaped through the ordeal of its religious and historical experience to be the bearer of the oracles of God, the mediator of the Covenant, the servant of the Lord. All this was done to Israel not primarily for its own sake but for the sake of other peoples who are no less than Jews the children of God, but that representative or vicarious function with which Israel's physical and spiritual existence was inescapably tied up made it a people apart, a consecrated 'peculiar' people, stamped with the seal of God's Word.

The rôle for which Israel was elected was agonisingly difficult: to be the human bearer of divine revelation and thus to suffer from its flame as no other people has ever had to suffer. Through the initiative and providence of God, Israel became the people where God's revelation of himself was earthed in the clay of humanity in such a way that through the responses it evoked, restructured and assimilated to itself as part of its own movement, it was translated into basic patterns of human understanding and articulation which could be available for all men and all ages. Thus in the course of Israel's history a two-way movement of the profoundest and most intimate nature was maintained between God and Israel within which the Word of God struggled with Israel's ways of life and thought and worship in order to break through the barriers of naturalistic and pagan convention that hindered knowledge of the living God, and used the reactions of succeeding generations whether of assent or dissent, obedience or disobedience, apostasy or reform, as instruments for ever-deepening penetration into Israel's existence and as the means through which it became understandable and communicable as God's Word to man.

The Old Testament Scriptures do not hesitate to record that in the long history of its partnership with God, in the mediation of divine revelation and reconciliation, Israel proved to be disobedient and rebellious again and again. But it is important to see that this obstinate behaviour on Israel's part was an inescapable and essential ingredient in its vicarious mission, for it was with Israel in its capacity as a representative of human nature in its stubborn estrangement from God, and with Israel precisely in its sinful existence, that God bound himself for ever in a covenant or partnership of steadfast love. And it is also important to see that, if the very intimacy of God's relations with Israel had the effect of intensifying the stubbornness of its self-will in a refusal of God, even that was intended in order that God might make it serve the purpose of his love in revealing himself and giving himself to man in spite of man's refusal of divine grace. The faithfulness of God is not robbed of its effect by the faithlessness of his people, for he will not let them go but binds them even more closely to himself through all divine judgement and rejection that they may finally be restored and reaffirmed in the fulness of his love.

Such was the extremely difficult rôle for which Israel was chosen in its partnership with God in his self-revelation to mankind. If again and again Israel was disobedient and rejected the claims of God's love, in a profound sense it *had* to do so in our place and for our sakes. And if in the process of mediating divine revelation Israel became blind to the way of God's grace — 'Who is blind but my servant?' (Isa. 42:19) — it *had* to become blind that we might see. And whenever Israel found itself overwhelmed in the horror of divine rejection — 'My God, my God, why hast thou forsaken me?' (Ps. 22:1) — that too *had* to take place, that the world might be reconciled to God. These harrowing experiences belong to the very essence of Israel's story in its covenanted partnership with God as the bearer of divine revelation. And that is how we Christians must still look upon Israel, from the perspective of the Cross of Christ — *Eli, Eli, Lama sabachthani?* (Matt. 27:46; Mark 15:34) — where the vicarious passion of Israel, the servant of the Lord, was gathered up fulfilled and transcended in the atoning passion of God

D

incarnate offered on behalf of Israel and all other peoples. Thus
Israel had and continues to have an inner organic bond with
Jesus Christ which is not shared by any other people, though it is
clearly reflected in the Virgin Mary. It is in the light of that bond
that our understanding of Israel must still be guided, and it is in
virtue of that bond consummated in the crucifixion and
resurrection of Christ that Israel's experience of abandonment,
above all in the pogroms and extermination camps of modern
Europe, points ahead to its own resurrection and reaffirmation in
the fullness of the Covenant and its divine promises.

2. *Israel is the only people with messianic promise*

As Gentiles we were 'without Christ', as St. Paul reminds us,
'being aliens from the commonwealth of Israel, and strangers from
the convenants of promise, having no hope, and without God in
the world' (Eph. 2:11). All these privileges belong to Israel (Rom.
9:4f.). Our Lord himself, as reported by St. John, made this quite
clear in the words: 'You do not know whom you worship, but we
know whom we worship, for salvation is of the Jews' (John 4:22).
Gentiles are saved, they are with God, they have Christ, they are
included in the covenant promises, they have hope, only as they
are incorporated into Israel, the one People of God, and that
happens, to refer to St. Paul again, as, in union with Christ, we,
who were far away, have been brought near through the shedding
of Christ's blood. 'For Christ himself is our peace who has made
us, Jews and Gentiles, one in his flesh by breaking down the wall
of partition (*fragmos*) between us. He annulled the law in its rules
and regulations in order to create the two into one new humanity
in himself thus making peace, and reconciled both in one body to
God through the cross and thereby killed the enmity between
them. And so Christ came and preached the good news of peace
to all, to you Gentiles who were far away from God and to the
Jews who were near to him, for through him we both have access
in one Spirit to the Father' (Eph. 2:12–19).

The picture that St. Paul has in mind in this passage is of the
barrier wall that was erected round the holy precincts of the
Temple to keep out all Gentiles, unbelievers and excommunicated
people, from joining with faithful Jews as they drew near to God
in worship and sacrifice. That is the barrier, together with the
legal ordinances which gave effect to it, that has been abolished
through the sacrifice of Christ on the Cross. Even before the
Cross, however, as we read in the Gospels, Jesus was at work

breaking down the *fragmos* as again and again he deliberately had table fellowship with those who were excommunicated from the Temple or who, for one reason or another, were beyond the barrier and excluded from drawing near to God, and thus he became the means in his own flesh and blood whereby sinners and outcasts might be included again within the profound partnership between God and his people, that is, the partnership made flesh in Jesus and established through a new universal covenant, in the shedding of his blood in atoning sacrifice on the Cross. It is on that ground, St. Paul claimed, that Gentiles are no longer to be regarded by Jews as foreigners or strangers but as fellow-citizens with God's people, and members of the family of God, for they too are now included within the messianic promises of God to Israel. Thus, far from being cancelled, the covenanted relation between God and Israel remains in force but as the core of a wider communion or partnership between God and all who draw near to him through the blood of Christ.

In the Epistle to the Romans St. Paul set out his argument in another way, through an analogy taken from horticulture in the grafting of a shoot from one tree on to another. If in their rejection of Jesus as the Messiah Jews appear to have broken themselves off as natural branches from the trunk of Israel, and Gentiles like wild olive branches are grafted on to it, the trunk which gives all the branches their life remains. Thus the covenanted people of God as such is not discarded with the foundation and expansion of the Christian Church. What happened to the Jews, when, through their blindness, they rejected their Messiah, took place for our sake, that we Gentiles might through them be reconciled to God, but our reconciliation will not be fulfilled apart from the reconciliation of Israel also. The inner connection between Israel and Christ is so close and strong that St. Paul insists that it carries with it the restoration and resurrection of Israel. Thus on the one hand he can say: 'If when we were enemies we were reconciled by the death of his Son, how much more shall we be saved by his Life!' (Rom. 5:10). But on the other hand he can also say: 'For if their casting away [*i.e.*, of Jews] meant the reconciling of the world, what will their inclusion mean but life from the dead?' (Rom. 11:15). That is to say, the messianic blessings of God mediated through Israel are universal in their range, but they will be finally actualised only as the promises of the covenant are fulfilled in and through Israel. The divinely given pledges to Israel remain in force and God will keep faith with his ancient people: otherwise all would be lost and without hope and without God in the world. On the other hand, this implies that the Gentile Church may share in the fullness of God's messianic blessing promised through Israel, if it keeps faith with Israel, for otherwise it would fail to keep faith with God, the God and Father of our Lord Jesus Christ.

Now this is something which it is more imperative than ever for us to take seriously, namely, that the Christian Church is *Church* only in that it is grafted like branches onto the trunk of Israel, and that it is the trunk that bears the branches and not the branches the trunk (Rom. 11:18). Since this is the case, the deepest schism in the one People of God is the schism between the Christian and the Jewish Church, not that between East and West or Roman and Protestant Christianity. The bitter separation between the Catholic Church and the Synagogue that set in after the Bar Cochba revolt in the second century after Christ was one of the greatest tragedies in the whole of our history, not only for the people of God but for all western civilisation. Let us think, for example, of the problem created by the Papacy. If the Gentile branches were themselves broken off from the trunk of Israel into which they were ingrafted, they had to find some basic centre to give them coherence and structure if they were not to disappear. It was out of this kind of need that Rome emerged as a centre for the expanding Catholic Church. As such it steadily intruded into the place of Jerusalem as the mother of the faithful, and thus took over the rôle of Israel as the historical, spiritual and theological centre of the one People of God, the trunk which under God provided the unifying base for all the branches of the Christian Church. It was evidently in justification of its own claims that the Roman Church gave currency to the false idea that Israel was the People of God only according to the flesh and had to be replaced by the Church of Jesus Christ as the People of God according to the Spirit. Schism always gives rise to substitute-centres which require special pleading, but the proliferation of schism, whatever may be its alleged justification, must surely be traced back ultimately to the radical split between Gentile Christians and Jews. Only with the healing of that split in a deep-going reconciliation will all the other divisions with which we struggle in the ecumenical movement finally be overcome.

3. *Israel will have a critical place in the consummation of all things*

As we have just noted, Israel will have a basic part in the reunion of the fragmented Gentile Church. It is not too much to say that the whole future of ecumenism and evangelism depends on the relation of Jews to Jesus Christ as the messianic Saviour and King. Only through the double witness of Jews and Gentiles to Christ will the Gospel finally be extended to cover all the peoples of the earth and the scattered children of God be brought together into one compact people. Therein Israel will also have a basic part to play in the relation of the Church to *world humanity*, a concern which has more and more occupied the thought and work of ecumenists. That will not, and cannot, come about as many people today seem to think, through a deployment of political power-structures for spiritual ends backed up by a theology of politico-messianic liberation, if only because it is quite impossible in that way to rise above the nationalistic divisions in the base of operations or to escape from the subtle group-egoisms that underly their ideological justification. Ultimately, of course, the salvation and renewing of mankind depend on the reconciling and resurrecting power of Christ himself, but if the actual unification of world humanity is to come about it must involve at its very centre the reconciliation of Jew and Gentile in Jesus Christ. And how is that to take place except through the fulfilment of Israel's vicarious rôle which, precisely because God's covenant with Israel is not annulled, remains very much in force?

Let us recall again at this point the unceasing struggle in historic Israel between its divine calling to be the people of God and its worldly aspiration to be a nation like the other nations of mankind. So long as Israel behaves just like another nation and the distinctive partnership between God and Israel is not allowed to bite deeply into its existence, Israel's vicarious function does not become manifest. But the closer the covenant bonds between Israel and God are drawn, the more intense its interrelation with God becomes, and the more its very existence is implicated in the mediation of divine revelation and salvation to mankind, the more Israel seems to be forced into a position where it draws back from its calling and reacts against God, because our estranged human nature, our self-centredness and our self-will in Israel are brought into conflict with God's will. However, as we have seen, in the fulfilment of his covenant purpose God uses that very state of affairs to ground his self-giving to mankind in and through Israel more deeply than ever in human existence. That is precisely how we are to understand Israel's strange rejection of its own Messiah in the crucifixion of Christ, something which, in its service of God's covenant-will, to bring about the reconciliation of all mankind and in the fulfilment of its God-given vicarious mission, Israel *had* to do. Thus Israel's rejection of Christ implicated it in the depths of Christ's own vicarious passion and atoning reconciliation.

Now if Israel is to accept Jesus as the Christ, and in Jesus Christ is to participate in the universal reconciliation of mankind to God, Israel can only do this, not by avoiding but by fulfilling its vicarious rôle in relation to Jesus, and thereby taking Christ's Cross on itself. If we think of the destruction of Jerusalem in A.D. 70 and the end of the Jewish State in A.D. 135 as somehow *having* to follow upon the crucifixion of Jesus, must we not also think of the restoration of Israel as *having* to follow upon the resurrection of Jesus? But as the way to the resurrection lies through the darkness of the Cross, so the way to Israel's resurrection must lie through the darkness of its participation in the Cross, that is, in obedience to its divine vocation in the Christian era when Israel still has a vicarious mission to fulfil deep in the shadow of the Cross, even if it is not fully aware of it. It is by sharing with Jesus to the full his experience of abandonment — 'My God, my God, why has thou forsaken me?' — that Israel will also share to the full in the power of his resurrection. Is that not exactly what has been taking place? Where more fearfully or profoundly than in the terrible concentration camps of Europe and their indescribable holocaust of more than six million Jews have the people of Israel suffered such abandonment? And where have they shared more deeply, if inarticulately, in the unmitigated pain and sorrow of God who refused to hold himself aloof from the world's bitter violence and unappeasable agony but came into the midst of it in Jesus Christ his incarnate Son? Through the Cross God bore it all upon himself in atoning love in such a staggering way as to make it finally serve the purpose of his redemption and healing of the human race. When, therefore, has Israel ever been more ripe through the fulfilment of its vicarious mission for participation in the power of Christ's resurrection when 'all Israel', as St. Paul prophesied (Rom. 11:26), Israel as a complete entity, will be saved and restored, and thus play a decisive part in the consummation of God's revealing and reconciling activity in the history of mankind?

The establishment of the new State of Israel, following hard upon the most harrowing ordeal of suffering the Jews have known, is surely the most significant sign given by God in his providential dealings with his covenanted People since the destruction of Jerusalem in A.D. 70, for now Israel as a complete entity has been openly thrust into the very centre of world history where it must bear witness to the sovereign rule of the living God and give an account of its divine vocation among the nations and peoples of mankind. Now in Israel, where Israelis are committed to defend themselves as a nation from eradication, the ancient tension between the 'laic' nature of their covenanted existence and their 'ethnic' aspirations in the world has become sharper than ever. Now also, however, after the prolonged night of travail and affliction in holocaust, when multitudes of Jews were driven like lambs to the slaughter and cut off out of the land of the living and the very soul of Israel was poured out in death, the conception of the servant-Messiah, embodying the suffering spirit and vicarious mission of Israel, struggles with the conception of the hero-Messiah identified with a mighty political Deliverer out of Sion. What will emerge from this inner tension and conflict within the people of Israel? If its faith in the faithfulness of God and in the integrity of his covenant is to survive, Israel cannot continue to hold apart the God in whom it believes and the enormity of its own suffering and hurt but must surely allow them to come together in the very heart of its trust in the living God. And how is that to come about except through the Cross of Jesus Christ, accepted as the atoning and vicarious passion of God himself, which gives redemptive meaning to Israel's distinctive history and existence, because it takes up, fulfils and transcends its own vicarious mission for mankind? Then at last it may be that through a 'laic' restructuring of Israel's 'ethnic' actuality the way will be opened for the realisation among all peoples and nations of the long promised reconciliation and unification of humanity in the messianic Kingdom of divine Peace. It is surely to that point in the eschatological and teleological gathering up of God's interaction with mankind that Israel is steadily and relentlessly being thrust by the God of steadfast covenant love.

Now what does all this have to say to us? What do the People of Israel, and Israel in this astonishing new 'Exodus' experience, mean for the Christian Church today? One thing at least is clear: we must acknowledge both our immense debt to Israel and our abject shame for what Christian peoples have done to Israel. The time has come for the whole Church of Christ to recognise far more profoundly and sincerely that it is a debtor to Israel, for it could not exist as Church except as it is grafted on to the stock of Israel and except at the expense of Israel. Israel remains the servant of the Lord with a vicarious function to fulfil *even for the Christian Church*, so that without heeding Israel or listening to its witness the Christian Church cannot properly understand its own existence or mission. But the Church today cannot relate sincerely to Israel without acknowledging to the full the piled-up guilt of its rejection and persecution of Israel throughout the Christian centuries. It cannot brush off the abominable horror of the mass extermination of Jews in modern times simply by putting it down to the Nazis, for it had its poisonous roots in many centuries of anti-semitism fostered by the Christian Church and discloses a deep-seated enmity that must constantly be dug out and submitted to the flame of divine judgement in the Cross of Jesus Christ. In faithfulness to the God and Father of our Lord Jesus Christ the Christian Church can never be the same after the Holocaust, for all its understanding of divine revelation and salvation, mediated through Israel, must be, and cannot but be, affected by the *Eli, Eli, lama sabachthani?* in which Israel and Jesus Christ are for ever forged together in a new and quite irreversible way. The Christian Church and the Jewish Church are now harnessed together in the mysterious judgements of God for witness, service and mission in the accelerating rush of world-events toward the end-time, when Christ himself will come to take up his reign and make all things new.

Now let us consider three things we may learn today from and through Israel.

1. *Israel can help us understand Jesus*

In modern times immense effort has been devoted by Christian scholars to what has been called 'the quest of the historical Jesus', but Jesus has proved to be tantalisingly elusive to our historico-critical reconstructions. Now it is becoming more and more evident that our constant problem arises from the fact that by our very approach to Jesus we Gentilise him and obscure him, so that he keeps vanishing from our 'observations'. Behind this lie the many, many centuries of ethnic and cultural conditioning of Christianity. We see this very clearly, for example, in the Latinisation of the Christian faith which our Eastern Orthodox brethren are not slow to point out to us. And when we study the ways in which the Christian Church has developed in other countries in Asia or Africa we become aware that we have imposed western and European patterns of thought and culture upon the Christian Church and have thereby often obscured its essential nature and character.

All this applies to the instruments we Gentiles have evolved for interpretation of the Gospels as we seek to penetrate behind the early Christian Community to Jesus himself, but we fail again and again quite disastrously, for all we seem finally to do is to construct a picture of Jesus which fits into our own western cultural preconceptions. Thus we put a Gentile mask on the face of Jesus which both obscures him from ourselves and prevents our Jewish brethren from recognising in the Jesus of Christianity (the Jesus of our scholarly observations), the Christ who is their own covenanted Messiah. We are like the blind leading the blind, for we stumble about in the dark together. We need to strip away from 'the historical Jesus', that is, from the Jesus Christ of our historical reconstructions, our Gentile patterns of thought and behaviour which we have foisted on him, if he is to disclose himself to our inquiry as he really was and is. But how can we manage to do that without the help of our brethren the Jews themselves? How can we see Jesus the Jew from Bethlehem, Nazareth and Jerusalem, without the use of Jewish eyes?

I recall an experience I had many years ago while working with a Jewish scholar, in which I found that he could discern things in the New Testament which I could not see and which took me some time to see even with his help. I could not see them because I was looking through the lenses of Gentile spectacles which distorted what was there, so that I had to learn to take off the spectacles I did not even know I was wearing. That common study with my Jewish friend taught me the kind of cooperation between Christians and Jews which we desperately need to enable us to discard the unconscious anti-semitism that is embedded in our culture and puts blinkers on our eyes, preventing us from seeing Jesus as he is actually mediated to us in and through Israel. We need to go to school with the People of Israel, as it were, in order to share with them the training they were given by God through many, many centuries until a matrix of understanding and thought and worship was prepared in Israel appropriate for the reception of God's ultimate self-revelation in Jesus Christ.

Now it looks as though God himself has been taking a hand in our predicament, in a number of ways, but let me mention only one which is of particular concern to me, in the interrelation between theology and science. Again and again in the development of modern science the real 'break-through' in our knowledge of the created universe, which has affected the fundamental structure of scientific thought, has been due to Jews. How are we to understand this? Let us think of it in the following way. If we take the history of western Christianity we find that large tracts of it, in the Roman Catholic and Lutheran traditions above all, have abolished the second commandment:— that is, the command forbidding Jews to conceive of God in terms of any kind of image. One of the other commandments, of course, usually the tenth, had to be divided into two in order to preserve the pattern of a 'decalogue'. This was no doubt influenced, but considerably reinforced by the classical Hellenic habit of 'thinking with the eyes', as Martin Buber used to speak of it, in contrast to the Hebraic way of thinking. Hence it is hardly surprising that western science has been so thoroughly 'observationalist' and 'phenomenalist' in its approach. But it is precisely at this point that modern science has had to break with that habit of thought, for the more deeply it has probed into the secrets of the universe, the more it has had to cope with what is inherently invisible and has had to find appropriate ways of thinking in terms of imageless relations and structures. This is where the Jewish mind has evidently had the advantage, through ingrained habits of thought that go back through the discipline of many, many generations in learning to think imagelessly of God. Our modern scientific advance has certainly benefited from it, not least in the Einsteinian development of relativity theory which has altered our whole outlook upon the universe.

I believe that biblical scholarship today can reap immense benefits from a rigorous scientific approach of this kind, pioneered by Jews, that operates with imageless ways of thought. This applies above all to the quest for the historical Jesus which for a hundred and fifty years has been dominated by the observationalism and phenomenalism of western culture and which breaks down again and again because the plastic images we use, in seeking to understand and interpret Jesus and the Gospel, are quite alien to the essential nature of God's revelation of himself in and through Israel.

2. *Israel can help us in understanding the atonement*

With the atonement we enter upon 'the holy of holies' of the Christian faith, the awesome unfathomable mystery of God incarnate racked in anguish, in Gethsemane and on the Cross, under the immeasureable weight of the world's sin and his own judgement upon it. Throughout history the Church's doctrine of atonement has constantly disintegrated, for the atoning sacrifice offered by Christ has a range and a depth that defy formal articulation. Were it not for the evangelical record of that last night when through a reconstruction of the Passover rite Jesus inaugurated the New Covenant in his body and blood, the Church would be completely bewildered. Quite evidently doctrinal formulation of the atonement needs to be recast again and again if its infinite truth in God is not to be obstructed from disclosing to us deeper aspects of itself, but what is so distressing to us is that an adequately coherent outline of its essential pattern keeps on eluding us. Is it not here also that Israel may help Christian understanding?

Let us recall the ancient rite enjoined by the Torah (Leviticus) for the annual renewal of the Covenant on the Day of Atonement when all Israel assembled before God, the only day each year when the high priest might pass through the veil in the Tabernacle and enter the Holy of Holies to make intercession and receive the divine peace. That rite has haunted the soul and memory of Israel since Mosaic times, making *Yom Kippur* still the most solemn and poignant in the Jewish liturgical year. Two goats were taken from the flock and presented before the Lord for a sin offering. One goat was killed and offered in holocaust on the altar as an atoning sacrifice for the people of Israel in expiation of their sins, and its blood was sprinkled before the propitiatory or mercy-seat of the divine presence, but it was also an act in atoning consecration of the very holy place itself. The other goat was made a living sacrifice. The high priest laid his hands on it, confessing over it all the iniquities, transgressions and sins of Israel, and then sent it away in utter rejection into the wilderness and released alive as a 'scapegoat' bearing and bearing away the guilt of the people. Each half of that mysterious ritual was incomplete without the other. How much Israel had to learn from the fact that both sacrifices were required, the sacrifice by blood and the living sacrifice, in liturgical witness to an atonement for sin which God himself alone could provide.

It is significant that both aspects of that atoning rite are reflected in the Isaianic account of the vicarious affliction of the 'suffering servant' (Isa. 53): the utter rejection of one despised and driven away as an unclean outcast on whom the iniquity of all has been laid, as well as the sacrificial death under judgement of the righteous one whose soul was made an offering for sin and who bearing the sin of many made intercession for the transgressors. But it is also significant that both these aspects of atonement, not least as they were personalised through the suffering servant, are reflected at awesome points in the Gospel presentation of the vicarious life and mission of Jesus the Son of

Man; for from his baptism in the river Jordan and his struggle with the evil one in the wilderness to his lonely death upon the Cross, the Lamb of God bore and bore away the sin of the world and the curse of its guilt, ridiculed and disowned by his brethren, the outcast of humanity. Apart from that matrix of atoning significance fostered through Israel's liturgy of sacrifice, the death of Jesus would remain a bewildering enigma. However, through it the self-interpreting passion of the Son of Man, crucified and risen, created a corresponding matrix of meaning in the witness of the early Church in terms of which it has been understood ever since, that is, as atoning reconciliation effected in the incarnate Person of the Son of God, the one Mediator between man and God, an act of sacrifice in blood perfected once and for all at Calvary but also a living sacrifice eternally availing for all mankind. Through the very fact that he remains an outcast from Israel, repudiated by his own, the despised and rejected of men, Jesus the anointed Servant of the Lord continues to bear the contempt and antagonism of the human heart to God and vanquishes it in the atoning love of God embodied in himself. It is as such that Jesus Christ is the Messianic Saviour of Jews and Gentiles alike, offensive though his crucifixion is to Jews and foolish weakness though it is to Gentiles.

However, when we consider the actual history of the world since New Testament times, we find the two-fold meaning of the atoning sacrifice of Christ unfolding itself but constantly tending to be split apart through the widening schism between the Christian Church and the Jewish Church. The Christian Church went out into history from the resurrection side of the Cross as the Church of the Lamb of God who has been slain but is now very much alive, with the message of universal salvation and reconciliation and the promise of a new humanity in the triumph of the Kingdom of Christ over all nations. The Jewish Church went out into history from the shadow side of the Cross to be scattered among the peoples and nations of mankind, where Jews were despised and rejected of men, the butt of their taunts, the scapegoat for all their ills, bearing mute and unwilling witness to the antagonism of man to God and thereby to the ineradicable reality of God for mankind. I believe that it is in the light of the subsequent history of Jews as well as Christians that we are enabled to grasp more of the profound significance of atoning reconciliation in and through Jesus Christ. We Christians need the Jews in their rejection by mankind to remind us that the Jew of Calvary is still the despised and rejected of men; we desperately need Israel in the frightful actualisation of its vicarious mission throughout the Christian era to teach us a deeper understanding of the suffering servant with which Jesus identified himself in his own vicarious passion. And that is now happening through Jewish and Christian reflection upon the Holocaust. But the Jews also need Christians to help them understand something of the finality of what took place in the crucifixion of Jesus which has ever since decisively affected their covenanted mission and their destiny in the mediation of divine revelation and reconciliation, and which they must surely take into their reckoning if they are to remain faithful to the faithfulness of God whose covenant has been cut into their flesh with the shedding of blood uninterruptedly from generation to generation but now in our time has for ever been burnt into the very existence of Israel by Holocaust. Only as Israel penetrates into the mystery of its own most harrowing suffering through the crucifixion of Jesus, who is not only the greatest of the Hebrew Prophets as Buber called him, but the very Holy One, the Redeemer of Israel, become incarnate, and only as the Christian Church acknowledges as never before the depth and continuity of Israel's divine calling in the Christian era together with the representative character of its rejection by the world but for the sake of the world, can Christians and Jews help each other to understand in a new way the atoning and living sacrifice which God himself has provided for mankind in Jesus Christ. Then Jews and Christians may advance together toward the fulfilment of God's redemptive purpose for both and for the whole human race.

3. *Israel can help us understand the interaction of God with the world*

One of the great problems of human civilisation in the east and in the west is what one may call a radical dualism in people's understanding of the relation of God and the world. This leads in different ways and in different cultures into some form of deism or some form of pantheism. It is a form of deism that lies behind the secularised outlook of the west, in which God is thought of as so detached from the world that he does not interact with it, so that the thought of God drops out of the picture as useless and unnecessary. It is a form of pantheism which has usually dominated the east, when God is regarded as so immanent in the being and process of all that is that he is reduced to some form of inertial presence who does not or cannot intervene in the inexorable wheel of events. But in contrast to all that, the Jews in ancient and modern times have always stood for a dynamic outlook upon God and the world which is essentially non-dualist. This is an outlook which conflicts sharply with both deism and pantheism, for it regards God as the mighty living acting God who created the universe out of nothing, continuously sustains it in its being and order and interacts with the life and history of mankind. It is that Hebraic and biblical understanding of the living God which lies behind the New Testament message about the Incarnation, as the Creator Word of God become flesh, and about the death and resurrection of Jesus, as the direct personal intervention of God himself in our human predicament, where we are trapped within our own sin and guilt and violence, in order to save us, and even rescue us, from the clutches of death itself. We cannot follow through here all the implications of this non-dualist world outlook which the Jews have handed down to us, but let us focus our attention on two points.

It is this Jewish outlook which is now in process of transforming the very foundations of our science. We have already noted that it is largely owing to Jews that we have learned to think in modern science in terms of imageless relations and structures, which cannot but have a beneficial effect in our interpretation of the New Testament message. That is to say, the Jews have taught us once again that the invisible things are not explained by the visible, but that the visible things are to be understood only by reference to the invisible. Even more basic than that, however, is the immense change which has been brought about from a dualist to a non-dualist or unitary way of knowing and thinking, that is, one in which we do not separate structure from matter or theoretical from empirical elements, for they belong naturally together. Along with this came an immense switch in our understanding of the universe. The Ptolemaic outlook which dominated science from late classical to modern times was radically dualist, for it divided sharply between a realm of physical events on earth and a realm of celestial events beyond. While that was overthrown by modern science, Newton elaborated another dualist outlook which gave rise to a closed mechanistic conception of the universe shutting out any thought of God as interacting in any dynamic way with our world. That is the narrow deterministic worldview which has helped to stifle belief in divine providence and to suffocate prayer and intercession and has undermined basic Christian beliefs in incarnation and atonement. Now, however, that whole mechanistic approach to the universe has itself been undermined and destroyed. This is due not least to Albert Einstein, the greatest scientist since Newton, who built into the fabric of our science a unitary way of thinking which is so characteristically Jewish and which is congenial to the biblical faith in the living God. Einstein himself claimed that he did not believe in a personal God who interacts providentially with mankind in history, but he did open the way for a new outlook, within which providence and prayer can once more be very much alive, and not least for many Jews who in a secular world seem to have lost touch with the living God.

It is in the light of this Jewish and biblical outlook upon God and the world that we must understand the Israeli concept of the *am ha'aretz*, the 'People of the Land', the deep interconnection between the People of Israel and the Holy Land. This is not easy for people in the east or the west who work with a dualist frame of thought at the back of their minds, for it makes them detach the concept of Israel as People from the concrete particularity of their existence in the space and time of this world where God has set them and preserves them. In the unitary outlook of the Jews, so powerfully represented in the Old Testament, the physical and the spiritual, the temporal and the eternal, the moral and the religious, are held inseparably together within the covenant faithfulness of God as it takes actual shape and form in the life and existence of Israel. There is an intrinsic relation between the People and the Land and also between the People and the Book. The uprooting of Israel from the physical location of God's self-revelation to and through them left its mark upon Judaism, particularly noticeable in a one-sided stress upon legal ordinance and a loss of the priestly and redemptive message of the Covenant except at rather attenuated points. But now in the return of Jews to the Holy Land there has come about a remarkable quickening of faith and a deep recovery of the sense of God's interaction with them in history which presses for fulfilment of the ancient promises of the Covenant. Thus it is not surprising to find in Israel today an eschatological excitement stirring in the depths of its soul and life brought on by the imminence of divine redemption, in which the land itself figures, as well as the people who dwell in it and make it blossom.

Throughout history the very existence of the Jews and their miraculous persistence in existence against all the forces that made for its complete eradication, bear incontestable witness not only to the living God, with whom the Jews have been uniquely and intimately bound up, but to the saving purpose of God for the human race, mediated in and through Israel. The Jews have always presented us with what John Macmurray used to call 'the clue to history'. Today, however, the intense actualisation, once again, of God's covenanted communion with the people of Israel within the land of promise, now called Israel, brings home to us in a new way not only the fact that the people and the land are woven indivisibly together in the fabric of Israel's vicarious mission and destiny among the peoples and nations of the earth, but also the fact that in this unitary spiritual and physical form Israel constitutes God's sign-post in the history of world-events, pointing ahead to a culmination in his saving interaction with mankind in space and time. From the perspective of the reconciliation of Jews and Christians in Jesus Christ, which we have already discussed, we cannot help but understand this in the light of the death and resurrection of Jesus Christ as entailing not only the redemption and resurrection of the People of the Land but the redemption and resurrection of all mankind.

It is highly significant that in the providence of God Jerusalem, the mother of faith in the living God, is once more the spiritual and physical centre of the people of Israel, and that is as it should be. But, as the mother of faith in the living God, Jerusalem is the appointed centre consecrated for ever by the death and resurrection of Jesus Christ for the one Church of God, Jewish and Christian, and the concrete pledge that Jesus Christ will come again to take up his Kingdom and reign in divine peace over all peoples and nations in a renewal of the creation which will far surpass anything that we can conceive in terms of human experience and history hitherto. Israel and Jerusalem do not and cannot tell us what God will actually do in the future. We can never anticipate God, as Jesus warned us. When God acts, he always takes us by surprise in breathtaking events. The startling reintegration of Jerusalem and Israel in our day, after nearly two millennia, is just one of these events, and as such it proclaims to the world in a dramatic way that the living God of Israel and of Jesus Christ will act and act decisively in human history in fulfilment of his universal purpose of love and peace.

Israel Today, in the Light of God's Word

DAVID W. TORRANCE

Israel today lies increasingly at the heart of world politics. This remarkable people has been threatened again and again throughout her long history with extinction at the hand of other hostile peoples, and never more so than during the Nazi Holocaust. Even during appalling suffering other nations have spurned and refused to comfort her, yet she has emerged in the Land of Promise, a people, virile and full of hope, the focus of world attention. This is a remarkable testimony to the Hand of God at work in his world and calling the nations to give account to him.

Whereas God is speaking to the nations through Israel, he is equally, through his servant Israel, speaking to his Church today.

No one can reasonably dispute that the Christian Church owes her spiritual heritage to Judaism. The Church owes to the Jews her understanding of God and his covenant of Grace with mankind and with all creation, her understanding of man as created in the image of God and the nature of God's salvation in Christ, the Scriptures of both the Old and New Testament and the glorious hope of things yet to come under the Hand of God. The churches have been very slow to accept, however, that God is speaking to his Church today, through Israel his covenant people, and that Israel has a continuing role in the purposes of God and continues to witness to God and that, too, the Church dependent on Israel's continued witness, for her understanding of important issues of her own faith. In comparatively recent years, however, churches in Western Europe, Protestant and Roman Catholic, and particularly in Germany, have begun to manifest a readiness to enter into dialogue with Jews and have, as a result, released some very helpful statements (see Appendix, 'Action by

the Churches', pages 135 following). From certain of these
statements, it is clear that churches have begun to take seriously the
continuing role of the Jews in history and their continuing
significance in salvation history.

The Bible contains important statements about the Jewish
people, which help us in some measure to understand some of the
things which have been happening to Israel and which we can
anticipate will yet happen. Certain of these passages have been
mentioned and helpfully considered in 'The Declaration of the
German Roman Catholic Bishops on the Church's Relationship
to Judaism', 28 April 1980 (see 'Christian Jewish Relations', no.
73, page 25 f.).

One important omission in the Declaration of the German
Roman Catholic Bishops, however, is any reference to the land.
This is mentioned by Sister Dr. Charlotte Klein, OLS, in her
'Critical Appreciation' of the Declaration (see *idem* page 43). 'The
Land is part of Jewish religious consciousness'. Their return to the
Promised Land is 'the consummation of Jewish hopes during the
last two thousand years'. Therefore, such an omission, Sister Klein
affirms, must surely go against the Vatican 'Guidelines' of
December 1974, which declares that Christians 'must strive to
learn by what essential traits the Jews define themselves in the
light of their own religious experience'. I would go further; such
an omission seems to indicate a failure to grasp the full
significance of God's promise to Israel, and that the Land belongs
to the content of that promise. 'The Lord said to Abraham ...
Now lift up your eyes and look from the place where you are,
northward and southward and eastward and westward; for all the
land which you see I will give to you and to your descendants for
ever' (Gen. 13:14, 15). 'He is mindful of his covenant for ever, of
the word that he commanded for a thousand generations, the
covenant which he made with Abraham, his sworn promise to
Isaac, which he confirmed to Jacob as a statute, to Israel as an
everlasting covenant, saying, "To you I will give the Land of
Canaan as your portion for an inheritance"' (Psalm 105:8–11).
The Land gives to God's covenant of Grace with Israel concrete
application, and likewise gives to God's covenant of Grace with
all mankind and with all creation, very definite literal application.

The Declaration of the Roman Catholic Bishops of Germany
recognises that a prophecy of the final restoration of Israel is
contained in Acts (1:6, 7). When the disciples came together they
asked Jesus, 'Lord, will you at this time restore the kingdom to
Israel?'. Jesus did not reject their question as wrong in itself, he

does not deny that there will be a future restoration of the kingdom to Israel, instead he says, 'It is not for you to know times or seasons which the Father has fixed by his own authority'. The restoration of that kingdom however is not possible without a restoration to the Land! It is therefore all the more surprising that, in the light of their own exegesis about the restoration of the kingdom to Israel, the Bishops have omitted any reference to the Land, in their Declaration.

Perhaps even more significant are the words of Jesus as he draws to the close of his earthly ministry, 'The great trumpet will sound, and he will send out his angels to the four corners of the earth, and they will gather his chosen people from one end of the world to the other. Let the fig-tree teach a lesson. When its branches become green and tender and it starts putting out leaves, you know that summer is near. In the same way, when you see all these things, you will know that the time is near, ready to begin' (Good News, Matt. 24:31–33, cp. Mark 13:27, 28; Luke 21:29–31). In the apocalyptic teaching in Matthew 24, Mark 13 and Luke 21, there is much that would seem to relate to the events that befell Jerusalem and the nation in A.D. 70. Equally, there is much that would seem to relate only to the End Times. These two strands of prophecy are interwoven in the one narrative. When our Lord spoke of gathering his chosen people from one end of the world to the other, this clearly refers, not to the events of A.D. 70 when his people were scattered to the ends of the earth, but to some future event when, under the Hand of God, they would return to the Land of Promise. In the establishment of the state of Israel, we see what seems to be a remarkable commencement of the fulfilment of this prophecy when Jews have come quite literally from north, south, east and west to their ancient homeland. The Lord said through Amos, 'I will plant them upon their land, and they shall never again be plucked up out of the land which I have given them' (Amos 9:15). If we interpret this prophecy about the future restoration of Israel in terms of today (and we cannot rightly relate it to any previous period in Israel's history), and if we see in present events the commencement of the fulfilment of this prophecy, then we can say that Israel will never again leave the Promised Land.

Jesus said, 'Let the fig-tree teach you a lesson'. In his helpful explanation of this passage, Lance Lambert, himself a Hebrew Christian, tells us, the fig-tree, along with the vine and olive tree, had often been used as a symbol in the Old Testament. It had been used firstly as a symbol of the Promised Land itself, of its plentiful abundance and fertility and of the possession of it (*e.g.*, Deut. 8:8; 1 Kings 4:25; 2 Kings 18:31; Haggai 2:19 and Zech. 3:10). Secondly it was used as a symbol of the covenant people of God and their fruitfulness (*e.g.*, Joel 1:7; Hosea 9:10, cp. Luke 13:6–9). By New Testament times, therefore, the fig-tree had associations in the popular mind with the land and the people of God, with both the nation and its national territory. The way in which the Lord Jesus used the fig-tree in the parable recorded in Luke 13:6–9 is surely conclusive evidence that he associated the fig-tree with the Jewish people. For the three years of his public ministry he had looked for fruit and found none. The 'acted' parable of Mark 11 (cp. Matt. 21) must be seen in this light ('Battle for Israel', page 93). The fig-tree withered from its roots (Mark 11:20) is Israel, along with her national territory, cursed because of her refusal to repent and her rejection of Jesus as Messiah. The fulfilment of this prophecy according to most commentators came in A.D. 70 with the destruction of both Jerusalem and the temple and the destruction of Israel as a nation for almost 2,000 years. Jesus however anticipated a remarkable recovery of this fig-tree which became dead all the way down to its roots. The day would come when in an astonishing way it would again sprout and send forth branches green and tender and covered with leaves. Here Jesus was anticipating the resurrection of the people and their restoration to the land. The present return to the land of a substantial remnant seems to mark the commencement of a remarkable fulfilment of Jesus' word.

To many theologians, accustomed to demythologise and to see only the ethical implications of the Word of God and not to see particular, material implications of that Word, the events of the Holocaust and the restoration to the land must be disturbing in the extreme. Accept the hand of God behind these events and we see in them a confirmation and unfolding of much that God has said through prophets and apostles. For many this must involve a reappraisal of the very nature of the Word of God and their understanding of it and a readiness to accept the Jewish position that, whereas prophecy has abiding spiritual value, it does have also a particular literal application. This acceptance of the practical and literal dimensions of the Word of God is so important to our understanding of the Incarnation, which was an event which took place at a particular time, in a particular place and in a particular people. Jesus was a Jew and remains for ever a Jew, a fulfilled and completed Jew. Our acceptance of the continuing place of the Jews in the on-going purposes of God and of the particular events that have happened to them as belonging to the unfolding of God's purpose, causes our understanding of the Incarnation, as it were, to be earthed. If, on the one hand, we do not accept the particular on-going witness of the Jews to God and do not accept the practical and literal dimension of the Word of God, which this acceptance demands, then we tend to spiritualise the Incarnation, in our understanding and more especially in our life and witness to Christ. From this follows all the problems with which we are confronted today in mission for we gentilise the Gospel. On the other hand when we accept the on-going witness of the Jews and the practical, literal application of prophecy in regard to them, then there is given to us a certain God-given unity of the secular and the spiritual, the things of time and the things of eternity, which has such far reaching consequences for the mission of the church.

Many people seem to be hindered in their acceptance of the restoration of Israel to the land as a fulfilment of the Word of God, by the actual events taking place in the Middle East today. They argue as follows. The great majority of Jews, either in the land of Israel or throughout the world, do not accept Jesus as Messiah and the majority remain, in some measure, agnostic: Israel's restoration to the land has brought about great suffering to many Arabs and unrest to the rest of the world: So many things that the government of Israel is doing do not seem in accord with the Word of God and with his love for the people of all nations: Whereas God loves the Jews, he loves the Arabs just as much. How then can we affirm that God, who is a God of love, is behind these events and that Israel's restoration to the Promised Land is a fulfilment of the Word of God? By way of answer I wish to state the following points.

First of all, God has called Israel and used Israel to testify to himself all through the years, despite her unbelief in Jesus and her rejection of him as Messiah. Accordingly, through the events of the Holocaust and through her restoration to the land, God is continuing to use Israel to call the attention of the nations to himself and to convince them that it is to God that they must give account. He and he alone is Lord of all history, the King and Judge of all nations.

Secondly, God's call of Israel to be his servant and chosen people and their restoration to the land, is God's way of working out his purposes of love and redemption for all the nations and for the world. It is because of his continuing love for the world, despite the world's sin and rejection of him, that God still continues to work out his purposes of love and redemption through the Jews.

Thirdly, Israel is called to be a people of God, separate from the other nations, in order, as God's servant, to be the instrument of blessing and salvation of the other nations. We cannot separate her being a people from her being a nation, yet her primary call is to be a people of God. Just as in the Old Testament, we see this tension between Israel's desire to be a nation like all the other nations of the world and her calling to be the people of God, so today we see this same tension as Israel struggles to be a nation, yet her primary calling is to be the people of God. Her struggle primarily to be a nation is a rejection of her calling, and many of the problems in the Middle East today and much of the suffering of both Jews and Arabs and others, follows as a result of her struggle primarily to be a nation. It is for the other nations and for the Church to help Israel to be the people of God and therefore a blessing and means of salvation for the world. The other nations, however, are just as sinful. Israel's sin is the sin of the other nations, and the Church, alas, in her blindness has failed to help Israel to be the people of God and therefore a blessing to both the Church and the world.

The other nations and the Church cannot rightly stand back from Israel in criticism and judgement of her. Judgement belongs solely to God. We all are equally involved in Israel's sin and rejection of her calling. Her sin is our sin, and her rejection of God's call is our rejection of God's call to obedience and love. We all are involved with Israel and have responsibility for helping her toward the path of obedience, for her sake and for the sake of us all. The salvation and peace of this world depend on it.

Fourthly, many things which are happening in the Middle East today are not in accord with God's will nor in accord with his love for all peoples. This flows from the fact that Israel has not yet embraced Jesus as her Messiah, neither have the Arab Muslims, nor have the other nations which seek to enter Middle East problems. As such, we are called, in understanding, in love and compassion, as Christians to enter into the sufferings, the injustices and fears of all parties in the Middle East, aware that all are equally precious in the sight of God. We are called to pray with deep concern for all, that they might recognise and accept the Living God, the Father of our Lord Jesus Christ, and submit to his way of salvation for them and for all people, that is, submit to his way of salvation which includes the restoration of his servant people to the Promised Land.

Fifthly, because there is a conflict between the rights of different peoples, there is no political solution and no human solution to the problems of the Middle East. The answer to the problems of the Middle East and of the world lies with God alone, and we, the Church, and the nations of the world, are called actively to seek God's solution and in so doing to recognise his plan for the Jews and their restoration to the Land, as belonging to his plan for the utlimate salvation of the world.

The Bible indicates that there will come mounting pressure against Israel and mounting opposition, from all the other nations of the world, as they continue to resist God. We in the Christian Church, however, are called to resist these pressures and to pray diligently and earnestly to seek to persuade the countries in which we live to resist these pressures against Israel, which are of a political, economic and military kind and are imposed by the nations, in their resistance to God. The resistance of the nations to God and his way of salvation is increasingly manifest in their opposition to Israel. Their attitude to Israel is the test of their attitude to God and the test whereby they will be blessed or judged by God. Such Scriptures as Zechariah 12 make it clear that God will judge every nation by its attitude to Israel. Nations that compromise over Israel will themselves be compromised; those that seek to break Israel will themselves be broken and nations that go against Israel will be opposed by God. This is again clearly stated by God in Isaiah 60:12, 'that nation and kingdom that will not serve thee shall perish, yea those nations shall be utterly wasted'. In Jeremiah 30:11, the Lord states the matter even more emphatically, 'for I am with thee, saith the Lord, to save thee: though I will make a full end of all nations whither I have scattered thee, yet I will not make a full end of thee' (Lance Lambert, 'Battle for Israel', page 76). The destiny of the Jews and the destiny of the world belong together and the peace and prosperity of Israel under God is essential for the peace and prosperity of the world.

Sixthly, Israel witnesses to a glorious hope. Her very presence in the world today and her restoration to the Promised Land testify to God's Grace and to his continuing determination to redeem the world. Despite the enormity and complexity of the problems that surround Israel, and despite the mounting opposition to Israel and to God by many people and nations, as a Christian Church we are called to go forward with this assured hope that God will triumph in the end and Israel will triumph and become the means of God's blessing and salvation for the world and all creation.

There are two events which have happened to the Jewish People and which more than any other since A.D. 70 testify before the nations to the Hand of God. These are the Holocaust and their return to the Promised Land. Israel's sufferings can only rightly be understood in terms of God's covenant with her and her call to be God's servant before the nations. Her rejection by the nations of the world is a living demonstration of the nations' rejection of God. Her unspeakable sufferings during the Holocaust when almost one half of the total population of the Jews was affected and one third was wiped out, give to the nations of the world the foremost visible demonstration of the sufferings of Christ. Her dereliction portrays his dereliction on the cross, and portrays the sufferings of a world without God and anticipates the sufferings yet to come of all who finally reject Christ. On the other hand, her resurrection from the gates of death and the restoration of a substantial remnant to the Promised Land, when Jews have come from all over the world to become a virile, vigorous people, testifies in a remarkable way to the Divine Hand at work in grace and salvation, and love.

God said, through his servant Paul, in Romans 8:37–39, 'No, in all these things we are more than conquerors through him who loved us. For I am sure that neither death, nor life, nor angels, nor principalities, nor things present, nor things to come, nor powers, nor height, nor depth, nor anything else in all creation, will be able to separate us from the love of God in Christ Jesus our Lord.' Paul was writing to Jewish Christians in Rome. and immediately in chapters 9, 10, 11, that followed, he illustrates this fact of God's ever embracing love, in regard to Israel. 'I ask, then, has God rejected his people? By no means! I myself am an Israelite, a descendant of Abraham, a member of the tribe of Benjamin. God has not rejected his people whom he foreknew … So I ask, have they stumbled so as to fall? By no means! But through their trespass salvation has come to the Gentiles, so as to make Israel jealous. Now if their trespass means riches for the world, and if their failure means riches for the Gentiles, how much more will their full inclusion mean!' (11:1, 2, 11, 12). In Israel's preservation from death and in her restoration to the Land, we see a remarkable confirmation of God's Word that nothing can separate her from the love of God and in all things she is more than conqueror through Christ Jesus, even although she does not yet know him.

In these same chapters of Romans, Paul anticipates Israel's restoration and the blessings which this restoration will bring to

ISRAEL TODAY, IN THE LIGHT OF GOD'S WORD   113

the Gentile nations. 'For if their rejection means the reconciliation of the world, what will their acceptance mean but life from the dead' (11:15). As the German Roman Catholic Bishops have said (*idem*, page 34), 'We Christians have to take seriously the prediction of the apostle about Israel's final salvation, though we do not know clearly how God will save "all Israel" '. The bishops link the final salvation of Israel with the prophecy of the final restoration of Israel which underlies Acts 1:6–8, and which has been referred to above. The bishops also link, and I believe rightly, Israel's final salvation with a prophecy contained in Acts 3. 'A restoration of the promised kingdom, as already the prophets of the old covenant announced it, is certainly coming, though we do not precisely know in what manner. According to Acts 3:19–21, the Jews should repent and turn to Jesus "that your sins may be blotted out, that times of refreshing may come ... and that he may send the Christ appointed for you, Jesus, whom the heavens must receive until the time for establishing all that God spake by the mouth of his holy prophets from of old". According to this text the returning Christ is also destined for Israel, for its "refreshing". The Jews too, with all the redeemed, will then be "refreshed" and liberated from their sufferings and sins' (*idem*, page 34).

Jesus also, I believe, refers to the restoration of Israel when he says in Luke 21:24, 'Jerusalem will be trodden down by the Gentiles, until the times of the Gentiles are fulfilled'. These words clearly imply that a time will come when Jerusalem will not be trodden down by the Gentiles and when Jerusalem will be restored and Israel will again be a people of God in the Promised Land. Again Jesus said in Matthew 23:29, 'For I tell you, you will not see me again, until you say, "Blessed be he who comes in the name of the Lord".' By that word 'until', Jesus implies that the day will come when in fact Israel will say, 'Welcome in the name of the Lord' or 'Blessed be he who comes in the name of the Lord'. Undoubtedly for Israel to welcome Jesus as Lord and Messiah, there will be a complete change of heart on the part of Israel. This surely is anticipated in that remarkable prophecy stated in Zechariah 12:10–13:1, 'And I will pour out on the house of David and the inhabitants of Jerusalem a spirit of compassion and supplication, so that, when they look on him whom they have pierced, they shall mourn for him, as one mourns for an only child, and weep bitterly over him, as one weeps over a first-born. On that day the mourning in Jerusalem will be as great as the mourning for Hadad-rimmon in the plain of Megiddo. The

land shall mourn, each family by itself. ... On that day there shall
be a fountain opened for the house of David and the inhabitants
of Jerusalem to cleanse them from sin and uncleanness' (cp.
Ezekiel 36, 37 and 39:25–29).

We might liken Israel's welcome of Jesus as Messiah to
another Pentecost, when through Israel will flow great blessing
on all the nations of the earth. 'If their trespass means riches for the
world, and if their failure means riches for the Gentiles, how much
more will their full inclusion mean! ... O the depth of the riches
and wisdom and knowledge of God!' (Rom. 11:12, 33).

The Messianic fulfilment of the Jewish faith

MARK KINZER

The Jewish Christian is for many people an anomaly and enigma. His identity often seems incomprehensible to both his non-Messianic Jewish brethren and his Messianic gentile brethren. The Jewish form of incomprehension was passed on faithfully to me in my younger years. I recall being unable to distinguish between the words '*goy*' ('gentile') and 'Christian'; in my mind both words referred to all of those who were not Jews. The 'Christian' form of incomprehension is reflected in the questions many gentile believers ask me: 'So you are a convert from Judaism?' or 'So you were formerly a Jew?' The man who insists that he is a Jewish Christian looks to all the world as one who is trying to walk along a fence with a leg on each side, or as one who answers 'yes' and 'no' to the same question.

There are obvious historical explanations for this inability to yoke together the words 'Jew' and 'Christian'. Nonetheless, one cannot dismiss Jewish Christianity on historical or logical grounds. Jesus was a Jew, the apostles were Jews, the New Testament is a patently Jewish book, and the early Messianic congregation saw the unity of Jew and Gentile within its halls as the paramount sign of God's having reconciled the world to himself (Eph. 2:11–22). Even the non-Messianic Jew cannot fault the logic: If Jesus was indeed the Messiah, then a Jew is obligated to follow him, and can only experience the fullness of Judaism as a result. One can argue with the premise, but not with the inevitability of the conclusion.

The fulfilment of Judaism in Jesus the Messiah is to me both a theological and an experiential reality, a truth I believe and a truth I live. I am a Jew, seeking to follow Torah (the Jewish law) and living today a more Jewish life than ever before; I am also a Christian, believing that Jesus fulfils the promises made to my ancestors, and experiencing the fruits that come from a relationship with him.

Background

My immediate family memory goes back only two generations. Just before World War I my grandparents made the long ocean voyage from the east European *shtetl* (Jewish village) to the great American metropolis. My mother's father was a humble carpenter, a jovial and simple man. My paternal grandfather was a learned and pious talmudic scholar. The rabbis would sit at his side and seek his opinion on abstruse matters of Jewish law. Though both of these men lived far beyond their allotted time of three score and ten years, a gulf separated their universe from mine—a gulf of language, culture, age, and world-view. I lived in the same house with each of them for a time, but I never really knew them.

My father was a kind man with few spiritual inclinations but with a passionate attachment to the synagogue and to Zionism. Through most of my youth he would drive twice daily to the *shul* (synagogue) to attend the morning and evening services. As President or Vice-president of the congregation he would devote several full evenings each week to committee meetings and practical management of the building. He would also contribute generously to the Jewish National Fund and other Zionist causes. Though usually mild and reasonable, he could be inflamed to a fever pitch at the mere mention of the state of Israel.

My mother's temperament was of a more intuitive bent. She believed deeply in God and in prayer, yet she had little knowledge of the scripture or of Jewish tradition. She concentrated her prayer and her energy rather on raising the three unruly youths to whom she had given birth.

My two older brothers and I responded to my parents' faith with undisguised condescension. We were living in a new age and a new culture, and the old ways were clearly unsuitable. We would sit together in the synagogue on the High Holy Days and joke about the operatic falsettos of the cantor or the spiritual apathy of the congregation. We were unimpressed with Judaism as we knew it—a ritualistic faith based on a language that few understood and a set of spiritual realities that few experienced. After celebrating our Bar Mitzvah's[1] in our thirteenth years, we all scrupulously avoided religion in any form.

Of course, I did have other obsessions. In my early years my life gained meaning from one main source—sports. My brothers and I ate, drank, and slept sports. We played them in the streets and fields, read about them in the newspapers, watched them on television, attended them at the stadiums and arenas, and talked about them everywhere. As I grew older I discovered another source of joy and purpose—music. Again I dove in with gusto, playing, singing, and listening, until even in sleep my head vibrated with Chopin and Brahms and B. B. King. Finally, I stumbled upon what was to become my greatest passion— philosophy. It all began when I pulled from the shelf of our local library a volume of Plato's *Dialogues*. I read it quickly, and was immediately conquered. Spinoza and Aristotle soon followed. Philosophy led to psychology, and I rapidly digested morsels from Freud, Jung, Fromm, and R. D. Lang. I had already read Dostoyevski and Tolstoy, and now I appreciated them even more. My mind had come alive with a hunger for knowledge and truth, and the passion was not less strong for being intellectual rather than physical.

At this time I had an ambivalent attitude toward Jesus—a mixture of fascination, attraction, fear, and hostility that is common to many Jewish people. On the one hand, the very name of Jesus could cause me to cringe with apprehension and animosity. There was something alien and threatening in that name; it was associated not so much with a person as with ideas, institutions, and an ancient enmity which I did not understand. My mother once told me how she came home crying after her first day in a gentile primary school and asked her parents, 'Who is Jesus? They said I killed Jesus! Whom did I kill?' Such incidents leave their mark. Even many Jews who have never personally experienced the hostility of Christians still react with irrational fear and anger at the mention of the name of Jesus.

On the other hand, the man Jesus fascinated me. Something about his teaching and his life caught my imagination and impressed me deeply. One night I stayed up till three A.M. watching a movie on television based on the life of Christ. I was so affected that I asked a gentile friend the next day if I could borrow her Bible. I wanted to read the first-hand accounts of the life of this remarkable man. Unfortunately the bible was in King James English, and I began with the first chapter of Matthew— sixteen verses of 'begats'. My zeal quickly waned, and I returned the bible to my friend in as unused a condition as it was when I received it.

Reversal

The most significant year of my life began as I left my parents' household and enrolled at the University of Michigan in Ann Arbor. I had been eagerly awaiting this transition for many years. I looked forward to being independent of my parents and their authority. Even more, I looked forward to the academic environment of intellectual and social ferment that awaited me in Ann Arbor. I wanted to meet other seekers who could aid me in my quest for knowledge and truth. Hidden in me beneath many layers of youthful pretence and egoism lay an intense desire for that which was right and true. I was a product of the late 60s, and the idealism of those years left an imprint on my mind.

The disillusionment of my first year at school hit me harder because of my high expectations. There were several reasons for this disillusionment. First, I found the huge university bureaucracy oppressive and stifling. Like most freshmen, I lived in a residence hall which housed close to a thousand students. I developed personal relationships with few of my classmates and none of my instructors. Secondly, I soon discovered that at the university, knowledge was fragmented into a multitude of discrete yet warring compartments. My quest for an integrated world-view was frustrated on every side. Each of my professors was eloquent, knowledgeable, and persuasive; unfortunately, they all disagreed with one another. Thirdly, I found few people who were actually concerned with life's meaning and purpose. For years the main philosophical question that troubled me was the question of death. I was not so much afraid of death as I was unwilling to ignore it. What was the meaning of my work, my morals, my body, my relationships of love and friendship if all were destined to end in dust? I quickly found that very few people were concerned about such things, even at the university. Finally, I began to grow more conscious of my own shortcomings. My ideals were high, but my ability to live up to these ideals was substantially lower. In particular, I began to see some of my closest relationships deteriorate, and I knew that I was largely to blame. Therefore, the university sent me home for the summer disheartened, disillusioned, and slightly confused.

For three years much of my life had revolved around three close friends. We were all agnostics, and we were proud of our unbelief. During these years we were never apart from one another. I now decided that it was time for me to make a break with my past stabilities — especially the camaraderie of my friends.

I needed to make up my mind decisively about what I thought, what I believed, and where I was headed. As an initial step in this direction, I purchased a back-pack and reserved a seat on a cheap chartered flight to Europe. This would allow me to be away from my friends and family, visit some places I always wanted to see, and make some fundamental decisions about the direction of my life.

The next seven weeks proved to be a turning point. Every book I picked up seemed to speak about the reality of God and of Jesus Christ. I visited the magnificent cathedrals of Europe and marvelled at the centuries of energy, treasure, and genius that men devoted to the glory of their God. A man approached me as I was eating lunch behind a Viennese palace and started speaking in German; as I told him that I did not speak his language, he broke out into a broad Kansas smile and began to speak to me in my native tongue about Jesus the Messiah. I spent a weekend with a Christian couple in Worcester, England, who talked with me about the Lord at great length and refreshed me with loving hospitality. They gave me a book which spoke of God as a personal and powerful being who ruled the world yet wanted us to know him consciously and intimately. I had been seeking an ultimate source of meaning, a foundational principle that could organise and integrate the field of human knowledge, an ethical system that was lofty yet liveable; but I was totally unprepared for this type of God, who was less concerned that we pursue him and more concerned that we let ourselves be found.

The straw that broke the camel's back awaited me as I returned home. In the seven weeks that I had been gone all three of my friends had become Christians. Their experiences and lines of thought paralleled my own. With this fact, I was finished. I could not resist and still maintain my integrity. I now began to pray, read scripture, and meet occasionally with other believers. Every day I found new confirmations of my still slightly half-hearted faith. Prayer was answered; scripture blazed like a torch before my eyes and enlightened my mind with unexpected truths; my life and character started to undergo a radical change. This was an entirely new world, full of powers and principalities beyond my imagining.

I had sought the truth, and it had seized me. I had longed for a comprehensive intellectual system, and instead found myself face to face with a person who was more than a person. This new faith had intellectual solidity, but it soared far beyond the realms of philosophy. The quest had ended where it had begun—with the

God of Israel. He had summoned me, and there was no possible response other than the response of my fathers: 'Here am I'.

A Messianic Judaism

How could I reconcile my new faith with my former aversion to 'Christianity', that cluster of ideas and institutions and historical events that I had once associated with the name of Jesus? My initial approach was simple: I was not becoming a 'Christian' in *that* sense. I was not joining myself to some entity called 'Christendom', but was merely believing that Jesus was the Messiah and deciding to follow him. In many ways I still identified 'Christianity' with the *goyim* (gentiles), and I was determined not to subject myself to a process of gentilisation. My attitude has mellowed over the years as I have learned to appreciate many aspects of the gentile Christian heritage, but that early determination to live as a Jewish follower of Jesus—a Jewish Christian—has remained the same.

My first Christian teacher was a Jewish man who was raised in an orthodox home. He had become a believer in Yeshua (Jesus) at the age of nineteen, and had been serving the Lord faithfully for over twenty years. His wife was also a Jewish believer in Yeshua. They lived their lives in a fully Jewish way—their children went to Hebrew school, and their son was Bar Mitzvahed in my father's synagogue. This man taught me a basic principle that I have never forgotten: accept your gentile brethren as your family in the Lord, but never abandon your Jewish life or identity.

The application of this principle had a striking impact on my parents. As can be imagined, at first they were appalled at my new religious convictions. My mother responded with vehement objections. My father, seeing that I would not change my mind, and wanting to calm my mother's agitated emotions, followed his usual course of trying to make the best of a bad situation: 'Look at it this way Marion—at least now he believes in God'. However, after several weeks they began to notice some things that surprised them both. First of all, I had clearly not forfeited my Judaism. In fact, I was more concerned about Jewish things than I had ever been before. I accompanied my father to synagogue, and peppered him with questions about Jewish life. I insisted that I was not departing from my heritage, but instead was returning to it. Secondly, they noticed changes in my way of relating to them. I was less rebellious, more respectful, more eager to help around the house. Something significant had obviously happened in my life.

The outcome of this summer at home was more dramatic than I had expected. Four months after I had professed faith in Yeshua my mother received a vision of the Lord and heard him call her name. She responded, and also became a follower of the Messiah. She has remained steadfast in her faith to this day.

In my first few years as a Christian I would at times grow fearful of losing my Jewish identity. Would my Judaism erode before the powerful assimilating forces of the gentile world and the gentile church? I no longer have such fears. Experience has confirmed what I already knew to be true theologically—faith in the Messiah is the fulfilment of Judaism.

I have experienced this fulfilment in many ways. First and most importantly, I have entered into an experienced personal relationship with the God of Abraham, Isaac, and Jacob. This is the God whom Jesus reveals in unique fashion (Matt. 22:32). He is not Marduk, Moloch, or Baal, but the God of my fathers. When my brothers and I were children my father wrote a prayer that he taught us and recited with us every night before going to sleep. We irreverently rattled it off as quickly as we could and never really understood its contents, but I still have it memorised today:

> The Lord is my shepherd, I shall not want.
> He is my rock, my fortress, my shield, my guide, my
> guardian, my deliverer, my protector, my redeemer, my
> saviour.
> He is the great God of Abraham, Isaac, Jacob, and Moses.
> He is the creator of all living things, in heaven and on earth.
> He is the maker of miracles and wonders.
> He is the God in whom I trust. Amen.

This is the same God whom I now confess, know, love, and serve. He is the source of the Jewish people, the covenant with Abraham, the promise of the land, the holy Torah, and the Messianic deliverance. He is the God of my fathers.

Secondly, faith in the Messiah has led me to a great love and reverence for the Hebrew scriptures, the Tanach (a Hebrew acronym for the Law-Torah, the Prophets-Nevi'im, and the Writings-Chetuvim). The scriptures are the true foundation of Jewish life. In Genesis (Bereshit) we read of God's irrevocable promise to Abraham and his children. In the subsequent books of Moses we read of the deliverance from Egypt, the covenant on Sinai, and the giving of the Torah. In the Psalms .(Tehillim) we

E

have the ancient prayers of Israel that have expressed for millennia the Jewish people's worship of God and longing for redemption. In the Prophets (Nevi'im) we read about the promised consolation of Israel, the hope that has sustained this people through times of darkest night. As a son of Abraham by faith and by circumcision, I have realised that the scriptures are my most precious heritage and possession. They tie me to the God of my fathers, but they also tie me indissolubly to the fathers themselves, those of my people among whom this book emerged and who have lived and died for this book and the way of life enshrined in it. Faith in the Messiah has brought me to a love and understanding of the Jewish scriptures that has confirmed me unalterably in my identity as a son of Israel.

Thirdly, my faith in the Messiah has planted in me a great zeal for Torah. This is certainly a point of controversy among both Messianic Jews and Gentiles, but I can only express here my own opinion and experience. I believe that Messianic Jews can and should (when possible) observe the Law of Moses, ceremonial as well as moral. My conviction is based largely on the evidence for early Messianic Jewish practice found in the New Testament writings. For example, in Acts 21:20–4 we have the following description of James's address to Paul and his co-workers upon their arrival in Jerusalem:

> You see, brothers, how many thousands there are among the Jews of those who have believed; they are all zealous for the law, and they have been told about you that you teach all the Jews who are among the Gentiles to forsake Moses, telling them not to circumcise their children or observe the customs. What then is to be done? They will certainly hear that you have come. Do therefore what we tell you. We have four men who are under a vow; take these men and purify yourself along with them and pay their expenses, so that they may shave their heads. Thus all will know that there is nothing in what they have been told about you but that you yourself live in observance of the law.

Paul followed James's suggestion in order to demonstrate that these rumours were false. Paul observed the ceremonial law, even as did the pious Messianic congregation of Jerusalem.

Of course, many complex questions now arise. How does one interpret the law? Should a Jewish Christian follow the traditional rabbinic interpretation and embellishment of the law? How much freedom does the Jewish Christian have in regard to Mosaic ceremonial injunctions? This is only the beginning of the questions. Such complex issues are very important, but my main point here is simple and elementary: I love Torah, believe that it has implications for the lives of all Jews, and strive to follow it according to the teaching and example of Yeshua and his disciples. Faith in the Messiah has not alienated me from the way of life given by God to my forefathers any more than it alienated the Apostle Paul from Torah.

Fourthly, my new knowledge of God has unlocked for me the immense treasury of Jewish worship. The Siddur Avodat Israel, the Jewish prayer book, abounds in the praise of God as do few books I have ever read. The core of the Siddur goes back to the time of Yeshua and reflects something of the way he must have prayed. As I pray daily from the Siddur I experience communion with Yeshua and am able to join my voice with Jewish saints, past and present, who have offered to God acceptable sacrifices of praise and thanksgiving. These prayers, which were once so meaningless to me, now embody and express what I have come to know in personal experience.

In addition to the daily pattern of worship found in the Siddur, I have also come to appreciate Shabbat (the Sabbath) and the Festivals. I can recall my first experience of the feast of Succoth (Tabernacles) after coming to believe in the Messiah. As I worshipped in the synagogue and waved my lulav (palm branch) and sang the Hallel (Psalms 113–118) and the great 'Hoshanah' (Hosanna), my mind was drawn to Yeshua's grand entry to Jerusalem at the beginning of the last week before his death. I also meditated on the promise of his coming again in royal splendour, and how it would fulfil both Palm Sunday and the prophetic significance of Succoth. I have had other such experiences and insights as I have celebrated Shabbat (Sabbath), Pesach (Passover), Shavuoth (Pentecost), Chanukah (Dedication), Rosh Hoshana (New Year), and Yom Kippur (Day of Atonement). Regular synagogue attendance and familiarity with Jewish prayer has also deepened my capacity to celebrate these feasts adequately.

Fifthly, my new appreciation for the Hebrew scriptures and Hebrew worship has given birth to a great love for the Hebrew language. I am not a Hebrew scholar, but I can pray and read with understanding. The more I use the language, the more it seems to me that it was fashioned with the worship and service of God in view. It is vivid, concrete, musical, and flowing with oriental richness. Ancient Hebrew is not a language like Greek that easily lends itself to metaphysical speculation. But it is a language that easily flows with the praises of God, and the richness of Hebrew worship is incomparable.

Sixthly, faith in the Messiah has given me a new love for the Jewish people. I once viewed the Jewish people as merely another ethnic grouping with its own customs, language, and history. I was not ashamed to call myself a Jew, but I was just as at home in modern American culture as I was in Jewish culture. Now I realise that I belong to a people which has a special call and destiny, not because of its great intrinsic worth or unique genius, but because of its election by God. I am humbled and ashamed at my people's consistent failings, but I am also grateful for God's continued faithfulness and love 'for the sake of their forefathers' (Rom. 11:28). I identify with Israel as my people, and like Paul, 'my heart's desire and prayer to God for them is that they may be saved' (Rom. 10:1).

Seventhly and finally, faith in the Messiah has brought me to a new love and appreciation for my own family. I am grateful for my parents and their faith, and for my grandparents and their faith. I am especially grateful for my grandfather and his life of devotion to God. I delight in hearing stories about him from my parents; he was a man full of wisdom, faith, zeal, and charity. My faith in the Messiah has made me eager to imitate him.

I have often heard an accusation made by non-Messianic Jewish leaders that is thoroughly contradicted in my own experience. According to these leaders, Jewish Christians only live a sham-Jewish way of life. They adopt Jewish customs, not out of genuine personal conviction, but only that they may deceive unsuspecting Jews into accepting the Messianic claims of Jesus. Perhaps some Jewish Christians have done this, but my experience has been entirely different. I am a Jew, and I want to live as a Jew, even if I am the only Jew in a city and have no hopes of persuading some of my brothers regarding the messiahship of Yeshua. The scriptures, worship, language, and destiny of Israel, and above all the God and Messiah of Israel are all part of my inheritance as a son of Abraham, and I have laid claim to that inheritance, for the God of Israel has laid claim to me.

Yeshua the Nazarene is the fulfilment of Judaism. He is the Jew *par excellence*, the personal embodiment of the people of Israel. Like the patriarchs and kings, and yet in even greater fashion, the Messiah *is* Israel, he is the personal head and representative and source and ruler of this people. This is the key to interpreting the

THE MESSIANIC FULFILMENT OF THE JEWISH FAITH 125

great Suffering Servant passage of Isa. 53—the Servant refers both to the people Israel (as the Jewish interpretation states) and to a personal Messiah (as the Christian interpretation states). If this is true, then how can one lose one's Judaism by following this Jew who embodies and personifies the entire Jewish people? In fact, how can one be fully a Jew without following him?

Indeed, faith in the Messiah has fulfilled my Judaism. To be more precise, it has brought me *back* to the God of Israel whom I abandoned in my youth. I was an assimilated Jew, independent, cynical, and unbelieving, yet hungry for knowledge and truth, and Yeshua revealed himself to me as the wisdom and the power of God. To be even more precise, faith in the Messiah has brought me *forward* to a new Judaism consummated in the death and resurrection of Yeshua and already bringing forth the first-fruits of the life of the age to come.

NOTE
1. A Jewish rite celebrating a boy's coming of age and his assumption of the full responsibilities of manhood.

Christ, the fulfilment of the Jewish faith

JOHANNA-RUTH DOBSCHINER

When asked if I would be a contributor to this volume, compiled by 'learned men', and express myself with regards to the above heading, it seemed as if I were back at school working on a project for my Finals.

Writing my autobiography, *Selected to Live*, presented no problem, for not being an authoress absolved me from 'keeping to the rules' or 'presenting a readable, gripping story'. All it required was: a talk on paper! It was the Lord God Himself who, for reasons only known to Himself, graciously breathed His Spirit into those pages.

But here, I am faced with some real deep thinking. Here, I must give a reason for the life and hope which is now within me. Here, I must stretch as a bridge between the Church, in which I now find myself, and the Jewish life and faith into which I was born. Believe me, if only I could be that bridge, it then would be so easy for both Jewish people and my brothers and sisters in Christ to identify with the reality of Paul's words in Eph. 2:14–18:

> He [Christ] is our Peace, Who has made the two one and has destroyed the barrier, the dividing wall of hostility, by abolishing in his flesh the law with its commandments and regulations. His purpose was to create in Himself one new man out of the two, thus making peace, and in this one body to reconcile both of them to God through the Cross, by which He put to death their hostility. He came and preached peace to you who were far away and peace to those who were near. For through Him we both have access to the Father by one Spirit.

The truth is indeed that 'in Christ' this one-ness and beauty of love and comfort is portrayed. It is a phenomenon which Christ wished to make known to His contemporaries, when He told them, 'By *this* shall

all men know that you are My disciples, if you love each other' (John 13:35). But truth and reality are often far removed from each other within the concept of our theme. The shores of Judaism and Christianity know few bridges.

However, it is delightful and most impressive to have met numerous draughtsmen, architects and builders, as well as the countless numbers known throughout past centuries in the pages of our history books, who supervised meticulously the building of those bridges. Even at this present time, I find myself among such great and dedicated men, within the pages of this volume.

Let me say at the very outset of my reflections, that I speak not for every Jewish believer, as each Hebrew-Christian has reached his or her moment of God's revelation along a most unique and personal pathway. Some have begun their journey from atheism or agnosticism, while others traced their Messiah through the pages of the Old Testament, being finally faced with the Christ as He reveals Himself within the pages of the New Testament.

It is this New Testament which became such a puzzlement to me during those early days of faith in and dedication to Christ, as Lord. How could anyone, I reasoned, without a Jewish background, its culture and tradition, anyone who was unfamiliar with God's dealings among ancient Israel, be interested and finally accept the outline of New Testament teaching as truth? How humble and yet how brave were those Gentile believers, I contemplated, to worship the God of *our* fathers, through the Messiah of Bethlehem and Calvary.

Since those early days, opportunity was afforded to me to familiarise myself in this and other countries, with this entirely new set-up in which I found myself. As I shared my treasured new Salvation, I also was able to learn a lot from those who had travelled this road long before me. My side of the coin was: to find a way of coping with the most extraordinary and outlandish attitudes of Gentile believers towards God's ancient soil — the soil on which He sowed for the final harvest to be. Matt. 25:31–46. Finally I became convinced, and still am, that the majority of Gentile Christians simply 'do-not-know' or have never been taught the relevance and proper place of Israel in God's Plan of Salvation. Yes, the more I read the New Testament as the natural outflow and continuation of the Old Testament, the more I marvel at the degree of blindness which has equally fallen on the Church of Jesus Christ, due to misinformed teaching and influences, even since kindergarten stage. Keeping this in mind, how is it possible for a Jewish person to remain placid when visiting a Christian place of worship — listening to hymns and Bible readings which mention Israel as land or people — and then be confronted with the extraordinary transformation when his so-familiar names suddenly mean 'Gentile believers' and 'The Church'?

Messianic believer, Hebrew-Christian, or whatever a Jewish believer may call himself, it becomes a deeply wounding and bewildering impact when singly, among a full congregation of Gentile believers, he hears a Bible reading which begins with the words, 'Ye men of Israel', without explanation of the true origin and setting of that Bible portion. How effective and timely it would be if the clergy of all denominations would lead their people in intercession for 'the children of Israel', as mentioned in Old and New Testaments, when appropriate Bible readings and sermons call for clear distinctions in terms.

In our Churches, we have become so used to the words and phraseology as heard from our pulpits, that people who hear them, accept them without questioning nor understanding their irrelevance on occasions.

It is Christmas Eve. The Church is decorated with its season's trimmings and the inevitable tree. Christmas carols, so familiar, are sung with the same warmth and fervour today, as before the establishment of The State of Israel. No mention is made of the Israel of God in its present national setting. No prayers included, that they also may become aware that their Saviour has indeed come.

No desire of the Churches worldwide, to wrap themselves around that little nation which needs the warmth of those who profess to be filled with Him Who was born at Bethlehem, Who lived and loved and taught at Nazareth, and Who filled that land and the world with His love.

We sing about Him Who is born, 'born The King of Israel', without identifying Him to our congregations with the still Christ-less Israel, which as a nation has, as yet, no intention to examine that claim. But let us rejoice with the vast number of individual citizens who do.

Not only do we sing those outspoken Songs of Zion, but we read from the pages of Holy Writ and thus address *our* hearers as 'Ye men of Israel' or 'Fellow-Jews and all of you who are in Jerusalem' (Acts 2:14, 22); without remarking that these words were and *still are* meant for those, blinded by unbelief in Israel whether in or out of the land. A Jewish believer in Christ's existence and his Lordship is expected to come to terms with a bewildering terminology which meets him at so many angles within the Church.

A striking example for me personally was the above Christmas Eve Service to which I was invited. The first lesson to be read began with the words, 'Men of Israel and you [of the Gentiles] who fear God' ...

(Acts 13:26). There wasn't another Jewish believer in that Church, yet the whole lesson, yes indeed, the whole chapter, is a classic study of the individuality of believers, both of Jews and of Gentiles.

Barnabas and Saul arrived at Salamis and proclaimed the Word of God in the synagogues (v. 5); then they met a Jewish magician who misled his people, proclaiming himself as a prophet (v. 6). But the proconsul for whom he worked realised that his words and acts were not authentic and summoned Barnabas and Saul instead, in order to hear the Word of God, The Truth! He was astonished to hear the life-giving teaching of the risen Christ through the mouths of these Jewish men, as compared to the twisted-cloudy words he had heard previously from Elymas the magician.

On they travelled and their next stop in Antioch, Pisidia, found them right away in the local synagogue. As visitors, they were invited to speak words of encouragement to the people. Paul took the Word, as we read in v. 16, beginning with the words previously mentioned: 'Men of Israel and you [Gentiles] who worship God, listen to me!'

When words like these are read in our Churches, would it, even faintly, occur to the hearers that these words were, and still are, addressed to Jewish people who really are not present in our Churches? It is therefore from passages of Scripture such as these that we can re-educate our people to relate to the Jewish people within our community — that Christ is indeed the fulfilment of the Jewish Faith.

It is this widescale attitude of ignoring the origins of our faith and salvation, which robs the Christian Church and the individual believer of the riches which are theirs in Christ Jesus, the Christ Who was born and brought up in a Jewish setting, tradition and faith. It was He Who became that first Mediator, that Bridge, to span the two shores from Jew to Gentile, around the world.

> We tell you the good news: what God has promised our fathers (in Israel) he has fulfilled for us, their children, by raising up Jesus ... (v. 32). Therefore, my brothers (in Israel) I want you to know that through Jesus, the forgiveness of sins is proclaimed to you. Through Him, everyone who believes (Jew and Gentile) is justified from everything you could not be justified from, by the Law of Moses (vv. 38–39).

All this happened in the *synagogue*, we notice in v. 42. Actually, not only were they invited to come back on the next Sabbath Day, but after the service both Jews and devout converts followed Paul and Barnabas to receive extra teaching and encouragement. During the week, the address from the previous Sabbath Day was discussed in houses and clubs, yes, everywhere evidently where people met together. This is underlined by the words of v. 44, 'On the next Sabbath almost the whole city gathered to hear the Word of the Lord'. Obviously the opposition was just as much in evidence as those who drank and benefited from the life-giving words of the apostles. It was on this occasion Paul spoke those poignant and decisive words, which resulted in the eventual establishment of *synagogues* for the Gentiles: our present *Church*. Paul and Barnabas answered their Jewish hearers bodly:

> We had to speak the Word of God to you first. Since you reject it and do not consider yourselves worthy of eternal life, we *now* turn to the Gentiles. For this is what the Lord has commanded us [the Jews]: 'I have made you a light for the Gentiles, that you may bring salvation to the ends of the earth'. When the Gentiles heard this, they were glad and honoured the Word of the Lord, and *all* who were appointed for eternal life believed' (vv. 46–8).

What rich passages are lost to both Jews and Gentiles, because the relevance to *both* is overlooked and not taught in its proper setting. The Church of Jesus Christ as the Gentile body of believers has all the vitamins available with which to restore to Israel, the living Lord Himself. This chapter in question finishes with the statement: 'And the disciples were filled with joy and with the Holy Spirit' (v. 52). Throughout those 52 verses of chapter 13 you have found yourself among a majority of Jewish believers. Men who joyfully welcomed the Gentile enquirers and believers into their midst. Although there was this unequal balance in cultural as well as racial background, the Gentiles were overjoyed to be drawn into this rather strange religious setting.

Today, the rôles are reversed.

Repeatedly I hear of Jewish individuals who express some hesitance with regard to their early involvement in Church life. Oh yes, as previously mentioned, all the touches to make it a perfect setting are available! The building, the music, the robes for the clergy and choir, the hymns and psalms, and above all, the reading of the Law, the prophets and the riches of salvation from the New Testament. Everything sounds so homely, and yet ... its Jewishness is not understood, hence not mentioned in a complementary sense, to enrich the worshippers, each according to their own need. A Jewish visitor ought to blossom within a living and warm Church Fellowship. A Gentile believer should no longer divorce his Saviour from His brethren according to the flesh. On the contrary, he should express the joy of his faith with gratitude to Christ's kinsmen, who so long have been blind to Christ's true identity! All this is but a hypothetical issue and a total impossibility, unless we in our Churches are re-educated to know the origin of our inheritance.

Jesus still weeps over Jerusalem. He still longs for those lost sheep of the house of Israel. He still confronts Jewish people of all ages and nationalities with his Lordship as Redeemer of Mankind — Saviour of all! How He longs for channels among the Gentile believers to do unto the children of Israel what the children of Israel have done to the world during those early days, for due to their dedication, the Church worldwide exists.

The disciples were filled with joy and with the Holy Spirit! (Acts 13:52). May each reader use his joy and the ever-present Holy Spirit in his own life, to comfort, encourage and enlighten those grass-roots of our own faith.

When you examine my grammar, you will from time to time question the position from which I express my observations and feelings. I must confess that my personal sense of belonging within the Gentile Church has met with few difficulties throughout. To go a step further, I have *loved* my communion with my brothers and sisters of all the major denominations. Our unity, fellowship and expectancy from the Word of the Lord and the enlightenment of his Holy Spirit, has been unique, encouraging, and a foretaste of the communion of Saints. The privilege which has been mine within this ministry entrusted to me, has never been taken for granted. Hence, when I speak about 'our' outreach to the world at large and Israel in particular, I speak from among the ranks of the Gentile tradition.

Equally so, I must speak with the voice of my brothers and sisters according to the flesh, for they have few voices to raise on their behalf. Who can express better their feelings of mistrust towards those who 'call' themselves Christians, than one who understands and yet must worship within the Body of Christ, the Church. Who, better than a Jewish believer, can rouse the Church to their responsibility and Christ-like attitude to his brethren, according to the flesh. But let no-one, whether Gentile-Christian or Hebrew-Christian, speak or move in this area UNLESS prompted and called to do so by The Holy Spirit of God.

Jesus did encourage us to be peacemakers and we would thereby be known as 'the sons of God' (Matt. 5:9), but can we do anything at all without absolute union in and through our Lord? No way! John 15:4 and 5 is the key to everything which will succeed: Abide in Me and I will abide in you. You will not be able to bear fruit unless you remain in Me — apart from Me, you can do nothing!

Christ Jesus, born in Bethlehem as a babe, very God of very God, Son of God and Son of man, He indeed has *proved* Himself within my life and in the lives of countless other Jewish people throughout the world. We know that this is He of whom Moses and the Prophets spoke. He lives and we shall live also, our lives already transformed and born again here and now, with the positive anticipation of our hereafter in his visible Presence.

Here and now we still move in areas of form and ritual of written statutes and 'order of services'. When this occurs, the old structure of Jewry and *our* normally set-services spring to mind. We are convinced that Christ came to set us *free* from such, in order to worship the Father in spirit and truth with a humility and joy which spring from the *heart* and *not* from a prescribed compulsion.

'The letter killeth, but the Spirit gives life', that Life with a capital 'L' which Jesus Christ obtained for us. In my early years I kept rigidly to the observances taught by my parents and elders. The Prayer Book was our central source of worship. Thereby and through its pages, we were enabled to approach the unseen, great and majestic God of our Fathers — that God, who evidently could commune without the slightest difficulty with such key figures as the Patriarchs, Moses, the Judges and the Prophets. *They* seemed to express themselves from the depth of their being, either in exuberant joy or in brokenhearted sorrow. Also, their worship language was sincere and their expressions of repentance came from a heart which overflowed with shame and godly sorrow, out of which flowed that healthy desire to know the certainty of God's forgiveness and acceptance. Not so with us, in *my* childhood Jewish tradition. We were bound by the centrality of page after page in our Prayer Book.

But Hallelujah, what brilliance of light, life and freedom, when the Messiah indeed proved Himself alive, real and THE Truth: through Him, our God became MY Father and *I* could speak with Him, yes, as His child.

Now I could come to Him, far, far easier than anyone who 'made prayers for me', to pray. I now approached that great Majesty, this Holy God, through a way which He Himself had provided for that purpose: The Messiah! He spoke devastating words, which in future, would annul any other way to God: '*I* am the Way, the Truth and the life. No one comes to the Father but *by Me*.'

And so, I came to the Father, bypassing the centrality of the Prayer Book, humbly approaching *My* Father: to worship, praise and pray. I learned to be free in His Spirit, because Jesus taught me to be bold when I approached the Throne.

If the Son has set you free, you are free indeed. How true these words have proved so far throughout my new life. Yet, this freedom, so great a heritage, was secured through the payment of an enormous price: the heart-rending event on Calvary, which led to the bewildering joy of the empty Tomb three days later, as promised. That event resulted in the rending of the Temple's veil, giving us all free access to the Father. Freedom to approach the Most High! A privilege which carries, as all privileges do, a great responsibility!

For, as Moses and Mirjam, David and Solomon, not only do I find myself at liberty to approach the eternal throne with humble-bold freedom, without the previous preparation to 'make-a-prayer', but like Moses and Mirjam, David and Solomon, Stephen, Peter, Paul and countless others throughout the ages, I may now come on behalf of others, to intercede. From the bondage of the letter, I was led into the joy and freedom of the Holy Spirit, knowing myself accepted by God, through this generous Grace, in Christ. To *speak* to Him! No more by a *prescribed method* which I had known since childhood.

Jesus, Messiah, my Lord and my God —

You came to meet with me and I know that You ARE and a rewarder of all who seek You with an honest heart. But now today, what have we done with You, Lord? The letter killeth, but the Spirit gives Life. Once more You have become part of a tradition, part of a programmed set-up of Church order and worship. Once more You have just got to 'take what's coming to You'. Most of the time You are not even given the chance to approach the expectant heart, for the order-of-service must go on. Once more, prepared prayers are directed towards You. Oh Lord, what have we done to You? You are unrecognisable! Have mercy on us all, Lord!

Are You moving from Church to Church now, seeking a place to rest? A place where all men will truly worship You? Worship YOU, Lord, really *worship* You? Are You bewildered, Lord, by the immense variety of form and ritual which has grown around You over the years, like the ever-growing ivy encircling a tree? At times it is hard to see You, Lord — even feel You, because of the density of that ivy.

It looks so beautiful, so lush; oh yes, it's so attractive, all those rituals which make up that 'service unto You'. Then, I am reminded of the Father Who spoke long before You were born, Lord, that 'man does look on the outward appearance', but You, You look on the heart.

Oh Lord, forgive us, your people, for framing You into Something or Someone. Stripping You from What and Who You really are! Forgive us, Lord, for the complicated way in which we have presented You to the world. Oh Lord, we truly repent. Lord forgive and have mercy on us, your ambassadors.

And so, we come to You, Lord, weak and helpless, confessing that we have failed You. Anoint us again and enable us to care for the sheep and lambs entrusted to us. No longer to lecture *at* them, but by Your grace and with Your help, take them along *with* us to worship at the crib; to repent with them at Calvary, receiving Your forgiveness; rejoicing *with them* at the open Tomb and to receive the Holy Spirit when You breathe on us all, when we approach You together in humility.

Oh Lord, let us become involved again, with YOU! Enable us, with simplicity, to open our lives to your indwelling Holy Presence, having no longer a form of godliness, and yet, the lack of life and power is so evident to all around, as well as to our own hearts.

Oh Lord, grant us another chance; to know *You* as Lord, Lord of our life. May *You* have all prime-priority, so that You will be recognised again by the world around us.

Oh Lord, we want to worship *Thee*, worship and adore Thee in truth, and let holiness gladden Your heart.

Lord, graciously renew us unto Thyself.

We are gratefully Yours.

Amen.

Appendix A(1)

Action by the Synod of the Protestant Church of the Rheinland

Editor's Note: The translation of this statement, together with the Translator's Note, was printed by Dr. Allan R. Brockway, in *The Church and the Jewish People* (Newsletter No. 1, June 1980) of the Programme Unit on Faith and Witness, World Council of Churches, and is published here by kind permission. The Evangelische Kirche Deutschlands is the Federation of the Lutheran, Reformed and United Churches in the Federal Republic of Germany.

Translator's Note: This is the translation of an official action taken by the regular Synod of the Protestant Church of the Rheinland, meeting in January 1980. This territorial church is the most populous of the 27 constituent units of the Evangelische Kirche Deutschlands. The statement begins by referring to action taken in the January 1978 Synod. The transition to the present position is made through reference to a study authorized by the Council of the E.K.D. and a position paper of one of its own committees. The statement opens, in classical Reformation style, with an appropriate text from the Bible. It is the most thorough-going statement yet made by any Christian judicatory to correct negative teaching about the Jewish people. Nes Ammim, to which reference is made, is a Christian *moshav* in the Galilee where volunteers from Europe and America work to help build up the Promised Land.

Franklin H. Littell

Toward renovation of the relationship of Christians and Jews

Thou bearest not the root, but the root thee (Rom. 11:18b).

1. In agreement with the 'Message to the Congregations concerning the Dialogue between Christians and Jews' from the provincial Synod of the Protestant Church in the Rheinland (12 January 1978), the provincial Synod accepts the historical necessity of attaining a new relationship of the church to the Jewish people.

2. The church is brought to this by four factors:
   (1) The recognition of Christian co-responsibility and guilt for the Holocaust — the defamation, persecution and murder of Jews in the Third Reich.

135

(2) The new biblical insights concerning the continuing significance of the Jewish people for salvation history (*e.g.*, Rom. 9–11), which have been attained in connection with the Church struggle.

(3) The insight that the continuing existence of the Jewish people, its return to the Land of Promise, and also the creation of the State of Israel, are signs of the faithfulness of God toward His people (*cf.* the study *Christians and Jews*, III, 3).

(4) The readiness of Jews, in spite of the Holocaust, to (engage in) encounter, common study and cooperation.

3. The provincial Synod welcomes the study 'Christians and Jews' from the Council of the Protestant Church in Germany (E.K.D.) and the more comprehensive and precise *Theses on the Renewal of the Relationship of Christians and Jews* of the Committee 'Christians and Jews' of the Protestant Church of the Rheinland.

The provincial Synod receives both thankfully and recommends to all congregations that the Study and the Theses be made the starting point of an intensive work on Judaism and the foundation of a new consciousness of the relationship of the church to the Jewish people.

4. In consequence the provincial Synod declares:

(1) Stricken, we confess the co-responsibility and guilt of German Christendom for the Holocaust (*cf.* Thesis I).

(2) We confess thankfully the 'Scriptures' of the Jewish people (Luke 24:27; 1 Cor. 15:3f.), our Old Testament, to be the common foundation for the faith and work of Jews and Christians (*cf.* Thesis II).

(3) We confess Jesus Christ the Jew, who as the Messiah of the Jews is the Saviour of the world and binds the peoples of the world to the people of God (*cf.* Thesis III).

(4) We believe in the permanent election of the Jewish people as the people of God and realise that through Jesus Christ the church is taken into the covenant of God with His people (cf. Thesis IV).

(5) We believe with the Jews that the unity of righteousness and love characterises the saving work of God in history. We believe with the Jews that righteousness and love are the admonitions of God for our whole life. As Christians we see both rooted and grounded in the work of God with the Jewish people and in the work of God through Jesus Christ (*cf.* Thesis V).

(6) We believe that in their calling Jews and Christians are always witnesses of God in the presence of the world and before each other. Therefore, we are convinced that the Church may not express its witness toward the Jewish people as it does its mission to the peoples of the world (*cf.* Thesis VI).

(7) Therefore, we declare:

Throughout centuries the word 'new' has been used against the Jewish people in biblical exegesis: the new covenant was understood as contrast to the old covenant, the new people of God as replacement of the old people of God. This obliviousness to the permanent election of the Jewish people and its relegation to non-existence marked Christian theology, church preaching and church work ever and again right to the present day. Thereby we have also made ourselves guilty of the physical elimination of the Jewish people.

Therefore, we want to perceive the unbreakable connection of the New Testament with the Old Testament in a new way, and learn to understand the relationship of the 'old' and 'new' from the standpoint of the promise: as a result of the promise, as fulfilment of the promise, as confirmation of the promise. 'New' means therefore no replacement of the 'old'. Hence we deny that the people Israel has been rejected by God or that it has been superseded by the church.

(8) As we are turning around we begin to discover what Christians and Jews both give witness to:

We both confess God as the creator of heaven and earth, and know that we are singled out in the ordinary life of the world by the same God by means of the blessing of Aaron.

We confess the common hope in a new heaven and a new earth and the power of this messianic hope for the witness and work of Christians and Jews for justice and peace in the world.

5. The provincial Synod recommends to the district synods the calling of a special officer of the Synod for Christian-Jewish dialogue.

The provincial Synod commissions the church leadership to constitute anew a committee 'Christians and Jews' and to invite Jews to work with this committee. It is to advise the church leadership in all questions concerning the relationship of the church and Jewry and to assist the congregations and church circles towards a deeper understanding of the new standpoint in the relationship of Jews and Christians.

The provincial Synod makes the church leadership responsible to consider in what form the Protestant Church of the Rheinland can undertake a special responsibility for the Christian settlement Nes Ammim in Israel, as other churches (e.g., in the Netherlands and in the German Federal Republic) have already done.

The provincial Synod makes the church leadership responsible to see to it that in church instruction, continuing education and advanced education the matter of 'Christians and Jews' shall be appropriately paid attention to.

The provincial Synod considers it desirable that a regular teaching post with the thematic 'Theology, Philosophy and History of Jewry' shall be established in the Wuppertal seminary and the Wuppertal general college, and requests the church leadership to consult with the Wuppertal seminary, the Wuppertal general college, and with the state of Nordrhein-Westfalen to this end.

Appendix A(2)

Christian/Jewish Dialogue: Report of the Overseas Council of the Church of Scotland

Editor's Note: The Overseas Council appointed a special group under the chairmanship of the Very Rev. Dr. T. F. Torrance to consider the theological implications of the Christian/Jewish Dialogue. This group consisted of the Chairman, the Rev. Dr. J. K. S. Reid, the Rev. Dr. George W. Anderson, and the Rev. Dr. George F. Knight. This Report was written by the Chairman and submitted on behalf of the group. It was considered by the Church and Israel Committee and by the Overseas Council. At its meeting on 18th March, 1980, the Overseas Council, on the recommendation of the Executive Committee, agreed to make the Report available to commissioners of the General Assembly meeting in Edinburgh in May 1980. Although further reports are awaited on this possible development, the General Assembly declared that it 'would welcome the appointment of a scholar to participate in Christian/Jewish Dialogue in Israel'. The General Assembly also approved 'the policy of working for reconciliation and understanding between Christian and Jew, and of opposing all forms of anti-Semitism'.

In May 1981, the General Assembly went further and affirmed that, 'They declare belief in the continuing place of God's people Israel within the divine purpose', and 'Instruct the Overseas Council to initiate Christian/Jewish consultations between the Church of Scotland and our Jewish Brethren; and urge the World Alliance of Reformed Churches to prosecute Christian/Jewish Dialogue at a world level'.

The Christian Church is inseparably bound up with the Gospel of Jesus Christ. By its very existence it is locked into the mission of Jesus himself to preach the Gospel, and can continue to exist only in so far as it continues to share in Jesus' own evangelical mission. How are we to think of this as bearing on the life and faith of the Jewish people, on Israel, today?

The Gospel can hardly be brought *to* Israel, for it derives *from* Israel. That means that the relation of the Christian Church and its mission to Israel must be quite unlike its relation to any other people or religion. Jews cannot be treated by Christians as unbelievers but only as brother believers with whom they are

139

privileged to share a common faith in God, and the same
promises of salvation. 'Salvation is of the Jews', as Jesus said.

On the other hand, the Christian Church has been entrusted
with only *one Gospel* which it may not desert or alter in any way,
as St. Paul insisted in his Epistle to the Galatians. Hence the
witness and proclamation of the Church cannot be changed or
diluted so as to omit what is distinctive and essential, such as the
uniqueness of Christ and his saving grace, or the Trinitarian basis
of faith and access to God. We must not forget that the New
Testament summons to the Church to remain faithful and
consistent in its witness to Christ and his Gospel took place
within the context of Judaism: there cannot be any doubt that
this summons remains valid today. The Christian Church is
obliged to witness to Christ and proclaim the Gospel to Israel
now as it was in New Testament times.

How can *both* these obligations be held together, without
letting one diminish the force of the other? *Only by taking
seriously the divine election and mission of Israel itself to the
world, and by incorporating the distinctive witness of the Christian
Church within it.* This requires a mutual listening to one another
on the part of the Christian Church and Israel within the one
mission of the people of God to the world.

The mission of Israel

Within the universal covenant of God's grace, which takes in
the whole creation, Israel was called out from the other nations to
be the unique historical partner of God's personal and intimate
self-revelation, whereby knowledge and worship of the living God
might be earthed in human existence, given shape in human
understanding and speech, and be mediated to the human race at
large. This historical partnership between Israel and God took the
form of a particular covenant with concrete provisions, in which
Israel was given a special priestly status among the nations as
God's representative and messenger. By its nature this covenant
was not meant to be an end in itself, for through it Israel was
steadily and painfully moulded by God into being the instrument
of his saving purpose, and made to provide in its very existence
among the nations the basis and provisional form of a new
covenantal relationship with God which would include all
nations. Through this special covenant or partnership Israel was
called to fulfil a costly, vicarious function in God's promise of
universal blessing, which has put its stamp on the Jewish people,

for it was involvement in this divine mission that really constituted the identity and peculiar priestly nature of Israel.

This vicarious mission of Israel was the subject of considerable attention in the Isaianic prophecies, notably in the 'Servant' passages, in which it is shown how deeply Israel suffered and had to suffer in its vicarious mission as bearer of divine revelation, and mediator of the covenant on behalf of the race, bringing light to the Gentiles and salvation to the ends of the earth, but subject at the same time to divine judgements upon its own unfaithfulness and calamities at the hands of other nations. In the heart of this presentation the notions of the suffering Servant, the Holy One of Israel and the Redeemer are drawn closely together in an enigmatically anonymous figure in whom the suffering ordeal and priestly destiny of Israel are gathered up, personified and infiltrated with universal significance, and made to point ahead to the consummation of God's redemptive purpose of peace in a triumphant Messianic era which will transcend the history of Israel itself.

In the course of this special partnership between Israel and God it is prophesied that the covenant relationship will change and a new covenant will be made with Israel — this is not an abrogation of the old covenant but a fulfilment of it in which its essential pattern, 'I will be your God, you will be my people', is raised to a higher level of intimacy and communion with God through the pouring out of his own Spirit upon his people.

The mission of Jesus and his Church

When we turn from the Old to the New Testament, we find that it is in connection with this alteration in the structure of the covenant through fulfilment of its universal Messianic purpose that the Christian Gospel is proclaimed. Jesus identified himself with the vicarious role of the Servant, showing that his own mission as Son of Man was fulfilled under the constraint of the redemptive and Messianic purpose of God embodied in the history and destiny of Israel. Jesus claimed that with him the promised era of the Kingdom had arrived and was being inaugurated through him — the blessing, the good news, the mission, the sin-bearing, the new covenant with God, and everything else spoken of by the prophets, were now coming to their fulfilment. He brought his earthly ministry to its climax in the week of his crucifixion, exhibiting beforehand the saving significance of his passion when, during his last Passover celebration with his disciples, he substituted himself as the sacrifice, and solemnly inaugurated the new covenant in his body and blood, and thereby also the new order of redemption for mankind. Charged with that destiny and significance Jesus went forth to the Cross, acting the part of the Servant by taking the sins of Israel on himself as at once the Priest and the victim, but also as the Lamb of God bearing away the sins of the world, in a decisive act of self-offering and vicarious intercession, which was stamped with the seal of God's complete approval in his raising Jesus from the dead. Then the vicarious mission of Jesus as Redeemer, in fulfilment of the divine necessity that burdened the destiny of Israel, was finally established in its triumphant consummation.

With the coming of the Holy Spirit at Pentecost the new covenant inaugurated by Jesus was actualised in the people of the Covenant which now took the form of the Christian Church, aware of itself as charged with world-mission. While it was inevitable that there took place a breach between the Christian Church and official Judaism which had denied its election at the decisive moment of its destiny in the crucifixion of the Messiah, the Church was deeply conscious that the crucifixion of Jesus was foreordained by God and was thus included within Israel's destined calling to act in a representative capacity for all nations. The crucifixion was seen, therefore, not as ground for a rupture with Judaism but for deeper solidarity, so that provision was made at the Apostolic Council in the 15th chapter of Acts, for measures to preserve the solidarity even between Gentile Christians and Israel.

It was given to St. Paul to provide the theological basis for the orientation of the life and mission of the Church in respect of its derivation from Israel. He insisted by word and by practice that the Gospel must be taken to the Jew first and then to the Gentile. The ground for that lay in the fact that the Church of Christ has no separate calling or independence of its own. In two passages of far-reaching importance he laid down the position which constitutes the charter for Church/Israel relations, Romans 9–11, and Ephesians 2. The Churches are like wild branches grafted on to the trunk of Israel in order to share its spiritual life and strength; but as branches they do not support the trunk, for it is the trunk that supports them. It is only through the union of the Christian Church in Christ with Israel that Christians can belong to the one people of God. Gentiles themselves are without hope and without God in the world, for they are aliens from the promises and the covenants. Israel alone is the people of God, the bearer of divine revelation and the promise of salvation, the one people with Messianic destiny, so that in order to share in the saving purpose of God, Gentiles must be incorporated into the commonwealth of Israel. In no sense does the Church replace Israel and its mission in the divine calling. It is only through assimilation into Israel that the Church may share in the divine mission and be engaged in the universalising of that mission to all the world — although the final success of that universalisation will depend, St. Paul argued, on the inclusion of Israel as a collective entity within the fullness of the reconciliation of the world in Christ.

The witness of the Christian Church to the Jewish Church

Sympathy and Understanding.

(a) Since there is only one Covenant of grace and only one people of God, the separation of the Christian Church from the Jewish Church represents the deepest schism there could be. So long as that split remains in force Jews and Christians have a distorted understanding of one another. This is nowhere more evident than in regard to who *Jesus* was and is. When the Gentile Church is cut off from Israel, it is in a measure cut off from Jesus, which helps to explain why Christians almost inevitably approaching Jesus from their own cultural assumptions put a Gentile mask over the face of Jesus, and thereby obscure and obstruct their own witness to Christ, making it impossible for their Jewish brethren to accept this 'Gentilised Christ'. At the same time the real Jesus eludes the Gentile quest, for he cannot be properly understood or interpreted by the conceptual instruments Christians bring to him.

(b) Christian people have traditionally held that the covenant between God and Israel has been abrogated and replaced with the new covenant in Christ, so that they regard the Jews as the people of God 'after the flesh' but look upon the Christian Church as the people of God 'after the Spirit'. That is a tragic mistake which insults the Jews and slanders the divine calling and election of Israel. It is essential to genuine Christian witness that we accept that the covenanted partnership between God and Israel remains in force and will remain in force until the consummation of God's kingdom. This means that we must think of the people of Israel as continuing to fulfil their vicarious function in God's calling; and it means that we cannot expect

Jews to become Christains in the same sense that we are, for they could only become followers of Christ as Lord and Saviour within the obedience laid upon them by God in the covenant bond which God has not revoked. This needs much more attention than Christians have yet given to it.

(c) It is important for Christians to understand the deep inner tension in which Jews are caught up through their vicarious mission. By creation Israel is a nation (*ethnos*) among other nations; but by divine election Israel is a church (*laos*), a people peculiarly related to God. This tension Israel has all through its history found well-nigh intolerable, but it has greatly increased with the setting up of the state of Israel in the Holy Land. Modern Israel is like a woman in the last stages of her travail, as a new reality struggles to be born. God is still creatively at work in Israel, fearfully and wonderfully giving substance and shape to the structure of the people of God as it will be finally manifest in the consummation of his Kingdom.

(d) Christians must also try to understand sympathetically what happened to Israel after the crucifixion of Jesus and the subsequent destruction of Jerusalem and the Temple. There took place a retreat from the priestly, redemptive orientation of Israel which is so strongly emphasised in the Old Testament, and thereby Israel has resiled from essential elements in its mission to humanity as a whole. Rabbinic Judaism has had to offer extensive reinterpretations of the Old Testament to bring it into line with Israel's *de facto* development as a severely ethicised religion, but thereby, as St. Paul saw so clearly even in his day, there is considerable contrast between the moral righteousness of Judaism and the righteousness that comes from the grace of God as it is proclaimed in the Gospel. There are deep changes now going on in Israel, not least in connection with the revitalisation of many biblical doctrines in the rediscovered connection between the People of God and the Holy Land, which are already bridging this gap between Jews and Christians, and they have to do with a deeper sense once more of Israel's vicarious function and divine mission.

Christian witness to Israel

It is St. Paul who has shown the Christian Church how to bear witness to Christ in the world, in relation to Israel as well as to Gentile nations. 'I am not ashamed of the Gospel of Christ: for it is the power of God unto salvation to everyone who believes; to the Jew first and also to the Gentile' (Rom. 1:16). Behind this lies the teaching of our Lord himself (Luke 24:47; Acts 1:8), but as St. Paul knew, the stumbling block was the Cross of Christ (1 Cor. 12:3) and the point on which the witness must pivot is the resurrection of Jesus as he knew in his own experience. Clearly the Christian Church must bear witness to Israel quite specifically about the crucifixion and resurrection of Jesus Christ: all Christian witness must be Christologically grounded and orientated. It must be proclamation of the Gospel of the unconditional love and forgiveness of God equally to Jews and Gentiles on the basis of the one covenant of grace mediated to us through Israel. Hence Christian witness must be related to the fact that in the existence and imperishable continuity of Israel God has set up among the nations and in the midst of world history a sign and testimony to his judgement and mercy toward all mankind.

What forms should this witness take?

(1) *The witness of the Christian Church must take a corporate form.*

If we follow the teaching of St. Paul in Rom. 9–11, the following lines of guidance may be traced out.

(*a*) The witness must be directed toward 'all Israel', *i.e.*, to Israel as a collective entity, not just to individual Jews. Since Jews cannot become Christians by excising themselves from the special covenant God has established with them in Israel, the Christian witness must bear upon Israel as a whole, in the hope that Israel as a collective entity will participate in the restructuring of the covenant relations that took place in and through Christ and the pouring out of his Holy Spirit.

(*b*) The witness must be linked to the fulfilment of Christian mission in the heart of world history, for then it bears directly upon Israel's own function and mission as it witnesses to the mighty acts of God in history and points ahead to the coming day of the Lord when all history and all mankind will be brought to their appointed consummation. The dramatic and historically unexpected restoration of Israel to the promised land falls within this witness of Israel to the coming day of the Lord. The Christian witness must be linked with that of Israel, but since it is bound up with the passion and resurrection of Christ its task is to direct attention to the final Advent of Christ which will usher in the great day of the Lord and the Messianic age. St. Paul argues that it will be the manifestation of God's work in the Church toward that supreme end that will make Israel 'jealous', provoking it to mutual partnership with the mission of the Church toward all mankind.

(c) The witness of the Christian Church to Israel must be bound up with the actualisation of reconciliation within the Christian community itself. The splintering of the Church's witness through the divisions of the Church shatters its effectiveness, and makes our Jewish brethren call in question the sincerity of our belief in the atoning reconciliation in the Cross of Christ. The actualisation of reconciliation within the Church is integral to the fullness of reconciliation in which Israel as a whole will participate, and it is only when that happens that the final fulfilment of God's reconciling purpose will affect all humanity.

(2) *The Christian Church must learn to share, and be seen to share, in the mission of Israel, if it is to bear effective witness to Israel.*

This will involve at least three lines of assimilation in witness and activity.

(a) The Christian Church must range itself alongside of Israel as *people of the Word of God.* Israel is the community called out of the nations through being directly addressed by the Word of God, summoned to hear and obey it. In Israel God's Word created a *community of reciprocity*, creatively begetting in Israel's historical dialogue and partnership with God a developing response to God which was taken up into the address of the Word, sanctified and assimilated into its mode and form as God's Word to Israel. Thus in a profound sense the Word of God within history took the existence-form of Israel, constituting Israel the great prophetic Word of God addressed to mankind. It was out of that reciprocity that the Old Testament Scriptures were generated as the continuing medium of God's revelation to Israel and through Israel to mankind. It was the temptation of Judaism, however, under the Scribes and in Rabbinic Judaism to concentrate on the sentence, the word and the letter of the Scriptures, thereby abstracting the written form of revelation from the Word as the living personal mode of God's self-communication, and becoming trapped in a legalistic relation to the Torah. While the temptation of the Christian Church has been in the other direction, to interpret the Scriptures in terms of its own autonomous tradition and self-understanding, thereby losing the substance of the objective Word as mediated through the word of revelation, it has a brotherly duty to fulfil in witness to Israel by proclaiming to them the Word of the Gospel, that whoever calls on the name of the Lord will be saved. How can they believe unless they hear, and how can they hear without a preacher? asked St. Paul (Rom. 10:12–18). It will be by bringing the Word of the Gospel to Israel that they may be helped to recover the creative source of their life in the living Word of God and really become the people of the living Word.

(b) The Christian Church must align itself more closely with the divine vocation and mission of Israel to mankind by *incorporating its own distinctive witness within it*. The crux of the matter was stated bý St. Peter when he described the Church of Jesus Christ precisely in terms of the priestly and holy nation in terms applied in the Old Testament to Israel, God's 'peculiar people' (1 Pet. 2:9–10). The temptation of the Christian Church is to shrink from being set apart like that, in a desire to be assimilated into general human society and culture. Israel's temptation is rather different, to withdraw into its narrow, particular self-identity, separated from all other nations, but it thereby loses its representative and priestly status and function. Christians and Jews clearly need one another if they are to fulfil their God-given world-mission. The special contribution of the Christian Church would be to help Israel to be more faithful to its representative status and significance, and to fulfil its priestly mission in the midst of mankind. Christians, for their part, must recognise that they have contributed to the separatism of Israel through the anti-semitism in Western Christian culture, and have thereby thickened, as it were, the veil over the Jewish mind (of which St. Paul spoke) evident when Jews read the Old Testament (2 Cor. 3:13–16). If that veil is to be taken away in Christ, it must surely be in connection with Israel's recovery of its own priestly mission and a fresh understanding of their holy Scriptures in that light. How can the Church help Israel here, unless it stands by and supports Israel in its desperately lonely and costly vicarious mission and destiny?

(c) Where more effectively can the Church of Christ share in Israel's mission and bear witness to Israel than in connection with the indescribable horror of the Holocaust? That enormous sacrifice in Israel's life-blood it had to pay for its vicarious mission to mankind — a cost fearfully intensified by Christian refusal to listen to God's continuing Word to it through Israel and by its consequent anti-semitism. The Holocaust reveals the terrible depth to which God's Word through Israel had nevertheless penetrated into the existence of European man, but it must also be understood in relation to the blood of the covenant faithfulness of God sealed in the innermost destiny of Israel, so that Israel comes forth from the Holocaust as a people new-born from the grave. To the unappeasable agony of the question *why?* Christians can only point to the Cross of Christ, which speaks of God himself present in the depth of human violence and abandonment, giving the Cross its unconquerable power, for Jesus remains completely unavoidable even after the world had done its worst upon him. So with Israel: even when the world has done its worst to Israel, Israel remains an unavoidable factor in the heart of world history, in connection with which mankind has to reckon with the God to whom Israel is inseparably bound in covenant mission and purpose.

(3) *The Christian Church must engage in a deep-level theological dialogue with Israel.*

It was St. Paul himself (following St. Stephen) who started this dialogue and made it an essential part of his proclamation of the Gospel, as we can see in his habit of seeking out the leaders of the Synagogue in every city, for doctrinal discussion. The same deep-going clarification of basic theological issues is needed today, if we are to fulfil our Christian witness and mission. At no time in the whole history of Christian/Jewish relations has this been more needed, and at no time has the 'hour' been more opportune or promising, in view of the profound change in orientation that has taken place and is now continuing to take place in the Israel of the Holy Land.

(*a*) *Basic questions.* Doctrinal questions are inevitably interlocked with one another, so that discussion will have to move back and forth between them. The whole range of basic concepts in Judaism and Christianity will come up for discussion, but all that can be done here is to suggest a brief agenda of basic issues. The idea of the *Covenant* is certainly basic, in its relation to the creation on the one hand and in relation to the concrete instrumental forms of the covenant relationship on the other hand, bound up with God's self-revealing and self-giving to his people in history. The gathering up and fulfilment of its substance in Israel and its restructuring through the Incarnation require conjoint thinking by Jews and Christians, and embedded in all that is the concept of the *Word of God* and the reciprocal relations it creates and continues in the vicarious obedience of Israel and in the vicarious humanity of Christ which form the real text of the Old and New Testaments. Behind all lies the doctrine of *God* and the meaning of his *Oneness* for Jews and Christians, which cannot be divorced from the basic epistemological question of whether we know God in some measure as he is in himself or not — whether God is completely ineffable and unnameable, or whether he admits us into his own inner Communion, as Christians hold. It is St. Paul's teaching that both Jews and Gentiles have access to God through Christ and in his Spirit which will focus dialogue here, leading to reflection on the *Triunity* of God on the one hand, and, as bound up with the participation of God's love in our suffering, on the traditional notions of the immutability and impassibility of God, on the other hand. Clarification of the significance of *Jesus* himself is certainly paramount in importance, and cannot be evaded. The whole approach to new understanding of Jesus in his relation to the destiny and mission of Israel, and his exhibition of Israel's vicarious and priestly function in the heart of world history, has opened up in a new and exciting way in Israel itself — *cf.* here the notion of *die Heimholung Jesu ins Judentum* associated in some Kibbutzim with the reading of the New Testament Gospels. A very different issue (yet not unrelated to Christology) is the problem of the *objectivity of law*, to which great Jewish scientists have contributed immensely, but which is now a burning issue in the constitution of states, the power or authority of parliaments and law-making bodies, and not least in legal institutions and the general ethics of the society behind them. Since the Nuremberg trials at the end of the Second World War, the whole notion of positivist or statute law which gave cover for the legalisation of violence has been undermined and the concept of human rights has become dominant. But is justice grounded on what is intrinsically right and true? Do laws have ontological grounds in reality? Is it not divine justice that lies behind all human law and ethics? Natural science has had to face a similar issue over the status of natural law, and has had to reject the positivist and conventionalist position, on the ground of objective contingent order in the universe a notion that actually derives from Judaeo-Christian sources, not least from the understanding of the creation in the light of the incarnation of the Creator Word in Jesus Christ. Hence this would seem to provide ground for deep and promising dialogue with leading Jewish thinkers.

(*b*) *Instruments of dialogue.* If on-going dialogue of this kind is to succeed it requires the creation and publication of a *relevant literature.* This means that a long-term policy needs to be developed and put into operation. On the one hand, books and magazines are needed at a level where the imagination and devotion of Jews and Christians can be kindled, so that a climate of common concern and dedication may emerge, within which

deeper dialogue may be effective. On the other hand, basic work
needs to be done by people of a high calibre (and they need to be
quite first class to match Jewish interlocutors) who are trained
and supported by the Church for engagement with Jewish
thought, sacred and secular, in the actual context and life of Israel
today. This would best be achieved, in connection with the
Hebrew University in Jerusalem, through the activity of *full-time
scholars and theologians*, participating in University life and work
at all levels. An ecumenical group of Christian theologians would
thus constitute the pledge of Christian participation in basic
thought and mission in Israel, and would generate the kind of
literature needed for worldwide dialogue between Jews and
Christians.

Appendix A(3)

Declaration of the German Roman Catholic Bishops on the Church's Relationship to Judaism

Editor's note: This Declaration, *Erklärung über das Verhältnis der Kirche zum Judentum, 28 April 1980,* was published by the Secretariat of the German Bishops' Conference, Bonn, no. 26, 32 pp. It was published in English in a slightly shortened form in *Christian Jewish Relations,* no. 73, December 1980, by the Institute of Jewish Affairs. It is published here by kind permission.

I. Jesus Christ—Our access to Judaism

When we encounter Jesus Christ we encounter Judaism. According to the testimony of the New Testament he, the 'Son of David' (Rom. 1:3) and the 'Son of Abraham' (Mt. 1:1; *cf.* Heb. 7:14), was born, 'according to the flesh', of the people of Israel (Rom. 9:5). 'But when the time had fully come, God sent forth his Son, born of woman, born under the law' (Gal. 4:4). According to his human nature, Jesus of Nazareth was a Jew; his origin was Jewish. He is therefore rooted in the history of the people of Israel (*cf.* the genealogy of Jesus in Mt. 1:1–17; Lk. 3:23–30).

Today Jewish authors too discover the 'Jewishness' of Jesus. Martin Buber saw in Jesus his 'great brother';[1] Shalom ben Chorin confesses: 'Jesus is for me the eternal brother, not only a human brother but my Jewish brother. I feel his fraternal hand holding mine so that I might follow him.... His unconditional faith, the absolute trust in God the Father, the readiness to humble himself totally under God's will, that is the attitude in which Jesus is our model and which can be a bond between us Jews and Christians.'[2]

II. The church's spiritual heritage from Judaism

Because of his Jewish origin, Jesus Christ brought a rich spiritual heritage, the religious traditions of his people, to the gentile world. Therefore the Christian is linked by 'spiritual bonds ... to the offspring of Abraham'[3] and continually draws on this heritage.

1. First there are the Sacred Scriptures of Israel, called 'Old Testament' by Christians. When the New Testament refers to 'Scripture' or 'the Scriptures', or to that which is 'written' (e.g., Mt. 4:6; Mk. 1:2; Lk. 24:44–46; Jn. 19:36f.; 1 Cor. 15:3f; Cor. 4:13; Gal. 3:10, 13), it means the Old Testament. The Second Vatican Council teaches: 'In carefully planning and preparing the salvation of the whole human race, the God of supreme love, by a special dispensation, chose for Himself a people to whom he might entrust his promises .... The plan of salvation, foretold by the sacred authors, is found as the true word of God in the books of the Old Testament.'[4]

Thus the Old Testament is for Jews and Christians a common source of faith. In the Old Testament the God of revelation speaks, the God of Abraham, of Isaac and Jacob who is also the God of Jesus. The *Vatican Guidelines* of 1 December 1974 remark on this: 'An effort will be made to acquire a better understanding of whatever in the Old Testament retains its own perpetual value ... since that has not been cancelled by the later interpretation of the New Testament. Rather, the New Testament brings out the full meaning of the Old, while both Old and New illumine and explain each other.'[5] 'The Old Testament and the Jewish tradition founded upon it must not be set against the New Testament in such a way as to make the former seem to constitute a religion of only justice, fear and legalism, with no appeal to the love of God and neighbour (cf. Dt. 6:5; Lev. 19:18; Mt. 22:34–40).'[6] The Church has rightly always refused all attempts to exclude the Old Testament from the canon and to accept as valid only the New Testament.

2. The Sacred Scriptures of Israel testify before everything else to the existence of the one God: 'Hear, O Israel, the Lord our God, the Lord is one!' (Dt. 6:4). This sentence, the basic creed of the Jewish religion, is daily recited in the morning and evening service, at home as well as in the synagogue. Asked by the scribe: 'Which commandment is the first of all?', Jesus answered: 'The first is, "Hear, O Israel, the Lord our God, the Lord is One; and you shall love the Lord your God with all your heart, and with

all your soul and with all your mind, and with all your strength"'
(Mk. 12:29 f.). The Council teaches: 'To His people which He had
acquired for Himself, He so manifested Himself through words
and deeds as the one true and living God that Israel came to
know by experience the ways of God with men; and with God
Himself speaking to them through the mouth of the prophets,
Israel daily gained a deeper and clearer understanding of His
ways and made them more widely known among the nations' (*cf.*
Is. 21:28 f.; Jer. 3:17)'.[7]

3. This one God is also the creator of the whole world. This is
expressed with classic precision in the first verse of the Bible: 'In
the beginning God created heaven and 'earth' (Gen. 1:1). This
term stipulates that creator and creature are not identical or
interchangeable; it prevents a deification of the world. Thanks to
Jesus and the Church the Old Testament message of creation was
brought to the gentile nations. It enables mankind to gain its
right relationship to the world.

4. Of particular topical significance is the teaching of Israel's
Scriptures that man is the 'image' of God: 'Then God said: "Let
us make man in our image, after our likeness; and let them have
dominion over the fish of the sea, and over the birds of the air,
and over the cattle, and over all the earth, and over every
creeping thing that creeps upon the earth." So God created man
in his own image, in the image of God he created him; male and
female he created them' (Gen. 1:26 f.). 'God created man for
incorruption, and made him the image of his own eternity' (Wis.
2:23). The teaching that man was created in the image of God
implies the absolute dignity of the human person and what is
called today 'human rights.' According to the teaching of Judaism,
a murderer destroys the image of God.[8] Nobody may despise his
neighbour for he has been created in the image of God.[9] 'The
Lord created man with his own hands and made him similar to
his own countenance ... He who despises the countenance of
man despises the countenance of the Lord!'[10] Quite in accordance
with these convictions of Judaism the Epistle of James says: 'With
it (the tongue) we bless the Lord and Father and with it we curse
men, who are made in the likeness of God.' (Jam. 3:9).

5. Israel knows of its covenant relationship to God. The
covenant is both privilege and obligation. It demands Israel's
exclusive worship of God alone. The covenant formula reads:
'You will be my people and I shall be your God.' The prophets
warn Israel against breaking the covenant.

The Scriptures tell of previous covenants, *e.g.*, with Abraham

F

(*cf.* Gen. 15), where God assures Abraham that he will fulfil the
promise of the land; another instance is the covenant with Noah
(*cf.* Gen. 9:9–17). This covenant is universal, it includes the whole
earth (Gen. 9:13), 'all living creatures' (Gen. 9:10, 12, 15, 16), 'all
flesh on the earth' (Gen. 9:13). It is therefore possible to state:
'The history of nature and the history of man fundamentally
demonstrate God's unconditional Yes to his creation, to all life,
which cannot be shaken either by catastrophes in the course of
history or ... by crime, corruption or mankind's rebellion. God's
promise remains unshakable "as long as the earth will last".'[11]
God will save the world, even when the earth has again been
'polluted under its inhabitants, for they have transgressed the
laws, violated the statutes, broken the everlasting covenant' (Is.
24:5). God will fulfil what has been promised in Noah's covenant
concluded with the whole earth, with all mankind.

The guarantor of the final fulfilment of the covenant obligations
is the 'servant of God,' whom God chooses to be both the
'covenant for my people' and 'the light of the nations' (Is. 42:6).
According to the Christian faith he has come in Jesus Christ, who
has explicitly called his blood shed on the cross 'the blood of the
covenant shed for many' (Mk. 14:24; Mt. 26:28), and the cup he
offered he designated as 'the new covenant in my blood' (Lk.
22:20; 1 Cor. 11:25). Jesus uses concepts of Jewish tradition to
explain his death. Salvation is interpreted as a covenant by means
of which God has entered into a relationship of permanent fidelity
to Israel and the whole world. 'Covenant' means that God will not
forget his creation. The creator is also the redeemer (*cf.* Is. 54:5).

6. Until the present day the pious Jew is particularly concerned
to live according to the 'teaching' of God, called 'Torah' in
Hebrew. The Torah determines the daily life of the Jew before
God. The centre of the Torah is the decalogue, the ten
commandments. Jesus fully accepted the decalogue (*cf.* Mk.
10:19). The 'Ten Words' as they are called in the Old Testament,
are normative for the conscience of all men, not only Jews. They
became the guiding principle for the moral consciousness of
mankind. The ten commandments are that which, according to
St. Paul, is 'written into the heart (of all men) ... by nature'—
'their conscience also bears witness and their conflicting thoughts
accuse or perhaps excuse them' (Rom. 14f.); without their
observance there is no real life in society and no real relationship
to God. The experience of history shows that without a
conscience formed by the law of God 'man becomes a wolf for his
fellowmen'. Without it there is tyranny and despotism, disregard

for the human person and its freedom. The decalogue constitutes the basic rule of human behaviour; it is indispensable for all times.

The messianic hope also originates in Judaism. Its beginnings were already early on linked to the Davidic dynasty, see especially 2 Sam. 7:12–6: 'When your days are fulfilled and you lie down with your fathers, I will raise up your offspring after you, who shall come forth from your body and I will establish his kingdom. He shall build a house for my name, and I will establish the throne of his kingdom for ever. I will be his father and he shall be my son ... your house and your kingdom shall be made sure for ever before me; your throne shall be established for ever.' The prophets of Israel spoke frequently of the messianic expectation and testified to it in different forms. If we ask what impetus the messianic hope has given to the Gentiles we may list three:

i. The messianic idea explodes the cyclical view of history; world history does not move in a circle, nor is there a constant return of the same things. The messianic promise proves that history is moving towards a goal.

ii. The movement of history towards a God-given goal leads from despair to salvation.

iii. Salvation will be brought about by a definitive saviour, called 'Messiah.' Through Jesus of Nazareth, whom the Church acknowledges and proclaims as the promised Messiah, the messianic hope entered into the thought and hope of the nations, though in a different manner. Christian messianism caused at first a profound interiorization of man's relationship to God, but Jesus himself announced his return at the end of time as an event which will concern the whole world: 'And they will see the Son of man coming in the clouds with great power and glory' (Mk. 13:26).

Messianism in the world today is more powerful than ever, though frequently in a secular form. The world does not want to turn in a circle, people look forward to the future, towards a goal. Messianic faith is future-oriented, for it predicts the coming of a Saviour for Israel and the nations. The messianic hope contains also the longing for a just world and complete peace for mankind. The prophets of Israel announced this for the future salvation, often combining their prediction with a critique of the social evils of their times. The New Testament continues this. It proclaims the Christ as the one who will judge the earth with justice (Acts 17:31) and who will announce peace to those who are near and who are far (Eph. 2:17), i.e. to all men. Together with Israel the Church awaits a 'new heaven and a new earth, where justice will

dwell' (2 Peter 3:13). But Jesus also warned of false messiahs who
will seduce people with their ideologies (cf. Mk. 13:22 par.).
Messianism can be perverted. The Church must know this: 'Take
heed; I have told you all things beforehand' (Mk. 13:23).

8. Observant Jews pray and praise God. Of the great treasury
of the prayers of Israel the Church has inherited especially the
Psalms which play a large part in the liturgy and the office of the
Church. The 'Lord's Prayer', however much it bears the stamp of
Jesus' Spirit, especially when it addresses God as 'Father,' has its
origin in Jewish prayers. The Jew too asks for the coming of the
kingdom, desires the sanctification of the 'name' and tries to
accomplish the will of God; he too prays for the daily bread and
to be delivered from temptations. The two great prayers of the
Infancy Narrative of Jesus, used in the liturgy, the 'Benedictus'
(Lk. 1:68–79) and the 'Magnificat' (Lk. 1:46–55), are almost
entirely composed of terms and verses from the Old Testament.

9. Israel's basic attitudes before God—reverence, obedience,
knowledge of God, repentance, remembrance, love, trust, holiness,
praise of God and of his mighty deeds[12]—are also those of the
Christian community. They have not been invented by the Church
but belong to the spiritual dowry received by the Church from
Israel; the Church, in its turn, hands them on to the nations,
renewed and firmly rooted in Christ.

10. Some other events belonging to Israel's spiritual heritage
must be mentioned; in them the saving deeds of God for man are
experienced as a concrete historical reality, especially the
following which belong together: Exodus, Passover, suffering,
judgement, resurrection.

The Exodus is for Israel the decisive liberating act of God
which Israel remembers again and again, according to the
Scriptures.[13] Exodus signifies the liberation from the 'slavery' of
Egypt. 'We were slaves to Pharaoh in Egypt but the Lord our
God brought us forth from there with a strong hand and an
outstretched arm. For if the Holy One, blessed be He, had not
brought our ancestors out of Egypt, then we and our children and
our children's children would still be enslaved to Pharaoh in
Egypt.' Thus begins the answer given by the Passover community
to the question asked by its youngest member: 'Why is this night
so different from all other nights?'[14]

Exodus also signifies the wandering in the desert where Israel
encountered its God and experienced his help. Exodus is finally
also the way into freedom, prefigured by the entry into the land
which God had promised to Abraham and his descendants.

During the Exodus Israel also felt the bitterness of life, suffering (often self-inflicted) and judgement, and therefore they learnt that suffering is connected with salvation by God. Jewish tradition sees in the Exodus a sign of hope of definitive salvation by God—the raising from the dead at the end of time.

Jesus, leaving his village of Nazareth and his relatives, wandering through the country of Israel, on the road to the cross on Calvary, but also in his resurrection and his glorification, reflects in a unique manner the Exodus experience of his people.

'Contrary to other nations, the Jewish people does not remember the golden age of its power, does not claim divine descent, but thinks of itself as a nation of slaves who experience God's salvation. And they make present the past with gratitude and thanks-offering.[15] The Jewish religion is a 'religion of remembrance'; the concepts of 'to remember', and 'memory', play a central role in Israel's Bible. The Jewish feasts are days of remembrance. This is most obvious at Passover which reminds the Jews of the night of liberation and which, at the same time, points towards the hope for the time when they will be definitively liberated.[16] Jewish feasts are, so to speak, three-dimensional: they symbolize past, present and future redemption.

Without taking these elements into account one does not understand the great feasts of the Church's liturgical year, and particularly the Eucharist. There, too, past, present and future redemption belong essentially together, they, too, commemorate God's saving deeds. They are no substitute for Israel's feasts but they are significantly related to them.

Even though the Church is convinced that with the resurrection of Jesus from the dead the future *aion*—a term known to early Judaism—has already broken into this age, there still exists a hope common to Christian and Jewish eschatology, as the last articles of the creed express it. 'With the prophets and St. Paul the Church awaits that day, known to God alone, on which all peoples will address the Lord with one voice and "serve him shoulder to shoulder".'[17] 'The day' of the Lord plays an important part both in Israel's Bible and in the New Testament. According to the prophets and to the New Testament this 'day' encompasses the whole world; it means the end itself. Only God knows it and brings it about, a day of transition into final salvation and therefore a day of hope for Israel and the Church.

III. Basic statements of Scripture and the church on the relation between church and Judaism

1. *The testimony of the New Testament*

(a) The New Testament contains important statements on the Jewish people. The first apostles were almost all Jews; Jesus lived and died in the country of Israel; he is conscious of having been sent 'to the lost sheep of the house of Israel' (Mt. 15:24). The Good News, salvation through Jesus, is first announced to the Jews (*cf.* Mk. 7:27; Acts 2:39; 3:26; 10:42; 13:46; Rom. 1:16; 2:10). The problem of the salvation of the Jews intensely preoccupied the primitive church, especially the Jew, Paul, a former Pharisee.

(b) However it cannot be denied that the New Testament also contains critical statements on the Judaism of the time of Jesus and the early church. Jesus himself said: 'Jerusalem, Jerusalem, killing the prophets and stoning those who are sent to you! How often would I have gathered your children together as a hen gathers her brood under her wings, and you would not! Behold, your house is forsaken and desolate' (Mt. 23:37f.). Jesus calls the Pharisees 'the blind leading the blind' (Mt. 15:14) whose sin 'remains' (*cf.* Jn. 9:41). 'You are of your father the devil, and your will is to do your father's desires' (Jn. 8:44). Jesus asserts that there is a guilty attitude. Paul states that 'they have a zeal for God but it is not enlightened' (Rom. 10:2; he speaks of a 'failure', a 'hardening' (Rom. 11:8), a 'trespass' of Israel (Rom. 11:11) and of their 'rejection' by God (Rom. 11:15); the Jews are 'as regards the Gospel, enemies' (Rom. 11:28). They 'killed both the Lord Jesus and the prophets, and drove us out, and displease God and oppose all men by hindering us from speaking to the Gentiles that they may be saved—so as always to fill up the measure of their sins' (1 Thess. 2:15 f.). Paul also speaks of his persecutions by his fellow-Jews (*cf.* 2 Cor. 11:24, 26). Acts, too, tell of the great difficulties the Jews made for Christian missionaries (*cf.* Acts 13:15; 14:5, 19; 17:5–8; 18:12; 23:12).

These are facts which might throw an unfavourable light on the Jews. It must however be observed that these are past events which do not allow a general judgement on Judaism. Further, these negative statements on the Jews must not be considered in isolation but in the context of the many positive statements of the New Testament.

(c) To begin with we should remember the witness of John's Gospel: 'Salvation is from the Jews' (Jn. 4:22). Jesus, the Saviour, originated in Judaism. Paul's Letter to the Romans in particular contains these important statements: 'Then what advantage has the Jew? Or what is the value of circumcision? Much in every way. To begin with, the Jews are entrusted with the oracles of God' (Rom. 3:1 f.). These are the sacred Scriptures of Israel, called by Christians Old Testament. Later he says: 'They are Israelites, and to them belong the sonship, the glory, the covenants, the giving of the law, the worship and the promises; to them belong the patriarchs, and of their race, according to the flesh, is the Christ' (Rom. 9:4 f.). The advantages listed here by the apostle are also called their 'privileges' which God himself has bestowed on them. God does not take them back, for 'his gifts and his call are irrevocable.'[18]

In Romans 11:1 f, the apostle writes: 'I ask then, has God rejected his people? By no means! ... God has not rejected his people whom he foreknew.' He adds: 'Have they stumbled so as to fall? By no means!' (Rom. 11:11). Paul talks of the 'root' which carries the Church (Rom. 11:18). This refers to all the people of Israel, not only to the patriarchs. Not only the root is mentioned but also the 'cultivated olive tree' and its 'branches' (cf. Rom. 11:16–21).[19] The apostle stresses the 'root'— it is mentioned four times—because the tree receives its sap from the root and thus becomes 'rich', i.e., fertile. The Church of the gentiles has been grafted on to the good olive tree by God and thus, by God's grace, shares in the root and the fertility of the olive tree. Though the Jews fell against the 'stumbling block,' Jesus Christ (cf. Rom. 9:32), and remained 'hardened' against the Gospel (Rom. 11:7, 25), they are, according to the prediction of the apostle, not for ever excluded from salvation: 'For God has the power to graft them in again, for if you (the Gentiles) have been cut from what is by nature a wild olive tree, and grafted contrary to nature into a cultivated olive tree, how much more will these natural branches be grafted back into their own olive tree' (Rom. 11:23 f.). Continuing from there Paul speaks of a 'mystery' which refers to the final redemption of Israel which he makes known: 'A hardening has come upon part of Israel until the full number of the Gentiles comes in, and so all Israel will be saved; as it is written, "the deliverer will come from Zion, he will banish ungodliness from Jacob"' (Rom. 11:26 f.).

Paul sees the 'hardening' and the 'hostility' of Israel towards the Gospel in a unique dialectical relationship to the salvation of the Gentiles: 'So I ask, have they stumbled so as to fall? By no means! But through their trespass salvation has come to the Gentiles, so as to make Israel jealous. Now if their trespass means riches for the world, and if their failure means riches for the

Gentiles, how much more will their full inclusion mean!' (Rom.
11:11 f.). 'For if their rejection means the reconciliation of the
world, what will their acceptance mean but life from the dead?'
(Rom. 11:15). For a while God favours the Gentiles until, at the
end of time, he will have mercy upon all (*cf.* Rom. 11:32). Only
thus can the statements of the apostle to the Gentiles be
understood; the Jews have become the enemies of the Gospel
'because of you' (Rom. 11:28), *i.e.*, the Gentiles. There is no
thought in the Epistle to the Romans of sin and punishment. We
Christians have to take seriously the prediction of the apostle
about Israel's final salvation, though we do not know clearly how
God will save 'all Israel'. The Jews remain the 'beloved' of God
'because of their fathers' (Rom. 11:28).

Acts too has a prophecy of the final 'restoration' of Israel.
When the apostles ask Jesus: 'Will you now restore the kingdom
to Israel?', he does not reject the question as wrong in itself but
says that the Father alone has determined the time of the
restoration of the kingdom to Israel. The apostles as witnesses to
Jesus should proclaim the Gospel 'to the end of the earth' (Acts
1:6–8). A restoration of the promised kingdom, as already the
prophets of the old covenant announced it, is certainly coming,
though we do not precisely know in what manner. According to
Acts 3:19–21, the Jews should repent and turn to Jesus 'that your
sins may be blotted out, that times of refreshing may come ... and
that he may send the Christ appointed for you, Jesus, whom the
heavens must receive until the time for establishing all that God
spoke by the mouth of his holy prophets from of old.' According
to this text the returning Christ is also destined for Israel, for its
'refreshing.' The Jews, too, with all the redeemed, will then be
'refreshed' and liberated from their sufferings and sins. These
positive statements of the New Testament about the Jews and
their salvation should be taken into account by Christian
theology and proclamation much more strongly than before,
especially as Vatican II has expressly assumed this task.

2. *Statements of the Catholic Church*

(a) The Second Vatican Council has, in its Declaration *Nostra
Aetate*, made some basic statements on the relationship of the
Church to Judaism.

(Here follows the full text of the Declaration, n.4).

(b) On 1 December 1974 the Roman 'Guidelines and
Suggestions for Implementing the Conciliar Declaration *Nostra
Aetate* n.4' were issued. They call the Declaration 'an important

milestone in the history of Jewish-Catholic relations. They talk
about the 'gap' which 'divided Jews and Catholics more and more
deeply until they hardly knew each other.' It is stated there 'that
the spiritual bond and historical links binding the Church to
Judaism condemn (as opposed to the very spirit of Christianity)
all forms of antisemitism and discrimination'; further it is pointed
out these links 'render obligatory a better mutual understanding
and renewed mutual esteem.' The monologues should give way to
'dialogue', inspired by 'respect for the other as he is', and avoid all
aggressiveness. 'In order not to hurt (even involuntarily) those
taking part, it will be vital to guarantee not only tact but a great
openness of spirit and diffidence with respect to one's own
prejudices.' There follow references to the liturgical elements
common to both, to the permanent value of the Old Testament
and to its right interpretation by Christian theology. The new
attitude, introduced by the Council, must have its effect on
teaching and education. The God of Jews and Christians is the
'same God.' 'The history of Judaism did not end with the
destruction of Jerusalem, but rather went on to develop a
religious tradition. And, although we believe that the importance
and meaning of that tradition were deeply affected by the coming
of Christ, it is still nonetheless rich in religious values.'

(c) On 22 October 1974 Pope Paul VI established a
'Commission for the Religious Relations to Judaism,' which is
linked to the Secretariat for Christian Unity and which has a
number of Jewish members.

In his allocution to the representatives of Jewish organizations
on 12 March 1979, Pope John Paul II referred to the statement in
Nostra Aetate n.4 that the Council, as 'it searches into the
mystery of the Church, remembers the spiritual bonds which tie
the people of the New Covenant to the offsprings of Abraham.'
He stressed the 'Guidelines' of December 1974 and invited the
Church to 'brotherly dialogue', to a 'fertile collaboration' and to
the 'surmounting of every kind of prejudice and discrimination'
against the Jewish people.[20]

When he visited Auschwitz, on his trip to Poland, the Holy
Father remarked: 'I am standing with you, dear companions,
before the memorial tablet in Hebrew. This reminds us of the
people whose sons and daughters were destined for total
extermination. Abraham, the father of our faith, as Paul of Tarsus
calls him (Rom. 4:12), is the original ancestor of this people. This
very nation who received from God the commandment "thou
shalt not kill" had to experience in their own existence and to a

truly extraordinary degree what it means to kill. No one ought to pass this memorial with indifference.'[21]

(d) The General Synod of the Dioceses of the Federal Republic of Germany has in its Resolution 'Our Hope' (IV, 2) emphatically asked for a 'new relationship to the faith of the Jewish people.' Important suggestions have been made by the Declaration of the French Episcopal Commission for the Relation to Judaism.[22] The paper of the Workshop 'Jews and Christians' of the Central Committee of German Catholics called 'Basic Theological Issues of the Jewish-Christian Dialogue' is also helpful.

3. Statements of other Churches

We gratefully remember the statements released by Protestants on the topic of Church and Judaism: 'People, Land and State. An attempt at a Theological Reflection by the Dutch Reformed Church.'[23] 'Christians and Jews. A Study of the Council of the Evangelical Church in Germany' (Gütersloh 1975), with the working paper 'Christians and Jews. A Study of the Council of the Evangelical Church in Germany.'[24] 'Reflections on the Problem Church/Israel,' published by the Board of the Swiss Evangelical Church, May 1977.[25] 'For the Renewal of the Relationship between Christian and Jews,' Working Papers for the members of the Synods and Presbyteries of the Evangelical Church in the Rhineland (Düsseldorf 1980).

Thus Christians today are remembering more intensely than before their 'roots,' their 'origin in Abraham.' They gain a new relationship to their elder brother, the Jewish people—surely a blessing for both. Contempt and disdain have been replaced by mutual respect and sympathy. There is no room left for any form of 'antisemitism.'

IV. Religious differences

In the dialogue between Jews and Christians religious differences, distinguishing and also separating, must be openly admitted. Only then is dialogue in truth and sincerity possible. The following in particular have to be kept in mind.

1. First one must state the Christian conviction that with Jesus of Nazareth the time has been fulfilled and the kingdom of God has come close (cf. Mk. 1:15). For Christians Jesus is the promised Messiah, with him the last era of history has arrived, the kingdom of God has broken into 'this aion,' the miracles of Jesus are the 'signs' pointing to the coming fulfilment, the forces of God's saving future are already at work, especially in the

sacraments of the Church, the final decisions are made. Christ is our peace, our reconciliation, our life. Certainly, Christians, too, know that in Jesus of Nazareth not all the promises of the prophets of the old covenant have been fulfilled: total justice has not at all been restored in the world, peace among the nations is not yet a reality, death still exercises his destructive power. The Christian must understand when Jews point to the still absent fulfilment of the prophecies and therefore cannot recognize' the promised one in Jesus of Nazareth.

2. The strongest bond between Christians and Jews is also that which separates them most. The Christian faith in Jesus who, as the crucified and risen Christ, is not only the promised Messiah but more than that: he is acknowledged and proclaimed as the consubstantial Son of God, and this appears to many Jews radically un-Jewish. They consider this a contradiction to, if not a blasphemy of, strict monotheism which the observant Jew daily professes in the 'Shema Israel.' The Christian ought to understand this, even if he sees no contradiction to monotheism in the dogma that Jesus is the Son of God. For him the confession of faith in the Trinity signifies an enhancement of God's unity, a mystery in which he believes and which he adores.

3. Jesus did not 'abolish' the law but 'fulfil' it (*cf.* Mt. 5:17), though he has at times vigorously criticized the legal practice of his people. He has emphasized the twofold law of love (*cf.* Mk. 12:30) and has summarized the many rules and prohibitions of the Torah and of the so-called 'tradition of the Fathers' (the rabbinic interpretation, called *Halakah* in Hebrew) in the law of love. After the crucifixion and the resurrection Paul, and the early Church with him, was convinced that man's road to salvation does no longer consist in doing the 'works of the Law' (Rom. 2:15, 3:20; Gal. 2:16; 3:2, 5, 10), but exclusively in faith in the crucified and risen Christ. The Christian, according to the teaching of the apostle and also of the first Apostolic Council (Acts 15:1–35), is, unlike the Jew, no longer obliged to keep the laws of the Torah; this however does not mean that the Christian may lead a life without laws. He is all the more obliged to observe the 'law of Christ' (Gal. 6:2) culminating in the law of love in which the Law finds its 'fulfilment' (*cf.* Gal. 5:14; Rom. 13:8–10). These religious differences must be openly discussed in Jewish-Christian dialogue.

V. A change of attitude towards Judaism

Far too frequently the Church has spoken in a false and

164   APPENDIX A(3)

distorting manner about Judaism, especially in sermons and catechetics. This resulted in wrong attitudes. Wherever false judgements have been made and wrong attitudes have been the consequence an immediate correction is necessary. The following should be particularly kept in mind:

1. The Term 'the Jews,' often used in St. John's Gospel, has frequently led to a theological anti-Judaism because it was uncritically assumed that it referred to the whole Jewish people at the time of Jesus; in reality 'the Jews' here mean usually the leaders of contemporary Judaism hostile to Jesus, especially the high-priests.[26] It should further be taken into account that the evangelist reflects on the events at the time of Jesus much later, towards the end of the first century and he sees them in a universal, cosmic perspective. Thus 'the Jews'—as far as a negative accent is intended—become the representatives of a 'cosmos' hostile to God. The evangelist speaks of that 'world' which does not want to know God and Christ. Thus the Johannine Gospel considers the trial of Jesus as a 'universal trial', i.e., of the powers of darkness against the divine light. This has nothing to do with 'anti-Judaism.'

2. The Gospels use of the term 'the Pharisees' is somewhat similar. An investigation of the statements on the Pharisees in the Gospels and of the traditional material used there shows unequivocally that the Pharisees were increasingly portrayed as the particular enemies of Jesus. This happened in the course of the painful and difficult separation which, after Easter, separated the Church from Israel. At the time of Jesus, as well as later, the Pharisees were a highly organized influential group within contemporary Judaism with whom Jesus came into conflict because of the interpretation of the Law. They were men of deep piety. It is the task of our modern exegesis, of religious teaching and preaching to talk about the Pharisees so as to do them justice.

3. The pious Jew rejoices in the Torah. At the end of the Feast of Tabernacles he celebrates a special holy day, 'Joy in the Torah.' 'I will delight in thy statutes; I will not forget thy word' (Ps. 119:14). 'O, how I love thy law! It is my meditation all the day' (ib. 97). For the Jew the Torah is a grace, not a heavy burden.[27] The observance of the Torah does not mean for him an 'accumulation of merits', or a 'performance' which could by itself lead him to God. Up to the present time the Jewish observance of the Law comprises three elements: trust, practice and the sanctification of daily life.[28] The pious Jew does not conceive faith

in the one God without the obedient realization in daily life of
God's commandments in the Torah. Life according to the Torah,
sanctifies the day, this is the true meaning of Torah; he who
submits himself daily and in all things to the yoke of the law,
sanctifies the ordinary day and the whole life with all its relations
and manifestations. The Jewish philosopher Ernst Simon
formulates it thus: 'The Jewish law proposes a way of life of
partial asceticism. No sector of existence, no part of the world is
excluded, none is for limitless permissiveness.'[29] The celebrated
teacher of early Judaism, Rabbi Jokanan ben Zakai (1st century
A.D.), has said: 'If you have kept the Torah, don't be proud of it,
because for this purpose you have been created.'[30] The Christian
must consider this if he wants to judge the Jew rightly.

4. Jews ought not to be called 'deicides.' The Council teaches:
'while it is true that the Jewish authorities and those who
followed their lead pressed for the death of Christ (cf. Jn. 19:6),
nevertheless what happened in his passion cannot be charged
against all the Jews, without distinction, then alive, nor against
the Jews of today.'[31] Instead of accusing others of the guilt for
Jesus' crucifixion we should think of our own sins because of
which we all become guilty of his death. The Roman Catechism
teaches that no single person but all men are guilty of Jesus'
death. 'This guilt seems more enormous in us than in the Jews,
since according to the testimony of the apostle (Paul) "had they
known it, they would never have crucified the Lord of glory" (1
Cor. 2:8); while we, on the contrary, professing to know him, yet
denying him by our actions, seem in some sort to lay violent
hands on him.'[32] Jesus' violent death is the cause of the terrible
deterioration of the relations between Church and Judaism. It is
the task of exact historical research, of Christian theology and of
dialogue to do away with this heritage of the past and to do
justice to Judaism. This is what the Church challenges us to do.[33]
Though the Church was already separated from Israel in the 1st
century A.D., the salvational significance of Israel and God's
promise of redemption for Israel remain valid. We are not
allowed to speculate as to its time, because the salvation of Israel,
just as the salvation of all nations, is God's own secret (Rom.
11:25f.).

5. Antisemitism, still existing in various forms among
Christians, must be replaced by a dialogue based on mutual love
and understanding. 'The spiritual bonds and historical links
binding the Church to Judaism condemn (as opposed to the very
spirit of Christianity) all forms of antisemitism and

discrimination.'[34] Antisemitism is not only directed against the message but finally against the person of Jesus Christ himself.

Though we must stress that Auschwitz was a result of a total negation of both Jewish and Christian faith, the terrible events of Auschwitz and the concentration camps should shake us Christians and move us to examine our conscience and to repent.

6. We must ever again respond to the demand of the Good Friday liturgy: 'Let us pray for the Jewish people, the first to hear the word of God, that they may continue to grow in the love of his name and in faithfulness to his covenant.' One of the duties of Christians towards the Jews is the continual prayer for the millions murdered in the course of history, asking God at the same time to forgive the many failures and omissions of which Christians have been guilty in their attitude towards Jews.

7. In Germany there is a particular reason why we should ask God and our Jewish brethren for forgiveness. We may remember gratefully how many Christians, often at great sacrifice, stood up for Jews, but we ought not and do not want to forget or to repress the memory of what has been done to the Jews by our own nation. We remind you of what the Bishops' Conference at Fulda (1945) declared at its first meeting after the war: 'Many Germans, even from amidst our own ranks, were seduced by the false doctrines of National Socialism and remained indifferent to the crimes against human freedom and dignity; many, by their attitude, aided and abetted the crimes, many were criminals, themselves. A heavy responsibility lies on those who, because of their position, could have known what was going on in our midst and who had the influence to prevent such crimes but did not do so. Because of their attitude they made those atrocities possible and thus became guilty too.'[35]

We confess again: 'Innumerable men and women were murdered in our midst because they belonged to the people who gave birth to the Messiah. We ask the Lord: "Lead all to understanding and repentance who, in our midst, have been guilty, by their actions, omissions or silence. Lead them to understand and repent so that they might atone for their sins. Forgive us because of your Son, in your immense mercy, the immeasurable guilt which no human effort can expiate."'[36]

VI. Common tasks

1. The pious Jew wants, in his daily life, to practise God's law laid down in the Torah. He is interested in the 'doing.' In the teaching of Jesus the term 'to do' plays a central role, as the

Gospels indicate. Both the commandments of the Torah and those of Jesus concern the will of God. The Psalmist prays: 'I delight to do thy will, O my God; thy law is within my heart' (Ps. 40:8); Jesus teaches: 'Not everyone who says to me "Lord, Lord" shall enter the kingdom of heaven, but he who does the will of my Father who is in heaven' (Mt. 7:21). He says of himself: 'It is meat and drink for me to do the will of him who sent me, and to accomplish his work' (Jn. 4:34). The realization of God's will in the world should therefore be the common programme of Jews and Christians.

2. On studying the prophets of Israel we are struck by their protest against any wrong, social and economic, and against all oppression, in the name of an ideology. Such a protest remains the task of both Church and Judaism. They protest against the many threats to freedom and in support of a true humanism and human rights, of fraternal love and peaceful community life; they protest against the spreading of lies about the world and history, against fascism, racism, communism and capitalism. The Jewish-Christian religion is therefore the anti-'opium' of the people.

3. Christians and Jews should stand together for what in Hebrew is called *shalom*. This is a comprehensive concept meaning peace, joy, freedom, reconciliation, community, harmony, justice, truth, communication, humanity. 'Shalom' will be realized when all relations exist in harmony, relations between God and man and man and his fellowmen. No limited, purely national peace should be our ideal. God wants no 'iron curtains'! The teaching in Israel's Scriptures of every man's likeness to God is proclaimed by the Gospel to all men: that all may know that they are brothers. Religions may thus no longer identify themselves with certain political systems. Judaism and Christianity should together steadfastly co-operate to establish total peace throughout the world.

4. By himself man is not able to bring final redemption to the world. Only God can do this; this is the conviction of believing Jews and Christians. Historical experience proves this. Neither through evolution nor through revolution does the world find its final salvation. Only God leads the world towards definitive redemption. He creates and bestows on men the 'new heaven and the new earth' for which both Jews and Christians are waiting (Is. 65:17; 66:22; Rev. 21:1).

5. St. Paul has formulated briefly the final goal of all secular and salvation history: 'God all in all' (1 Cor. 15:28). Jews and Christians can agree on this formula. 'God all in all' means: at the

end of time God, his being the God of all men, and the universality of salvation will be manifested to all. 'The last enemy to be destroyed is death' (1 Cor. 15:26). Thus the God whom Israel, Jesus and the Church proclaim will manifest himself. He will quicken the dead and so show his invincible power. 'We expect the resurrection of the dead and life of the world to come.' To profess this publicly to the world is the common task of Christians and Jews.

NOTES

1. M. Buber, *Werke I* (München/Heidelberg, 1962), 657.
2. Sh.Ben-Chorin, *Bruder Jesus, der Nazarener in jüdischer Sicht* (München, 1967) 12.
3. *Nostra Aetate*, no. 4.
4. *Constitution on Revelation* (Vatican II), no. 14.
5. Papal Commission for Religious Relations with the Jews, 'Guidelines and Suggestions for Implementing the Conciliar Declaration *Nostra Aetate*, no. 4.'
6. *Ibid.*
7. *Constitution on Revelation*, no. 14.
8. *Mekilta Bahodesh*, 88:72f.
9. *Ibid.*, 20:26.
10. Slav. En. 44:1.
11. C. Westermann, *Genesis I* (Neukirchen, 1974), 633f.
12. See F. Mussner, *Traktat über die Juden* (München, 1979), 103–20.
13. *Cf.* A. Friedlander, *Die Exodus-Tradition*, in J. Henrix and M. Stoehr (eds), *Exodus und Kreuz im ökumenischen Dialog zwischen Juden und Christen* (Aachen, 1978), 30–44.
14. *Ibid.*, 35.
15. *Ibid.*, 40.
16. *Cf.* N. Füglister, *Die Heilsbedeutung des Pascha* (München, 1963).
17. 'Guidelines'.
18. *Nostra Aetate*, *cf.* Rom. 11:28f.; see also *Constitution on the Church*, Vatican II, no. 16.
19. *Cf.* Mussner, 68–70.
20. *Osservatore Romano*, 30 March 1979. German, Weekly Edition.
21. Sermons and Allocutions of Pope John Paul II during his pilgrimage in Poland, published by the German Bishops' Conference.
22. *Freiburger Rundbrief*, (1973), no. 25.
23. Ibid., no. 23 (1971).
24. R. Rendtorff (ed.), Gütersloh 1979.
25. *Freiburger Rundbrief*, no. 29, (1977).
26. *Cf.* Mussner. 281–291.
27. *Cf.* H. Gross, 'Tora und Gnade im Alten Tesament', in: *Kairos*, NF 14 (1972); R. J. Werblowsky, 'Tora als Gnade', ibid., no. 15 (1973). E. L. Ehrlich, 'Tora im Judentum', in *Evangelische Theologie*, 37 (1977).
28. *Cf.* N. Oswald, 'Grundgedanken zu einer pharisäisch-rabbinischen Theologie', in *Kairos* 6 (1963).
29. E. Simon, *Brücken, Gesammelte Aufsätze* (Heidelberg, 1965).
30. *Abot*, II, 8.

31. *Nostra Aetate*, no. 4.
32. *The Roman Catechism of Trent*, I, ch. V, quest. 11.
33. *Nostra Aetate*, no. 4.
34. 'Guidelines'.
35. Pastoral Letter of the German Bishops, 23 August 1945.
36. Prayer for the murdered Jews and for their persecutors, to be said in all Catholic Churches in Germany, 11 June 1961. *Cf. Freiburger Rundbrief* no. 13 (1960/61).

Appendix A(4)

Anglicans and Jews

First Jewish-Anglican Consultation
Theme: 'Law and Religion in Contemporary Society'

The first Anglican-Jewish Consultation, lasting for three days, took place in November, 1980, at Amport House, Andover. It was chaired by the Archbishop of York and the Chief Rabbi and attended by 20 Christian and Jewish leaders. The aim of their discussion was to seek to 'offer guidance from within their religious traditions on urgent moral issues facing society today'.

The full test of this Consultation and the papers presented were published in *Christian Jewish Relations*, Volume 14 Number 1 (74), March 1981, which is available from the INSTITUTE OF JEWISH AFFAIRS, 11 Hertford Street, London W1Y 7DX. Tel. 01-491 3517.

Appendix B

CONTRIBUTORS
with selected Bibliography

The Revd George G. W. Anderson, D.D., Teol.D., F.B.A., F.R.S.E., Professor of Hebrew and Old Testament Studies, Edinburgh University: Member of the Consultation of the Church and the Jewish People (C.C.J.P.) of the World Council of Churches. Address: New College, Mound Place, Edinburgh EH1 2LX, Scotland, U.K.

The Revd Charles E. B. Cranfield, M.A., D.D., Emeritus Professor of Theology in the University of Durham. Author of *Romans*, The International Critical Commentary, volumes 1 and 2, edited by J. A. Emerton and C. B. E. Cranfield (T. & T. Clark). Address: 30 Western Hill, Durham City DH1 4RL, England, U.K.

Mrs Johanna-Ruth Dobschiner, R.G.N., Hebrew Christian. Author of *Selected to Live* (Pickering and Inglis). Address: 'Theodotion', 51 Stamperland Avenue, Clarkston, Glasgow G76 8EX, Scotland, U.K.

The Revd Henry L. Ellison, B.A., B.D., Hebrew Christian: Son of a Hebrew Christian missionary among the Jews; missionary in Romania, 1931–9; formerly Bible College Lecturer. Author of *The Christian Approach to the Jews* (U.S.C.L.); *Understanding a Jew* (Olive Press); *The Mystery of Israel* (Paternoster Press). Address: 14 Rosyl Avenue, Holcombe, Dawlish, Devon EX7 0LE, England, U.K.

The Revd Jakob Jocz, Ph.D., D.Litt., Hebrew Christian, Professor Emeritus of the Chair of Systematic Theology, University of Toronto, Canada. Author of *The Jewish People and Jesus Christ* (revised ed. Baker Book House, 1980); *The Jewish People and Jesus Christ After Auschwitz* (Baker Book House, 1981); *The Spiritual History of Israel* (Eyre and Spottiswoode, 1961); *Christians and Jews, Encounter and Mission* (S.P.C.K., 1966); *A Theology of Election, Israel and the Church* (S.P.C.K., 1958). Address: 60 Kendal Avenue, Toronto, Ontario M5R 1L9, Canada.

Mr Mark Kinzer, B.A., Hebrew Christian: Co-ordinator in the Word of God in an interdenominational Christian community in Ann Arbor, Michigan 48197, U.S.A. Author of *The Self-Image of a Christian.* Address: 212 Washtenaw, Ypsilanti, Michigan 48197, U.S.A.

The Very Revd George A. F. Knight, M.A., B.D., D.D.; 1935–1940, Director of the Church of Scotland Jewish Mission and School, Budapest, Hungary; 1941–42, engaged in Jewish-Christian work throughout Scotland; 1942–6, British Council of Churches Centre on Jews, London; 1947–65, Lecturer and Professor of Old Testament in Knox College, Dunedin, New Zealand, in St. Mary's and St. Salvator's Colleges, University of St. Andrews, Scotland and in Chicago, U.S.A.; 1965–72, Principal of the Pacific Theological College, Fiji. Author of *For Christians Only — About Jews* (Church of Scotland, 1943); *From Moses to Paul* (Lutterworth, 1949); *The Jews and New Zealand* (Presbyterian Church of New Zealand); *Jews and Christians: Preparation for Dialogue* (Westminster Press, 1965). Address: 3/20 Paunui Street, St. Heliers, Auckland 5, New Zealand.

The Revd Franklin H. Littell, B.A., B.D., Ph.D., D.Theol., Professor of Religion, Temple University (Philadelphia); Adjunct Professor, Hebrew University (Jerusalem); Chairman, National Institute on the Holocaust; President, National Christian Leadership Conference for Israel. Author of *The German Phoenix, the Crucifixion of the Jews*; Co-editor and contributor: *The German Church Struggle and the Holocaust, Reflections on the Holocaust.* Address: Temple University, College of Liberal Arts, Philadelphia, Pennsylvania 19122, U.S.A.

The Revd David H. S. Lyon, M.A., B.D., S.T.M., General Secretary, Overseas Council of the Church of Scotland. Address: Church of Scotland, Overseas Council, 121 George Street, Edinburgh EH2 4YN, Scotland, U.K.

The Revd Murdo A. MacLeod, M.A., Director and General Secretary, Christian Witness to Israel. Address: Seven Trees, 44 Lubbock Road, Chislehurst, Kent BR7 5JX, England, U.K.

The Revd John K. S. Reid, C.B.E., T.D., M.A., B.D., D.D., Professor Emeritus, Chair of Systematic Theology, University of Aberdeen. Address: 1 Camus Road, Edinburgh EH10 6RY, Scotland, U.K.

The Revd David W. Torrance, M.A., B.D. Minister of the Church of Scotland. Address: The Manse, Earlston, Berwickshire TD4 6DE, Scotland, U.K.

The Very Revd Thomas F. Torrance, M.B.E., D.Litt., D.D., Dr. Theol., D.Theol., Dr. Teol., F.R.S.E. Former Moderator of the General Assembly of the Church of Scotland: Professor Emeritus of the Chair of Systematic Theology, University of Edinburgh. Address: 37 Braid Farm Road, Edinburgh EH10 6LE, Scotland, U.K.

Appendix C

Churches and Addresses

Church of Scotland,
Overseas Council,
121 George Street,
Edinburgh EH2 4YN,
Scotland.

Deutsche Bischofskonferenz,
Sekretariat und Zentralstellen,
Kaiserstrasse 163,
5300 Bonn 1,
Germany.

Evangelische Kirche im Rheinland,
Das Landeskirchenamt,
Hans Böckler-Strasse 7,
Postfach 320340,
D 4000 Düsseldorf,
Germany.

Appendix D

Publications and Addresses

Christian Jewish Relations (*A Documentary Survey*),
The Institute of Jewish Affairs Ltd (in association with the World
Jewish Congress),
11 Hertford Street,
London W1Y 7DX, U.K.

Current Dialogue (continuing the quarterly Newsletter of the
Consultation on the Church and the Jewish People),
World Council of Churches,
Dialogue with People of Living Faiths and Ideologies,
150, route de Ferney,
P.O. Box 66,
1211 Geneva 20,
Switzerland.

*Lausanne Occasional Papers, no. 7, The Thailand Report:
Christian Witness to the Jewish People,*
Lausanne Committee for World Evangelisation,
P.O. Box 1100,
Wheaton,
Illinois 60187,
U.S.A.

Appendix E

World Jewish Communities

Editor's Note: These figures concerning world Jewish communities were kindly provided by the Jewish National Fund, Youth and Education Department, Harold Poster House, Kingsbury Circle, London NW9 9SP.

In view of the large movements of population in recent years and in many countries the difficulty of obtaining exact figures, Jewish population statistics must, in most cases, be based on estimates received from a variety of sources.

Estimates of the present world Jewish population give a total of about 14,161,000, including 2,200,000 in Russia. Over 3,693,000 are in Europe, almost 6,910,000 in North and South America, over 3,305,000 in Asia, including 3,254,000 in Israel, nearly 177,000 in Africa and about 76,000 in Australasia. The number of Jews in Moslem countries is about 75,000.

The number of Jews in the world before the outbreak of war in 1939 was estimated at a figure slightly under 17,000,000, of whom about 10,000,000 lived in Europe, 5,375,000 in North and South America (which seems to have been an overestimate), 830,000 in Asia, 600,000 in Africa, and less than 33,000 in Australasia. The difference between the pre-war and post-war figures is accounted for principally by the enormous losses suffered by the Jewish people between 1939 and 1945. Although estimates of Jews murdered by the Nazis and their collaborators vary, the number is commonly accepted to be 6,000,000.

From the seizure of power by Hitler until the outbreak of war in 1939, 80,000 refugees from Central Europe were admitted to Britain. During the six years of war, a further 70,000 were admitted and since the end of the war about 70,000 displaced persons as well as refugees from a number of other countries. Probably some 80 per cent of these were Jews. Many of these were, however, only temporary residents and as opportunity arose proceeded further.

Table I

POPULATION OF THE PRINCIPAL COUNTRIES

	Jewish	Total		Jewish	Total
Afghanistan	80	15,490,000	Indonesia	100	148,470,000
Albania	300	2,670,000	Iran	40,000	35,510,000
Algeria	700	19,130,000	Iraq	450	12,770,000
Argentina	400,000	26,730,000	Ireland	2,000	3,370,000
Australia	72,000	14,420,000	‡Israel (September,		
Austria	12,000	7,510,000	1980)	3,254,000	3,885,000
Bahamas	40	220,000	Italy	35,000	56,910,000
Bahrein	150	350,000	Jamaica	350	2,160,000
Barbados	50	270,000	Japan	700	115,870,000
Belgium	40,000	9,870,000	Kenya	300	15,320,000
Bolivia	750	5,430,000	Lebanon	60	3,090,000
Brazil	165,000	118,650,000	Libya	20	2,860,000
Bulgaria	5,100	8,810,000	Luxembourg	1,200	360,000
Burma	200	32,910,000	Malta	50	350,000
Canada	305,000	23,690,000	Mexico	43,000	69,380,000
Chile	30,000	10,920,000	Morocco	20,000	19,470,000
China	30	945,020,000	Netherlands	30,000	14,030,000
Colombia	15,000	26,360,000	New Zealand	4,500	3,100,000
Costa Rica	2,500	2,190,000	Norway	1,050	4,070,000
Cuba	1,200	9,850,000	Pakistan	250	76,770,000
Cyprus	30	620,000	Panama	3,000	1,880,000
Czechoslovakia	6,000	15,250,000	Paraguay	1,000	2,970,000
Denmark	8,000	5,120,000	Peru	5,500	17,290,000
Dominican Rep.	300	5,280,000	Philippines	200	47,720,000
Dutch Antilles	850	250,000	Poland	6,000	35,440,000
Ecuador	1,500	8,080,000	Portugal	300	9,870,000
Egypt	300	40,980,000	Puerto Rico	2,000	3,400,000
El Salvador	50	4,350,000	Romania	34,000	22,070,000
Ethiopia	28,000	30,420,000	Singapore	450	2,360,000
Finland	1,000	4,750,000	South Africa	115,000	28,480,000
France	700,000	53,480,000	Spain	12,000	38,180,000
*Germany, East	680	16,740,000	Sudan	50	17,870,000
†Germany, West	27,770	61,340,000	Surinam	650	380,000
Gibraltar	600	30,000	Sweden	16,000	8,300,000
Great Britain and			Switzerland	20,745	6,330,000
N. Ireland	410,000	55,820,000	Syria	4,000	8,350,000
Greece	4,875	9,360,000	Taiwan	70	13,142,000
Guatemala	1,500	6,620,000	Thailand	60	46,140,000
Haiti	100	4,920,000	Trinidad	750	1,130,000
Honduras	150	3,560,000	Tunisia	6,000	6,370,000
Hong Kong	200	4,710,000	Turkey	22,500	44,310,000
Hungary	90,000	10,700,000	Uruguay	50,000	2,910,000
India	6,200	650,980,000	U.S.A.	5,861,000	220,100,000

*Including East Berlin.
†Including West Berlin.   ‡Including Eastern Jerusalem.

	Jewish	Total		Jewish	Total
§U.S.S.R.	2,200,000	264,110,000	Venezuela	18,000	13,520,000
			Virgin Islands	450	92,000
			Yemen, North	2,000	7,000,000
			Yugoslavia	6,000	22,110,000
			Zaire	330	27,750,000
			Zambia	150	5,650,000
			Zimbabwe	1,950	7,140,000

§According to the 1979 official Soviet census there are 1,811,000 Jews in Russia, but some Western experts believe the real figure is much higher.

Table II

MAJOR CENTRES OF JEWISH POPULATION

EUROPE

Amsterdam	17,000	Lodz	1,500
Ankara	500	Lvov	25,000
Antwerp	13,000	Lyons	32,000
Athens	2,800	Madrid	3,500
Barcelona	3,000	Marseilles	85,000
Basle	2,570	Metz	2,500
Belgrade	1,550	Milan	10,000
Berlin, East	400	Minsk	45,000
Berlin, West	6,145	Moscow	285,000
Bordeaux	8,000	Munich	3,920
Brussels	24,000	Nancy	3,000
Bucharest	17,000	Nice	27,000
Budapest	80,000	Odessa	120,000
Cologne	1,245	Oslo	900
Copenhagen	6,600	Paris	380,000
Dublin	1,900	Prague	1,200
Düsseldorf	1,690	Riga	25,000
Florence	1,290	Rome	15,000
Frankfurt	4,930	Rotterdam	1,500
Geneva	4,300	Salonika	1,060
Gothenburg	1,600	Sofia	3,200
Grenoble	8,000	Stockholm	8,000
Hamburg	1,330	Strasbourg	8,000
Helsinki	800	Sverdlovsk	40,000
Istanbul	19,000	The Hague	2,500
Izmir	1,200	Toulouse	21,000
Jassy	500	Turin	1,630
Kazan	20,000	Vienna	10,000
Kharkov	80,000	Vilna	13,000
Kiev	152,000	Warsaw	2,000
Kishinev	50,000	Wroclaw	1,500
Kovno	5,500	Zagreb	1,300
Leningrad	165,000	Zhitomir	20,000
Lille	2,500	Zurich	6,700
Lisbon	350		

Table II — continued

ASIA

Bombay	3,600
Damascus	3,000
Shiraz	6,000
Tashkent	56,000
Tehran	30,000
Tokyo	450

ISRAEL

Acre	29,000
Afula	19,700
Ascalon	52,000
Ashdod	62,300
Bat Yam	130,100
Beersheba	107,000
Bnei Brak	89,600
Dimona	27,800
Elat	18,900
Givatayim	49,300
Hadera	37,800
Haifa	213,800
Herzlia	56,400
Holon	128,400
Jerusalem	287,400
Kiryat Atta	31,400
Kiryat Bialik	27,500
Kiryat Gat	24,300
Kiryat Motzkin	23,200
Kiryat Ono	22,500
Kiryat Yam	28,400
Kfar Saba	38,100
Lod	33,800
Nehariya	28,200
Netanya	95,900
Or Yehuda	19,400
Petah Tikva	117,000
Ramat Gan	120,400
Ramat Hasharon	30,100
Ramle	34,600
Ranana	29,700
Rehovot	63,700
Rishon le-Zion	87,800
Tel Aviv-Jaffa	328,100
Tiberias	28,300
Upper Nazareth	21,400

AMERICA

Atlanta	22,000
Baltimore	92,000
Boston	170,000
Buenos Aires	250,000
Buffalo (N.Y.)	22,000
Calgary (Alberta)	6,000
Chicago	253,000
Cincinnati	28,500
Cleveland	75,000
Dallas	20,000
Denver	40,000
Detroit	75,000
Edmonton (Alberta)	2,900
Elizabeth (New Jersey)	20,000
Fort Lauderdale	60,000
Halifax (N.S.)	1,500
Hamilton (Ont.)	5,000
Hartford (Conn.)	23,500
Hollywood (Florida)	55,000
Houston	27,000
Kansas City	20,000
London (Ont.)	1,760
Los Angeles	455,000
Mexico City	36,000
Miami	225,000
Milwaukee	23,900
Minneapolis	22,100
Montevideo	48,000
Montreal (Que.)	115,000
New Haven (Con.)	20,000
New York (Greater)	1,998,000
Newark and Essex Cnty.	95,000
Ottawa (Ont.)	7,500
Paterson (New Jersey)	26,000
Philadelphia	295,000
Phoenix	29,000
Pittsburgh	51,000
Rio de Janeiro	55,000
Rochester (N.Y.)	21,500
Rhode Island	22,000
St. Louis	60,000
San Diego	26,500
San Francisco	75,000
Santiago	25,000
São Paulo	75,000
Toronto (Ont.)	120,000
Vancouver (B.C.)	12,000
Washington, D.C.	160,000
Windsor (Ont.)	2,500
Winnipeg (Man.)	20,000

Table II—continued

AFRICA

Alexandria	100
Bulawayo	900
Cairo	170
Cape Town	24,000
Casablanca	14,000
Durban	5,000
Fez	4,000
Germiston	5,700
Johannesburg	56,000
Meknes	3,500
Port Elizabeth	2,500
Pretoria	3,500
Rabat	4,300
Salisbury	1,350
Tangier	3,000
Tunis	5,000

AUSTRALASIA

Adelaide	1,800
Auckland	2,350
Brisbane	1,500
Canberra	300
Hobart	50
Melbourne	36,000
Perth	3,000
Sydney	29,000
Wellington	1,800

Table III

JEWS IN BRITAIN AND NORTHERN IRELAND

The official census in Britain does not include an inquiry regarding religious affiliation, and the following figures are based on unofficial estimates. In arriving at the overall estimate of 450,000 for Great Britain, about 10 per cent has been added to the total of the figures given below to allow for Jews who have no known communal affiliation. A Board of Deputies survey, published in 1968, arrived at a total of 410,000, but did not include Jews without any Jewish affiliations.

	Jewish	Total		Jewish	Total
Aberdeen	30	208,570	Chelmsford	150	132,300
Ayr	40	48,021	Cheltenham	70	86,000
Barrow-in-Furness	19	72,200	Chester	70	116,200
Basildon	60	145,900	Colchester	100	135,400
Bedford	70	129,700	Coventry	150	337,000
Belfast	770	354,400	Crawley	50	71,500
Birmingham	6,000	1,041,000	Darlington	90	94,600
Blackburn	12	142,900	Derby	75	215,400
Blackpool	1,500	147,300	Dundee	80	191,517
Bognor	40	33,910	Eastbourne	90	71,900
Bournemouth	3,000	144,200	East Grinstead	40	23,000
Bradford	500	463,100	Edinburgh	700	463,923
Brighton			Exeter	25	95,300
and Hove	10,000	242,000	Gateshead	600	214,200
Bristol	410	411,000	Glasgow	13,400	809,000
Cambridge	250	102,300	Grimsby	130	91,900
Cardiff	2,000	278,400	Guildford	150	117,700
Chatham	200	59,060	Harrogate	250	113,800

Table III—continued

	Jewish	Total		Jewish	Total
Hastings	50	73,200	St. Albans	300	123,400
High Wycombe	60	60,510	St. Annes-on-Sea	700	29,980
Hoylake	58	32,450	Sheffield	1,400	547,900
Hull	2,000	285,970	Slough	130	98,000
Leeds	18,000	728,500	Southampton	120	210,300
Leicester	700	277,500	Southend		
Liverpool	5,950	528,000	and Westcliff	5,000	154,700
Llandudno			Southport	2,600	85,250
and Rhyl	85	38,250	South Shields	20	98,610
Llanelli	20	75,700	Staines	350	56,730
Luton	1,160	161,500	Stockport	220	291,100
London (Greater			Stoke-on-Trent	150	257,200
London Area)	280,000	6,970,100	Sunderland	845	300,200
Manchester			Swansea	240	187,700
and Salford	35,000	745,000	Swindon	30	90,330
Margate	350	49,730	Torbay	110	108,900
Middlesbrough	210	152,900	Tunbridge Wells	18	95,900
Newcastle-			Wallasey	100	96,070
upon-Tyne	2,000	291,600	Welwyn	195	93,600
Newport	100	133,100	Whitley Bay	85	37,590
Northampton	300	151,300	Wolverhampton	80	260,600
North Shields	16	66,300	Worcester	24	74,100
Norwich	170	119,800	Worthing	300	89,900
Nottingham	1,500	280,900	York	14	101,000
Oxford	600	127,700			
Peterborough	50	125,300			
Plymouth	175	256,400			
Pontypridd	20	34,390			
Portsmouth	490	191,400			
Preston	25	127,500			
Reading	1,000	138,700			
Reigate			Isle of Man	40	56,289
and Redhill	60	113,700	Jersey	80	72,532